An Illustrated History of
L.M.S.
WAGONS

R. J. Essery

Volume Two

Oxford Publishing Company

Copyright © R. J. Essery & Oxford Publishing Co. 1983

ISBN 0-86093-255-9

Typesetting by:
Aquarius Typesetting Services,
New Milton, Hants.

Printed in Great Britain by:
Balding & Mansell Ltd., Wisbech, Cambs.

The publisher wishes to point out that many of the drawings are of poor quality. This is due to the fact that the publisher has used the original Railway Companies' drawings for total authenticity.

Page 4 Caption

This picture of Toton, selected as the frontispiece for this volume, typifies the steam age of railways in so far as freight traffic is concerned. The wide expanse of sidings contain many varied types of vehicles and traffic and provide a sight not to be seen on the railways of today. On the original print, it is possible to see a number of interesting features. On the far right, there are a number of coke wagons forming part of a train while closer to the camera is a hopper wagon with a high load of slack. In the foreground, to the right, one can see timber roped into an open goods wagon, while the next vehicle, a private owner wagon, carries a load which cannot be clearly identified. In the immediate foreground, there is a roof with two differing rain strips and the plank lines can be seen through the roof canvas. Also in the foreground one can see an open wagon with a white effect caused by a previous load. To the left of the picture a low goods wagon carries a 'C' type container, while in front are mineral wagons. It should be noted how the loads lie in the vehicles. To the left are more mineral wagons, and again attention is drawn to the coal and how it lies in the wagon. The different types of coal should also be noted; the larger size for domestic use and the smaller for power stations. Also to the left of the picture one can see a Southern Railway covered goods van within a line of mineral wagons, and everywhere there is coal, mostly loaded into private owner vehicles.

Photograph British Rail

Title Page

A train of four wheel trolleys, location and date unknown. The vehicle nearest the camera is No. 299879 of diagram book, page 96B. Two further examples of this type will be found in **Plates 57 & 58**.

Photograph British Rail

Published by:
Oxford Publishing Company,
Link House,
West Street,
POOLE, Dorset.

Contents

Class 5, 4-6-0, No. 5335 heads a fitted freight train on the Western Division probably just prior to the outbreak of World War II. The train appears to consist almost entirely of 'BR' and 'BM' type containers and could well be carrying imported meat from the docks.

Photograph Photomatic

Introduction

Volume One comprised the 'standard' wagons in LMS diagram page order and, in many respects, was arranged as an 'illustrated diagram book'. A similar style has been adopted for the first part of this volume which has been divided into a number of sections as detailed in the index.

The introduction to Volume One included the various acknowledgements for both volumes and in presenting this second and final volume, dealing with LMS stock, I have endeavoured to provide sufficient information to enable modellers to build 'that particular vehicle'

Readers will note that, wherever possible, the LMS drawing numbers have been quoted so that, as and when they become available to modellers, identification of the correct drawing for each diagram will be possible.

A few slight errors may be found and most certainly there are some omissions. Pictures of every vehicle in various conditions are not available but, at least, it has been possible to use every picture which was available to tell the story. K. R. Morgan, my co-author of *The LMS Wagon*, published by David & Charles in 1977, has been kind enough to provide a section dealing with wagon construction and this useful addition, for modellers, forms part of the final section of this book.

Finally, my grateful thanks go to my wife, Wynne, who has turned my scrawl into a working manuscript, and to my son, Steven, who completed the typing.

R. J. Essery,
Orpington 1983

A train of special wagons hauled by an ex-Midland Railway 3F, 0-6-0. The vehicle next to the ex-MR 20 ton goods brake van, is an example of a 40 ton bogie trolley from diagram book, page 129.

Photograph British Rail

This illustrates an example from diagram book, page 137A showing a 70 ton twin girder truck, No. 5045, in service.

Photograph British Rail

This picture illustrates an example from diagram book, page 129, and is a 40 ton bogie trolley No. 245740.

Photograph British Rail

Chapter One Special Wagons

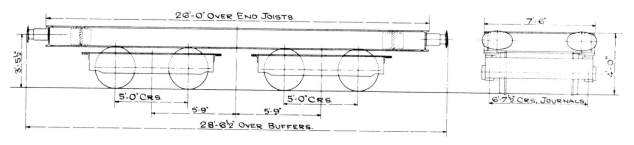

Figure 1

26'-0" OVER END JOISTS.

3'-5½"

5'-0" CRS.

5'-9" 5'-9"

5'-0" CRS.

28'-6½" OVER BUFFERS.

7'-6"

4'-0"

6'-7½" CRS, JOURNALS.

100 TON ARMOUR PLATE TRUCK

Figure 1

Drawing No. P3/2542   Diagram Book Page 2A

SCALE - 0 1 2 3 4 5 6 7 8 9 10 FEET.

Code: HAX
Lot number: 1061
Quantity: 1
Built: Derby 1937
Running number: 700200
Tare: 18 tons 19 cwt
      28 tons 14 cwt with 3" armour plate top.

The minimum curve that this truck will negotiate is 80 ft. radius. To be run with match trucks Nos. 116347/8 at Sheffield. For internal working only. All metal floor. Transferred to E/NE Region on 3rd February 1958 and coded ARM EU.

Plate 1   This illustrates the vehicle under test before being painted. A photograph, taken at Derby in 1964, shows it was still coded HAX with '100T M700200' shown over the extreme left hand wheel, HAX over the other wheel on the left hand bogie, and 'armour plate truck' over the inner wheel of the right hand bogie.

Photograph British Rail

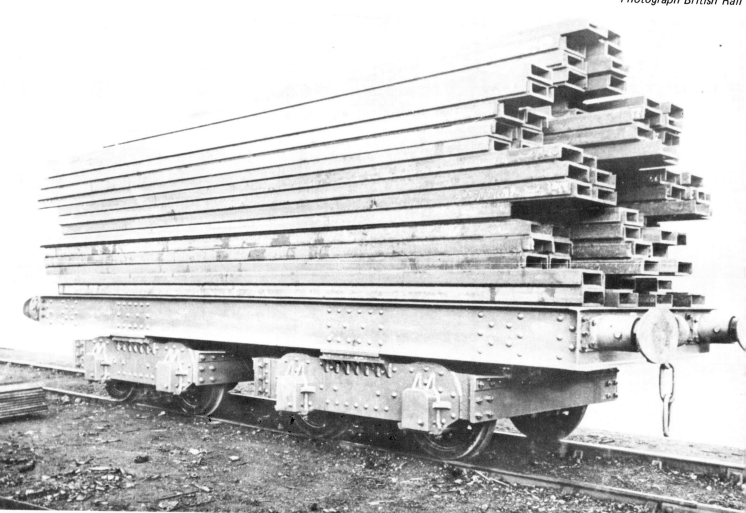

Plate 2 This ex-works photograph of No. 700227, in bauxite, is the only known photograph of one of these vehicles.

Photograph British Rail

Figure 2

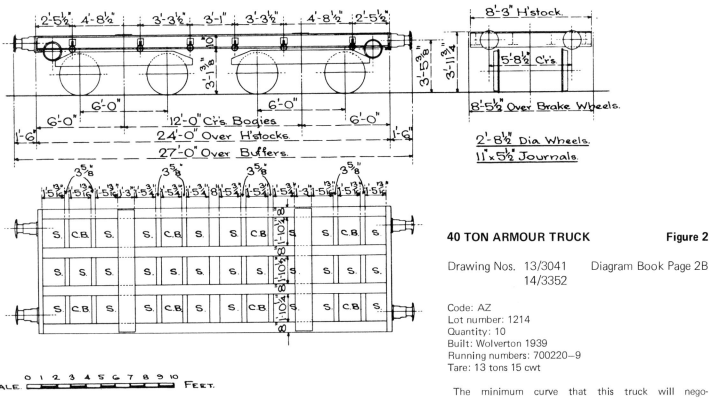

SCALE. 0 1 2 3 4 5 6 7 8 9 10 FEET.

S indicates space open to rail.
C.B. " chain box.

40 TON ARMOUR TRUCK **Figure 2**

Drawing Nos. 13/3041 Diagram Book Page 2B
14/3352

Code: AZ
Lot number: 1214
Quantity: 10
Built: Wolverton 1939
Running numbers: 700220—9
Tare: 13 tons 15 cwt

The minimum curve that this truck will negotiate is one chain. Binding chains: 4 sets, including
screw couplings. Steel floor. Transferred to E/NE
Region on 3rd February 1958. Coded EB.

55 TON ARMOUR PLATE TRUCK

Figure 3

Drawing No. 13/2528

Diagram Book Page 3A

Code: AE
Lot number: 1065; Quantity: 6; Built: Wolverton 1937; Running numbers: 700201—3 (LMS)
Lot number: 1144; Quantity: 4; Built: Wolverton 1939; Running numbers: 217329—31 and 217295 for L N E R
Tare: 16 tons 3 cwt

The minimum curve that the truck will negotiate is ¾ chain. All wood floor. Carrying capacity: 55 tons over not less than 16 ft. at centre. Transferred to E/NE Region on 3rd February 1959. Coded ARM E.

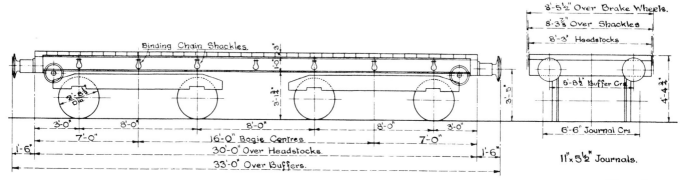

Figure 3

Scale 0 2 4 6 8 10 Feet.

Plate 3   This illustrates No. 700201 when first built in, what appears to be, bauxite livery.

Photograph British Rail

Plate 4   No. 217331 is an example of lot 1144, built for the L N E R.

Photograph British Rail

Plate 5 This shows a vehicle prior to painting and clearly illustrates how the bolsters were built up in the well.

Photograph British Rail

BOGIE BOLSTER 'B' TRUCK
(Converted from a 50 ton Warwell)

Figure 4

Drawing No. 13/6058

Diagram Book Page 5B

Code: Not recorded
Lot number: 1547
Quantity: 37 (Quantity was originally 38 but No. 721234 was broken up prior to 1961)
Built: Wolverton 1949
Running numbers: 721200—721237
Tare: 29 tons 5 cwt

The minimum curve that the trolley will negotiate is 2 chains. When two or more trolleys are coupled together, the minimum curve is 3 chains. Carrying capacity 30 tons. Fitted with screw type hand brake and A V B.

Plate 6 This picture has been selected to illustrate how the original lettering was displayed, and the legend reads 'Load to be evenly distributed on bolsters. No load on floor'.

Photograph British Rail

Figure 5

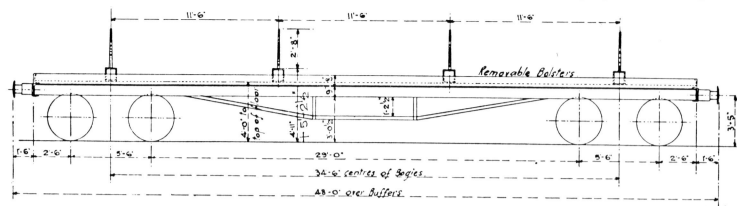

Scale 0 1 2 3 4 5 6 7 8 9 10 feet

Plate 7   This photograph shows No. 12312, a Midland Railway built truck, and has been included to illustrate the brake wheel originally used.

Photograph Author's Collection

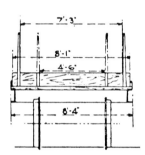

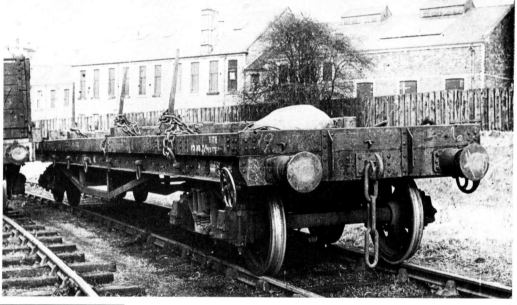

25 & 30 TON BOGIE BOLSTER TRUCKS   Figure 5

Drawing No. 6468   Diagram Book Pages 6 & 11

Code: BBS
Lot number: 287; Quantity: 89; Built: Wolverton 1926
Lot number: 348; Quantity: 50; Built: Metro C&W 1927
Lot number: 349; Quantity: 50; Built: Gloucester C&W 1927
Lot number: 392; Quantity: 88; Built: Wolverton 1928
Lot number: 759; Quantity: 50; Built: Wolverton 1934
Total quantity built: 327
Running numbers: Various including the block 290017—82
Full details are given in an *Illustrated History of Midland Wagons*, see below
Tare: 14 tons 11 cwt
   The minimum curve that the truck will negotiate is 1 chain. All wood floor.
Binding chains: 4 sets, including screw couplings.

   These 25 and 30 ton vehicles are a little confusing inasmuch as the Midland Railway built seemingly identical vehicles with these two carrying capacities. The LMS adopted the 30 ton vehicle as a standard design and built more than 200 before producing a new design in 1936. Full details of the Midland Railway vehicles will be found in an *Illustrated History of Midland Wagons, Volume Two,* Chapter 10, published by O.P.C., and the description here will deal only with the LMS vehicles. However, it should be noted that page 6 of the LMS 'Special Book' probably referred to the Midland-built vehicles while Page 11 covered the 30 ton trucks and included some Midland and all the LMS-built trucks.
   The Midland-built trucks were equipped with both a lever and wheel to apply the brakes, whereas the LMS-built vehicles were only equipped with a brake lever, see **Plate 9**.

Plate 8   This close up picture shows the arrangement of the brake lever used by the LMS on this otherwise Midland Railway design.

Photograph A. E. West

Plate 9 This illustrates truck No. 301326 in original condition. The painted number on the bolsters should be noted together with the general layout of the livery when compared with **Plate 10** which shows an alternative style on wagon No. 314064, still in grey body colour. When in bauxite, a layout similar to **Plate 19** (diagram book, page 18c) would have been employed.

Photographs British Rail and A. E. West

Figure 6

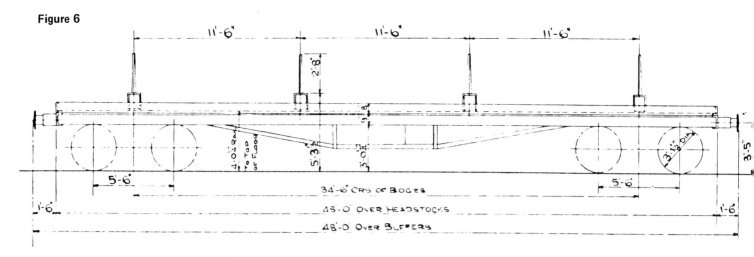

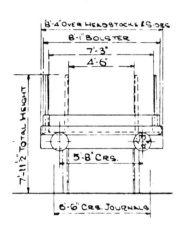

30 TON BOGIE BOLSTER TRUCK

Figure 6

Drawing No. 13/2228

Diagram Book Page 11A

Code: BBS
Lot number: 937; Quantity: 50; Built: Hurst Nelson 1936; Running numbers: 720500—49
Lot number: 983; Quantity: 25; Built: Hurst Nelson 1936; Running numbers: 720550—74
Total quantity built: 75
Tare: 15 tons 5 cwt 2 qtrs

The minimum curve that the truck will negotiate is 1 chain. Timber bolsters removable. Binding chains: 4 sets, including screw couplings.

Plate 11   This illustrates truck No. 720514 in original condition. The method of showing the running number, which is cut into the wooden bolster, should be noted. The tyres were painted white, probably only for the purpose of this photograph. In bauxite livery, the layout would be similar to that shown in **Plate 19**, (diagram book, page 18C) and B R livery **Plate 20** (also page 18C).

Photograph British Rail

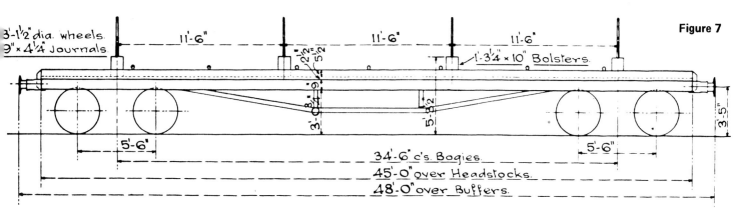

Figure 7

3'-1½" dia. wheels.
9" x 4¼" Journals.

11'-6" 11'-6" 11'-6"

1'-3¾ x 10" Bolsters.

34'-6" c's. Bogies.
45'-0" over Headstocks.
48'-0" over Buffers.

5'-6" 5'-6"

3'-5"

Scale 0 1 2 3 4 5 6 7 8 9 10 Feet.

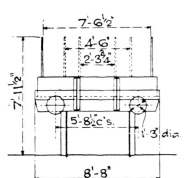

7'-6½"
4'-6"
2'-3¾"
7'-11½"
5'-8½" c's.
1'-3" dia.
8'-8"

30 TON BOGIE BOLSTER TRUCK

Figure 7

Drawing Nos. 13/3022
             13/2232

Diagram Book Page 11C

Code: BBS
Lot number: 1210
Quantity: 30
Built: Wolverton 1939
Running numbers: 720575–720604
Tare: 15 tons 9 cwt

The minimum curve that the truck will negotiate is 1 chain. All wood floor. Binding chains: 4 sets including screw couplings.

No pictures are known to exist for this diagram which was very similar to that in the diagram book, page 11B and the livery remarks for that page are applicable except that these trucks never ran in LMS grey livery.

30 TON BOGIE RAIL WAGON (ENGINEERS DEPT)
(Converted from Warwell)

Figure 8

Drawing No. 14/4460

Diagram Book Page 11D

Code: Not recorded
Lot number: 1497
Quantity: 50
Built: Derby and Wolverton 1947/8
Running numbers: 748300–748349 inclusive
Tare: 28 tons 17 cwt

Unlike the conversions allocated to diagram book, page 5B, these were for the Engineers Dept. and employed a flat deck arrangement.

The minimum curve that this wagon will negotiate is 2 chains. When two or more wagons are coupled together the minimum curve is 3 chains. Carrying capacity: 30 tons. Fitted with screw hand brake and AVB.

6'-4⅞" CRS
3'-8" CRS
7'-11¾" OVERALL
5'-3¾" RAIL-TOP OF BOLSTER
8'-0"
8'-3" MAX. WIDTH

11" x 5½" JOURNALS

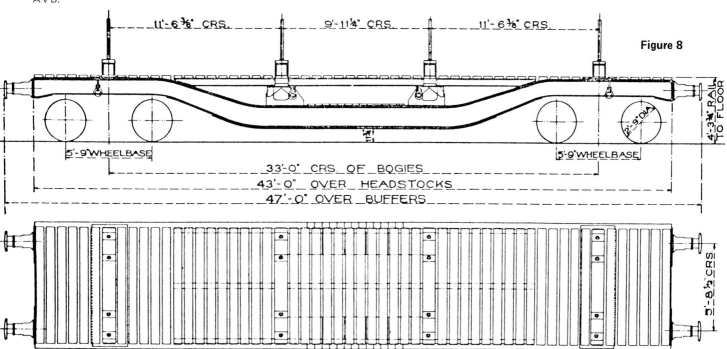

Figure 8

11'-6⅜" CRS. 9'-11¼" CRS. 11'-6⅜" CRS.

2'-9" DIA.
4'-3¾" RAIL TO FLOOR

5'-9" WHEELBASE 5'-9" WHEELBASE

33'-0" CRS OF BOGIES
43'-0" OVER HEADSTOCKS
47'-0" OVER BUFFERS

5'-8½" CRS

0 1 2 3 4 5 6 7 8 9 10
SCALE — FEET

Plate 12   An official picture of No. 748323 showing the livery when built. The legend reads 'Wire Permanent Way Stores Crewe when empty' and 'Load to be evenly distributed on bolsters, no load on floor'.

Photograph British Rail

Plate 13   A photograph of No. DM748309 in service c 1965. The body colour appears to be grey, and the running number etc. is painted on a black background.

Photograph Author's Collection

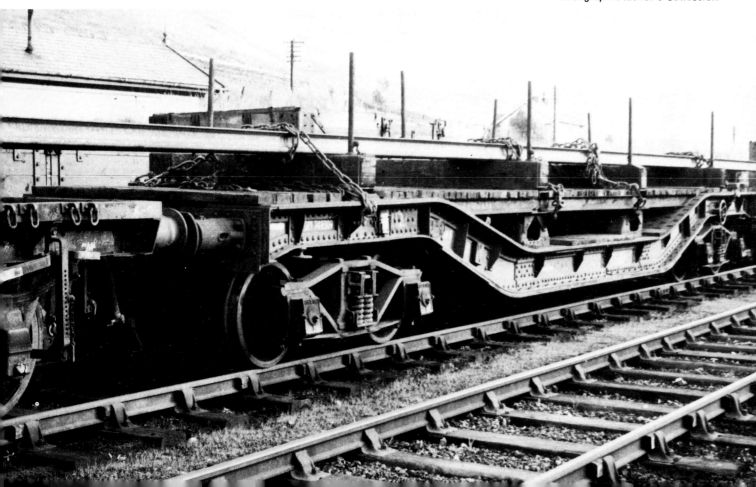

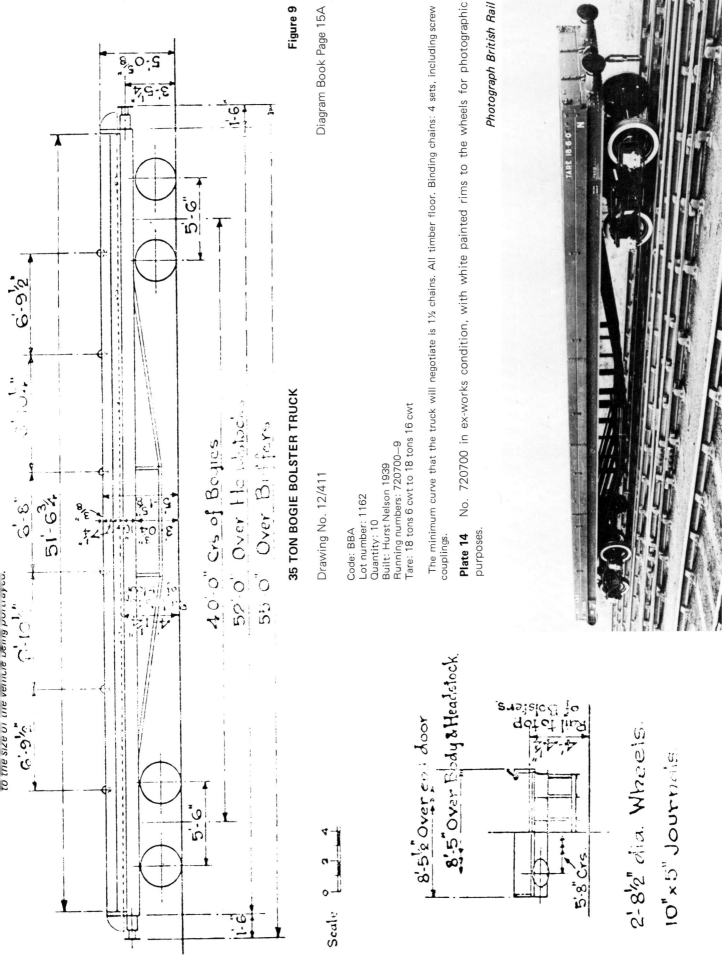

Figure 9

Diagram Book Page 15A

35 TON BOGIE BOLSTER TRUCK

Drawing No. 12/411

Code: BBA
Lot number: 1162
Quantity: 10
Built: Hurst Nelson 1939
Running numbers: 720700—9
Tare: 18 tons 6 cwt to 18 tons 16 cwt

The minimum curve that the truck will negotiate is 1½ chains. All timber floor. Binding chains: 4 sets, including screw couplings.

Plate 14 No. 720700 in ex-works condition, with white painted rims to the wheels for photographic purposes.

Photograph British Rail

Figure 10

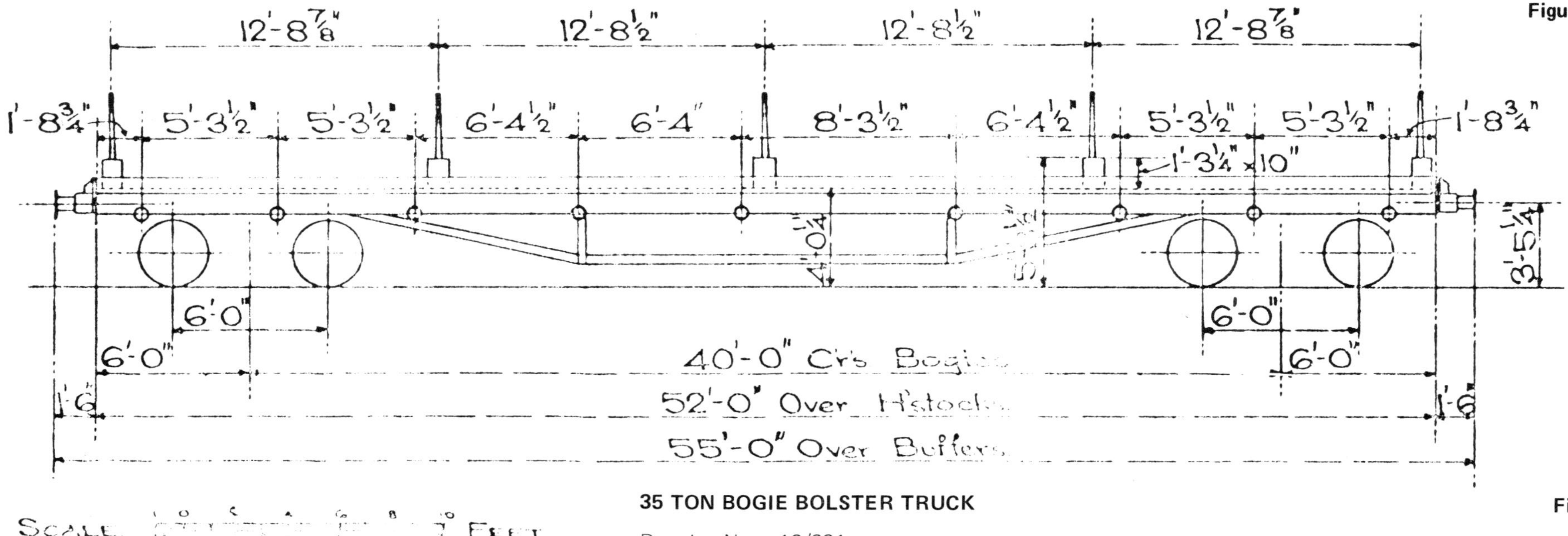

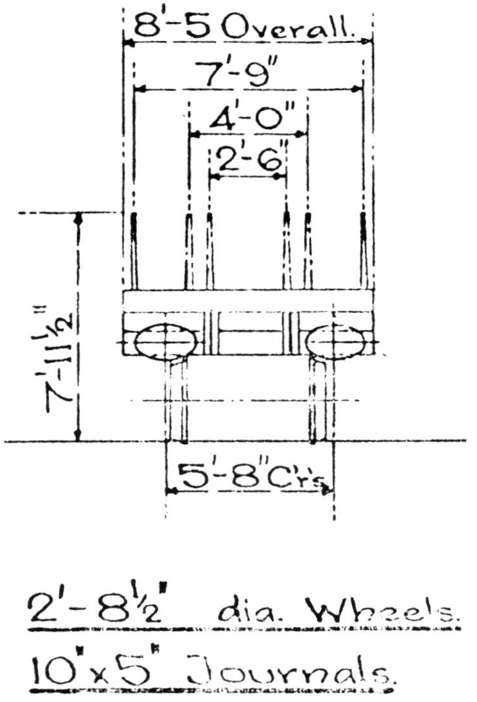

Figure 10

Diagram Book Page 15B

35 TON BOGIE BOLSTER TRUCK

Drawing Nos. 12/281
13/2077

Code: BBA
Lot number: 1211
Quantity: 20
Built: Wolverton 1940
Running numbers: 720710–29
Tare: 18 tons 13 cwt

The minimum curve that the truck will negotiate is 1½ chains. Binding chains: 4 sets, including screw couplings.

40'-0" Crs Bogie

52'-0" Over Headstocks

55'-0" Over Buffers

SCALE OF FEET

12'-8⅞" 12'-8½" 12'-8½" 12'-8½" 12'-8⅞"

5'-3½" 5'-3½" 6'-4½" 8'-3½" 6'-4" 6'-4½" 6'-4½" 5'-3½" 5'-3½"

1'-8¾"

3'-5¼"

6'-0" 6'-0" 6'-0" 6'-0" 6'-0"

1'-3¾" x 10"

8'-5 Overall
7'-9"
4'-0"
2'-6"
5'-8 Crs
7'-11½"

2'-8½" dia. Wheels

10" x 5" Journals.

Plate 15 This is No. 720717 in ex-works bauxite livery. No pictures of this vehicle in BR livery are known to the author.

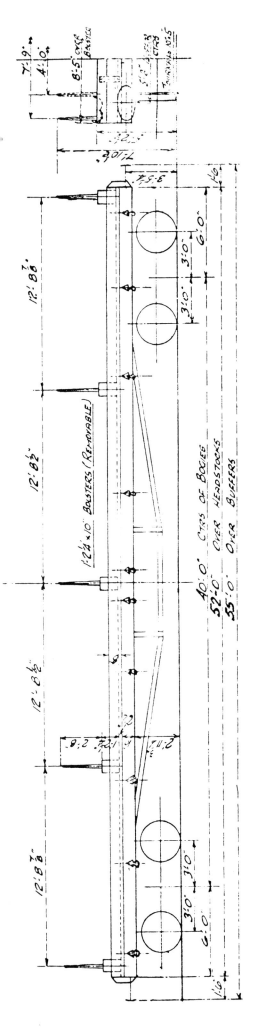

0 2 4 6 8 10 FEET

Plate 16 When photographed at Wolverton in 1936, No. 720007 was in original condition.
Photograph British Rail

40 TON BOGIE BOLSTER WAGON

Figure 11   Diagram Book Page 18A

Drawing Nos. 12/281
              13/2077

Code: BBZ
Lot number: 841
Quantity: 20
Built: Wolverton 1935
Running numbers: 720000—19
Tare: 18 tons 5 cwt

The minimum curve that the truck will negotiate is 1½ chains. Binding chains: 4 sets, complete with screw couplings.

These vehicles were similar to those on page 15B of the diagram book, except that they were originally painted in a grey body colour.

19

Figure 12

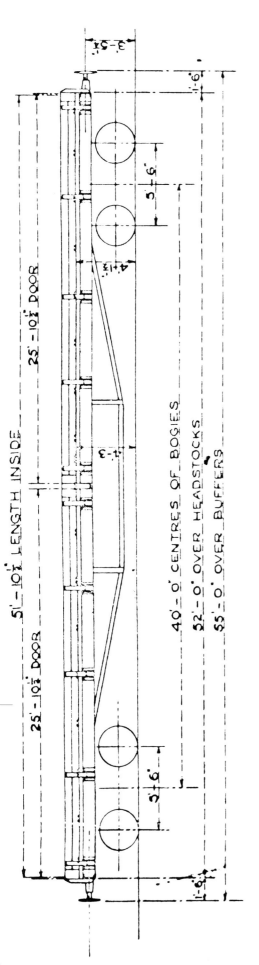

SCALE 0 1 2 3 4 5 6 7 8 9 10 FEET

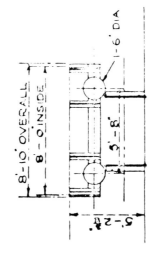

42 TON BOGIE PLATE WAGON

Drawing Nos. 14/2925
12/726

Figure 12

Diagram Book Page 18B

Code: Not recorded
Lot number: 1422; Quantity: 50; Built: Derby 1947; Running numbers 721500—721549
Lot number: 1455; Quantity: 20; Built: Derby 1947; Running numbers 721550—721569
Total quantity built: 70
Tare: 18 tons 17 cwt

The minimum curve that the truck will negotiate is 70ft. Carrying capacity: 42 tons. All wood floor. Drop sides.
This was not a bolster wagon and its original description was a bogie plate wagon. However, at least one was used as a trestle wagon, see **Plate 18**.

Plate 17 (below top) This illustrates a wagon in the original unpainted livery of 1949. The steelwork is painted and the wooden parts left bare.

Photograph British Rail

Plate 18 (below bottom) No. M721568, now coded 'Boplate E' and equipped with a trestle, is photographed at Horwich in 1965.

Photograph Author's Collection

Plate 18

Figure 13

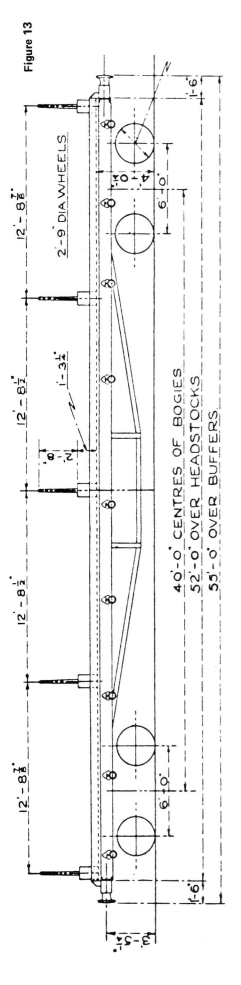

12'-8⅞"   12'-8½"   12'-8½"   12'-8⅞"   12'-8⅞"

2'-9 DIA WHEELS

40'-0' CENTRES OF BOGIES

52'-0' OVER HEADSTOCKS

55'-0' OVER BUFFERS.

SCALE   0 1 2 3 4 5 6 7 8 9 10   FEET

42 TON BOGIE BOLSTER TRUCK

Figure 13   Diagram Book Page 18C

Drawing Nos. 13/2077A
12/281G

Code: Not recorded
Lot number: 1513
Quantity: 66
Built: Derby 1948
Running numbers: 720020–720085 inclusive
Tare: 18 tons 12 cwt

The minimum curve that this truck will negotiate is 1½ chains. Binding chains: 4 sets including screw couplings.

Plate 19 (below)   No. 720026 is shown in final LMS bauxite livery. This picture should be compared with **Plate 20.**

The first of these trucks entered traffic in LMS bauxite livery, but a photograph exists to show M720060 in BR condition **(Plate 20)** and is probably the first vehicle so painted. Carrying capacity: 42 tons. All timber floor. Binding chains: 1½ chains. Carrying capacity: 42 tons. All timber floor. The lettering is central on the body side.

Photograph British Rail

10" x 5" JOURNALS.

2'·0" x 1'·2" BUFFERS.

Plate 20 (above) By this time the railways were nationalized and the difference in livery style should be noted. The lettering is at the bottom of the side, and the bolsters are unpainted.

Photograph British Rail

Plate 21 (below) This picture, taken at Coalville in 1964, has been included to illustrate the condition, after 16 years in traffic, of a BR wagon.

Photograph Author's Collection

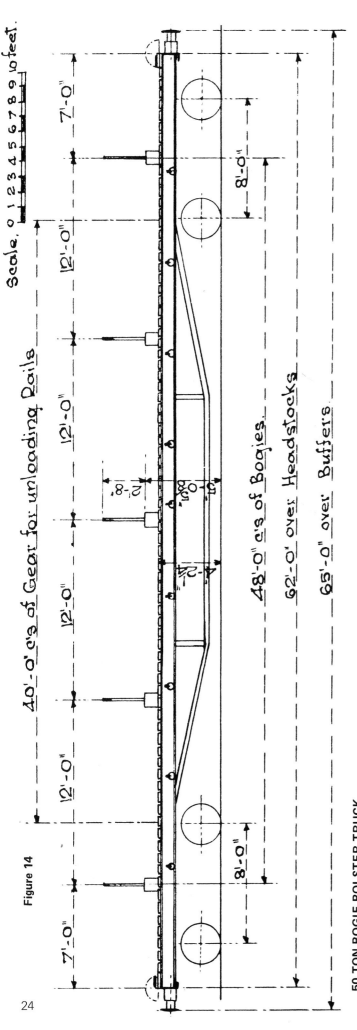

Scale. 0 1 2 3 4 5 6 7 8 9 10 feet.

Figure 14

40'-0" c's of Gear for unloading Rails

7'-0" | 12'-0" | 12'-0" | 12'-0" | 12'-0" | 7'-0"

8'-0"

2'-8'

8'-0"

48'-0" c's of Bogies.

62'-0" over Headstocks

65'-0" over Buffers

50 TON BOGIE BOLSTER TRUCK

Figure 14   Diagram Book Page 19A

Drawing No. 11/188

Code: BORAIL BBP (later coded BORAIL G by BR)
Lot number: 420
Quantity: 12
Built: Derby 1929
Running numbers: 168908–168919
Tare: 25 tons 5 cwt

The minimum curve that the truck will negotiate is 2½ chains. All wood floor. Binding chains: 4 sets, complete with screw couplings.

These vehicles were the first of a series of very similar 50 ton trucks built between 1929 and 1942 and allocated to diagram book pages 19A to 19G. The various slight differences will be seen on the diagram reproduced as **Figures 14 to 20.**

Plate 22   No. 168911, is pictured here, in original condition. Reference to **Plates 24, 26 & 27** should be made which will indicate LMS bauxite and BR livery styles.

Photograph British Rail

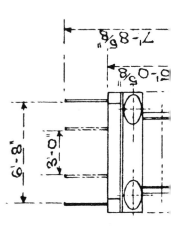

7'-8⅝"

10'-0⅝"

6'-8"

3'-0"

Figure 15 (Left diagram — side elevation)

7'-0" 12'-0" 12'-0" 12'-0" 12'-0" 7'-0"

8'-0"

8'-0"

2'-8"

5'-3½"

48'-0" c's of Bogies.

62'-0" over Headstocks.

65'-0" over Buffers.

Scale. 0 1 2 3 4 5 6 7 8 9 10 feet.

Figure 15

Diagram Book Page 19B

50 TON BOGIE BOLSTER TRUCK

Drawing No. 11/281B

Code: BBP (later coded BORAIL MB by British Rail)
Lot number: 988; Quantity: 8; Built: Fairfield 1936/7; Running numbers: 720900—7
Lot number: 1138; Quantity: 30; Built: Fairfield 1939; Running numbers: 720908—37
Total quantity built: 38
Tare: 24 tons 10 cwt

The minimum curve that the truck will negotiate is 2½ chains. All wood floor. Binding chains: 4 sets, complete with screw couplings. Regrettably, no pictures in LMS ownership are known to exist so the author cannot be certain if they (lot 988) entered traffic in grey or bauxite livery. However, two pictures in BR ownership have been included.

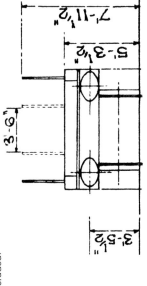

(End elevation dimensions)

7'-11½"

5'-3½"

3'-6"

3'-5½"

These photographs illustrate No. M721046 unloaded, in 1964, and No. M720918 loaded at Crewe in 1970. **Plate 23** in particular, shows the truss rods beneath the vehicle.

Plates 23 & 24

Photographs Author's Collection

Figure 16

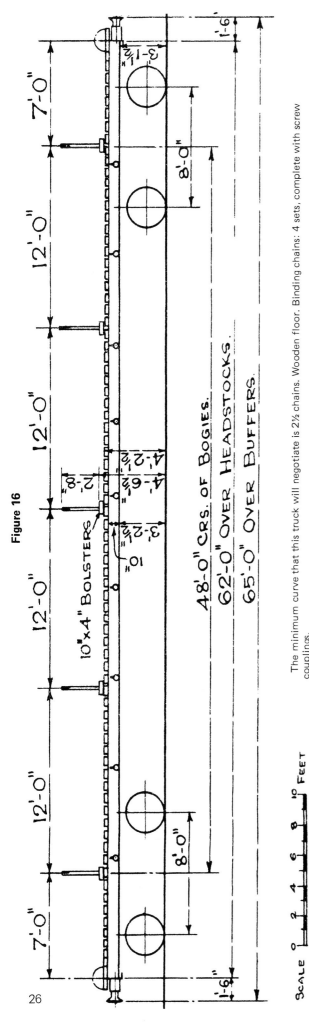

10"×4" BOLSTERS.

48'-0" CRS. OF BOGIES.

62'-0" OVER HEADSTOCKS.

65'-0" OVER BUFFERS.

SCALE 0 2 4 6 8 10 FEET

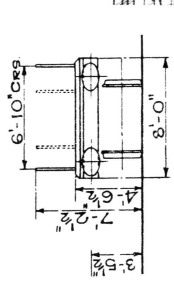

The minimum curve that this truck will negotiate is 2½ chains. Wooden floor. Binding chains: 4 sets, complete with screw couplings.

No official photographs appear to have been taken, but **Plate 25** illustrates No. DM748011 at Crewe in 1964. When built, they could have been in bauxite livery, although the first two could possibly have entered traffic painted in grey livery.

50 TON BOGIE RAIL WAGON (ENGINEERS DEPT)   **Figure 16**

Drawing Nos. 11/294
14/2945

Diagram Book Page 19C

Code: Not recorded
Lot number: 1080; Quantity: 2; Built: Wolverton
1937; Running numbers: 748000/1
Lot number: 1146; Quantity: 13; Built: Wolverton
1938/9; Running numbers: 748002–14
Total quantity built: 15
Tare: 23 tons 10 cwt

26

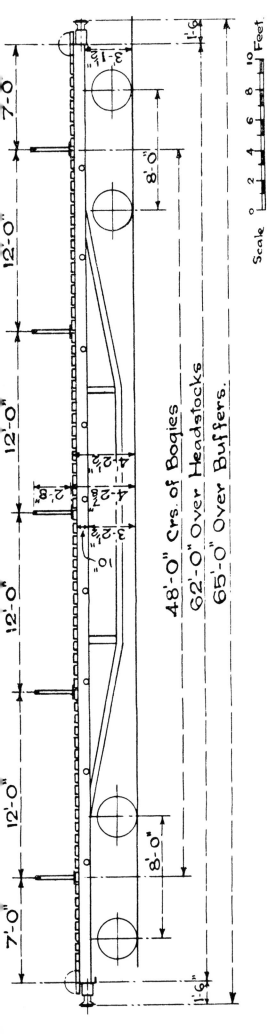

48'-0" Crs. of Bogies

62'-0" Over Headstocks

65'-0" Over Buffers.

Scale

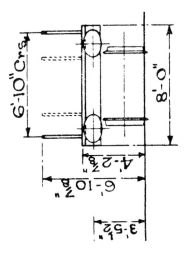

6'-10" Crs.

The author has no knowledge of any photographs of these vehicles, however, when first built, they would have entered traffic in the bauxite livery. **Plate 26** shows a similar vehicle in this style of painting.

Photograph Author's Collection

50 TON BOGIE RAIL WAGON (ENGINEERS DEPT)

Figure 17

Diagram Book Page 19D

Drawing Nos. 11/325
             14/2945A

Code: Not recorded
Lot number: 1159
Quantity: 25
Built: Wolverton 1939
Running numbers: 748015—39
Tare: 23 tons 5 cwt

The minimum curve that the truck will negotiate is 2½ chains. Wooden floor. Binding chains: 4 sets, complete with screw couplings.

Figure 17A This shows the method of loading and securing 50 tons of rails on a BBP.

27

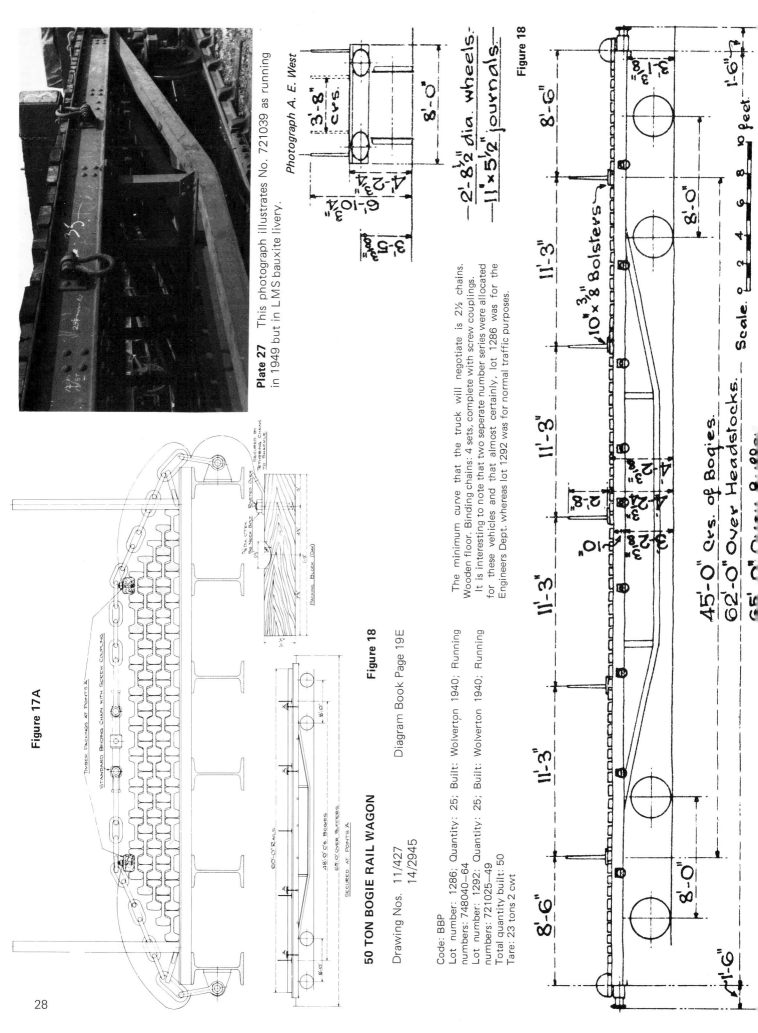

Figure 17A

Figure 18

50 TON BOGIE RAIL WAGON

Diagram Book Page 19E

Drawing Nos. 11/427
14/2945

Code: BBP
Lot number: 1286; Quantity: 25; Built: Wolverton 1940; Running numbers: 748040–64
Lot number: 1292; Quantity: 25; Built: Wolverton 1940; Running numbers: 721025–49
Total quantity built: 50
Tare: 23 tons 2 cwt

The minimum curve that the truck will negotiate is 2½ chains. Wooden floor. Binding chains: 4 sets, complete with screw couplings. It is interesting to note that two separate number series were allocated for these vehicles and that almost certainly, lot 1286 was for the Engineers Dept. whereas lot 1292 was for normal traffic purposes.

Plate 27 This photograph illustrates No. 721039 as running in 1949 but in LMS bauxite livery.

Photograph A. E. West

Figure 18

2'-8½" dia. wheels.
11" x 5½" journals.

Scale. 0 2 4 6 8 10 feet.

45'-0" Crs. of Bogies.
62'-0" Over Headstocks.
65'-0" Over Buffers.

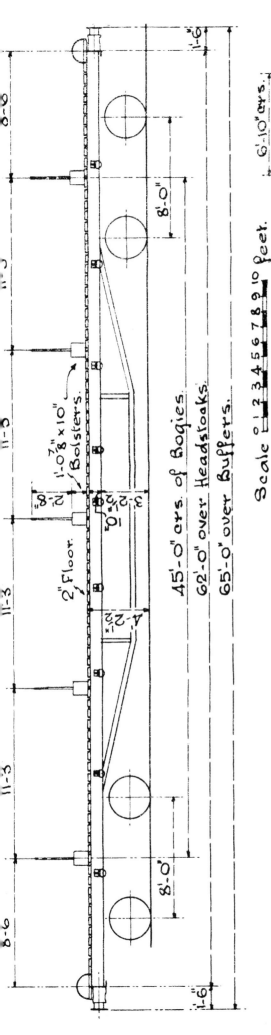

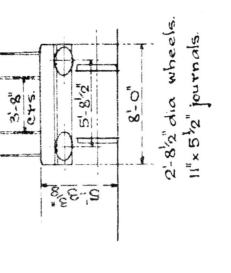

2'-8½" dia wheels.
11" x 5½" journals.

45'-0" crs. of Bogies.
62'-0" over Headstocks.
65'-0" over Buffers.

Scale 0 1 2 3 4 5 6 7 8 9 10 Feet.

50 TON BOGIE BOLSTER TRUCK

Figure 19

Drawing Nos. 11/438   Diagram Book Page 19F
14/2945

Code: BBP (later coded BORAIL MD by British Rail)
Lot number: 1293
Quantity: 25
Built: Wolverton 1941
Running numbers: 720938—62
Tare: 24 tons 18 cwt

Produced during wartime, these vehicles were not officially photographed and therefore no ex-works pictures are available. However, **Plate 28** illustrates No. M720941, in 1964, at Gloucester.

Photograph Author's Collection

The minimum curve that the truck will negotiate is 2½ chains. Wooden floor. Binding chains: 4 sets, complete with screw couplings.

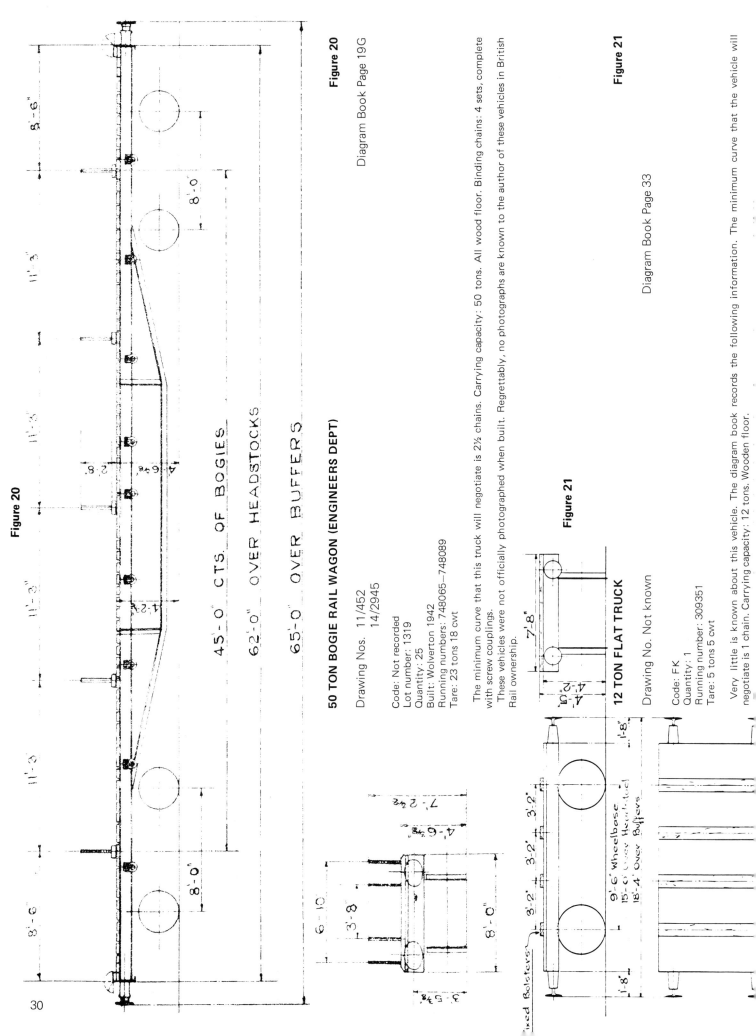

Figure 20

50 TON BOGIE RAIL WAGON (ENGINEERS DEPT)

Diagram Book Page 19G

Drawing Nos. 11/452
14/2945

Code: Not recorded
Lot number: 1319
Quantity: 25
Built: Wolverton 1942
Running numbers: 748065–748089
Tare: 23 tons 18 cwt

The minimum curve that this truck will negotiate is 2½ chains. Carrying capacity: 50 tons. All wood floor. Binding chains: 4 sets, complete with screw couplings.

These vehicles were not officially photographed when built. Regrettably, no photographs are known to the author of these vehicles in British Rail ownership.

Figure 21

12 TON FLAT TRUCK

Diagram Book Page 33

Drawing No. Not known

Code: FK
Quantity: 1
Running number: 309351
Tare: 5 tons 5 cwt

Very little is known about this vehicle. The diagram book records the following information. The minimum curve that the vehicle will negotiate is 1 chain. Carrying capacity: 12 tons. Wooden floor.

Figure 22

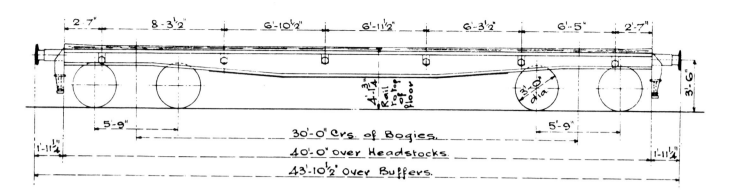

WARFLAT TRUCK FVF

Drawing No. Not known

Figure 22

Diagram Book Page 40A

Code: Not recorded
Quantity: 17
Running numbers: 66—68, 70/1, 73—6, 79, 82, 85—88 and 218*
Tare: 18 tons 3 cwt

The diagram contains the following information. The minimum curve that the truck will negotiate is 120ft. Carrying capacity: 45 tons over 30ft., 40 tons over 10ft. 6in. at centre. *Fully fitted with Westinghouse brake and hand brake, the remainder having hand brake and Westinghouse through pipe.

The author has no information other than that printed on the diagram and reproduced here. Whether these were built during World War I for the Ministry of Supply or another Government body, cannot be ascertained, but the basic measurements are identical to diagram book page 19. This shows a 40 ton bogie bolster truck, which was supposed to be an ex-Midland Railway vehicle and was possibly Government-built during World War I and then taken over by the Midland Railway. This is the more likely explanation but regrettably no confirmed photographs are known to the author.

Figure 23

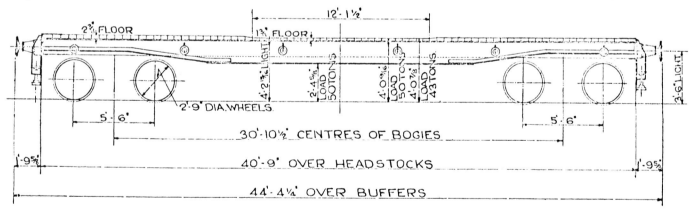

WARFLAT TRUCK USA FLAT

Drawing No. Not known

Figure 23

Diagram Book Page 40B

Code: Not recorded
Quantity: 50
Running numbers: 34800—34849 inclusive (LMS allocation 34815—34839 inclusive)
Tare: 15 tons 15 cwt

The minimum curve that the truck will negotiate is 120ft. Carrying capacity: 50 tons. Wood floor. AVB, Westinghouse and hand screw brake.

Even less is known about diagram book page 40B than page 40A, and the sum total is printed with the diagram. Unfortunately, no photographs appear to exist to illustrate these vehicles.

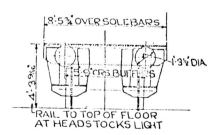

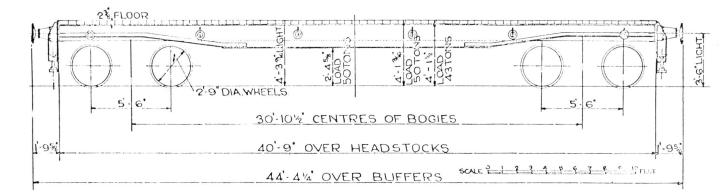

Figure 24

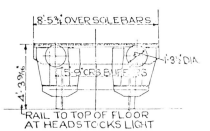

CASE TRUCK USA CASE

Figure 24

Drawing No. Not known

Diagram Book Page 40C

Code: Not recorded
Tare: 15 tons 15 cwt

The minimum curve that the truck will negotiate is 120 ft. Carrying capacity: 50 tons. Wood floor. A V B, Westinghouse and hand screw brake.

On diagram book page 40B, the quantity and running numbers were recorded, but this diagram is less illuminating and even this information is not available. Again, no photographs are known to exist to illustrate these vehicles.

Plate 29

Plate 30

Figure 25

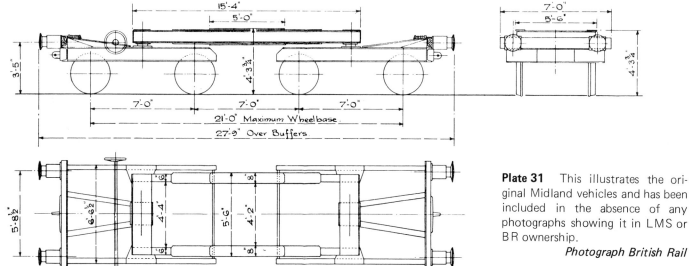

Plate 31 This illustrates the original Midland vehicles and has been included in the absence of any photographs showing it in LMS or BR ownership.

Photograph British Rail

35 TON GUN TRUCK

Figure 25

Diagram Book Page 41A

Code: GUNSET MB (later coded EB by British Rail)
Quantity: 1
Running number: 9696 (muzzle portion)
Tare: 10 tons 19 cwt 1 qtr

The minimum curve that the trolley will negotiate is 66 ft. Carrying capacity: 35 tons. The diagram contains a note to the effect that the vehicle was handed to the E/NE Region on 3rd February 1958.

This single vehicle was adapted from an ex-Midland Railway gunset built in 1912 and described in an *Illustrated History of Midland Wagons, Volume Two,* Chapter 10, published by O.P.C.

Plates 29 & 30 (left) Not withstanding the uncertainty in the author's mind about these vehicles in diagram book, pages 19, 40A, 40B and 40C, these two pictures have been included to indicate what was built at Derby in 1917. This information can be seen on the works plate on both vehicles. **Plate 29** shows No. 296959 in LMS grey livery. The code is BBZ and an unreadable plate, which resembles a building plate, can be seen on the solebar just to the left of the 'M'. This does not make a great deal of sense owing to the fact that a further plate states 'LMS built 1917'. In truth, it was probably constructed at Leeds Forge or at a similar works. The date of this picture is probably c 1924 and should be compared with **Plate 30** which shows No. 181992 carrying a January 1942 paint date and running in LMS bauxite livery.

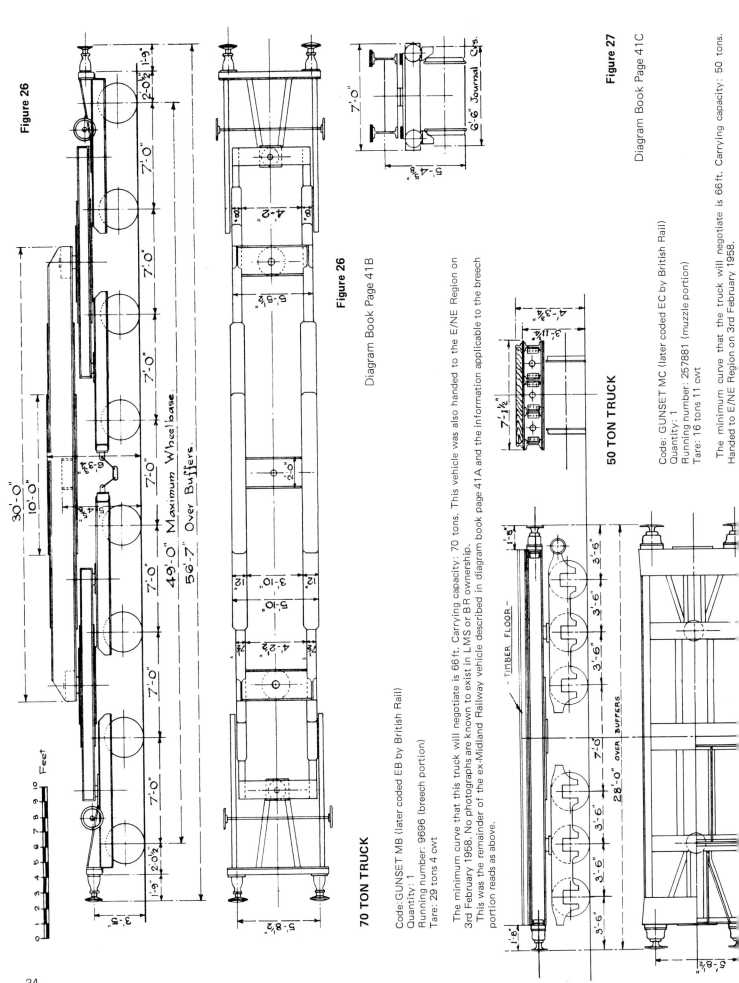

Figure 26

Feet

Figure 26

Diagram Book Page 41B

70 TON TRUCK

Code: GUNSET MB (later coded EB by British Rail)
Quantity: 1
Running number: 9696 (breech portion)
Tare: 29 tons 4 cwt

The minimum curve that this truck will negotiate is 66 ft. Carrying capacity: 70 tons. This vehicle was also handed to the E/NE Region on 3rd February 1958. No photographs are known to exist in LMS or BR ownership.
This was the remainder of the ex-Midland Railway vehicle described in diagram book page 41A and the information applicable to the breech portion reads as above.

Figure 27

Diagram Book Page 41C

50 TON TRUCK

Code: GUNSET MC (later coded EC by British Rail)
Quantity: 1
Running number: 257881 (muzzle portion)
Tare: 16 tons 11 cwt

The minimum curve that the truck will negotiate is 66 ft. Carrying capacity: 50 tons. Handed to E/NE Region on 3rd February 1958.

- TIMBER FLOOR -

34

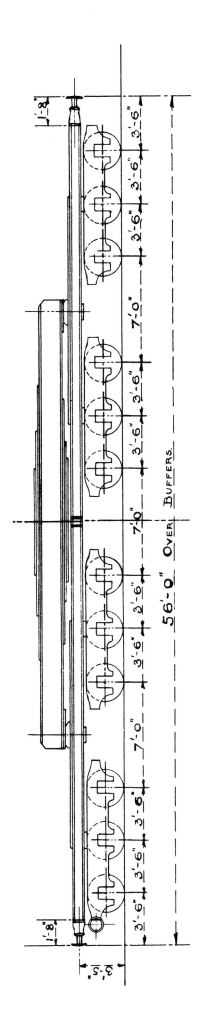

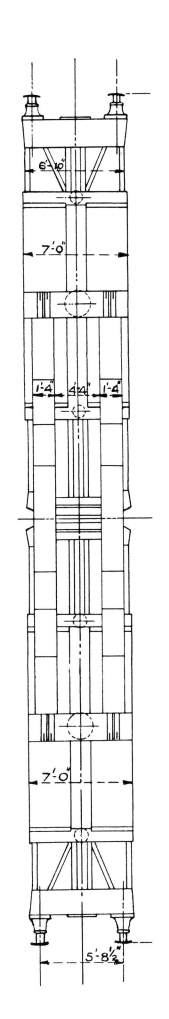

56'-0" OVER BUFFERS.

107 TON TRUCK

Figure 28

Diagram Book Page 41D

Code: GUNSET M (later coded EC by British Rail)

This forms the rest of the vehicle described in diagram book page 41C and the details are identical except that the carrying capacity was 107 tons and the tare weight 39 tons. It was transferred to the E/NE Region on 3rd February 1958.

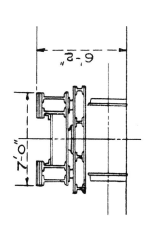

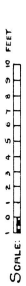

SCALE: 0 1 2 3 4 5 6 7 8 9 10 FEET

Drawing No. 6022   Diagram Book Page 52

Code: U10 (later coded LOWMAC MH by British Rail)
Lot number: 150; Quantity: 11; Built: Derby 1925
Lot number: 354; Quantity: 15; Built: Derby 1928
Lot number: 429; Quantity: 5; Built: Derby 1929
Running numbers: 18866, 19890, 23388, 30554, 30564, 34797, 50477, 77988, 80675, 96080, 117588, 178614, 178841, 179315, 189986–90, 294262, 297160, 297162, 300009/17/20/22/26/29/34/82
Total quantity built: 31
Tare: 10 tons 17 cwt (with baulks)
Tare: 8 tons 17 cwt (without baulks)

The minimum curve that the truck will negotiate is 1½ chains. All wood floor. Binding chains to be fitted if required.

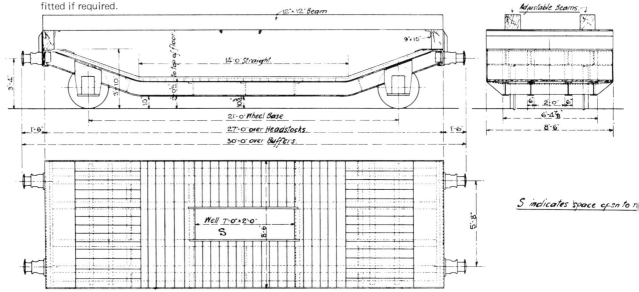

Plate 32   No. 19890 is shown here in ex-works condition. The arrangement of the floor can clearly be seen.

Photograph British Rail

Plate 33   No. M23388 of lot 150, in service at Rugby, in 1965. Note that the ends have been removed and 'the hole' filled in.

Photograph Author's Collection

Figure 30

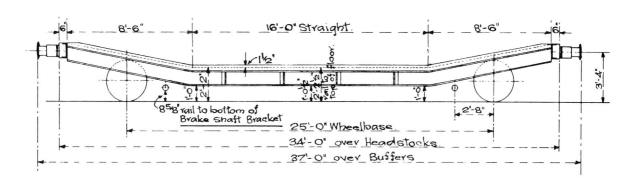

Scale 0 1 2 3 4 5 6 7 8 9 10 feet

20 TON IMPLEMENT TRUCK

Figure 30

Drawing No. 12/171

Diagram Book Page 52A

Code: U10 (later coded MJ by British Rail)
Lot number: 606; Quantity: 5; Built: Derby 1931; Running numbers: 299785—299789
Lot number: 607; Quantity: 5; Built: Derby 1931; Running numbers: 299789—299794
Lot number: 1018; Quantity: 10; Built R & W Maclenan 1937; Running numbers: 70060—9
Total quantity built: 20
Tare: 10 tons

   The minimum curve that this truck will negotiate is 2 chains. All wood floor. Binding chains: 2 sets, including screw couplings.

2'-8½" dia. wheels.

10" x 5" journals.

Plate 34   No. 299789, is pictured here, in original condition and this is the only photograph of this vehicle known to the author.

Photograph British Rail

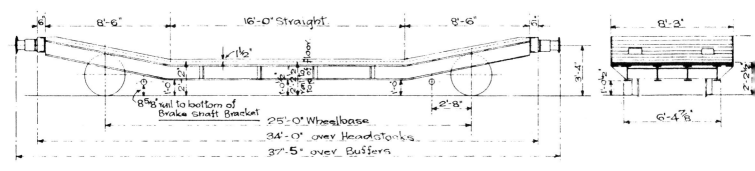

Scale 0 1 2 3 4 5 6 7 8 9 10 feet

20 TON IMPLEMENT TRUCK

Figure 31

Drawing No. 12/468

Diagram Book Page 52B

Code: U10 (later coded LOWMAC MK by British Rail)
Lot number: 1212
Quantity: 10
Built: Wolverton 1940
Running numbers: 700610—19
Tare: 10 tons 16 cwt

The minimum curve that the truck will negotiate is 2 chains. All wood floor. Binding chains: 2 sets, including screw couplings. Fully fitted and screw couplings. These vehicles never ran in LMS grey livery.

Plate 35 No. 700610 is pictured here in original condition.

Photograph British Rail

Plate 36 This shows the same vehicle as pictured in **Plate 35** at Coalville in 1964. It has been included to illustrate the method of construction and also shows the B R livery.

Photograph Author's Collection

Plates 37 & 38 These pictures show No. 700612 and another lowmac, and have been included to illustrate the top of these vehicles when empty. They were photographed at Wolverton in 1965.

Photographs Author's Collection

Drawing No. 15/721N   Diagram Book Page 54A

Code: U1R (later coded LOWMAC MO by British Rail)
Lot number: 1342
Quantity: 30
Built: LNER
Running numbers: 700700—700729
Tare: 13 tons 12 cwt

   The minimum curve that the truck will negotiate is 2 chains. Carrying capacity: 25 tons. Vacuum brake, independent RH lever brake at each side of truck. 4 binding chains. 16 lashing rings (12 on solebars, 4 on headstocks)
   These final 30 implement trucks were built for the LMS by the L N E R and no official ex-works photographs appear to have been taken. All the recorded details were taken from the diagram and two photographs, showing the vehicles in B R condition, have been selected to illustrate them.

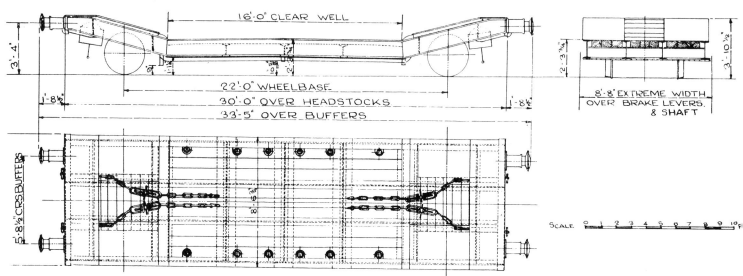

Plate 39   No. M700270 is pictured at Wolverton in 1965, whilst **Plate 40 (top right)** is a close up of one end of this vehicle.

Photographs Author's Collection

12 TON TRACTION TRUCK

Plate 40

Diagram Book Page 59

This was really a Midland Railway diagram and as such is illustrated in an ***Illustrated History of Midland Wagons, Volume Two,*** Chapter 9, published by OPC. Forty vehicles numbered 189431–70 were built at Wolverton, in 1929, to lot 408.

Plate 41   No. 189460 is photographed in December 1939 and appears to be in bauxite livery, but it is not possible to read the painting date.

Photograph A. E. West

Figure 33

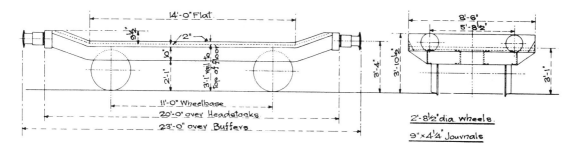

14'-0" Flat

2"

11'-0" Wheelbase
20'-0" over Headstocks
23'-0" over Buffers

2'-1"

3'-1" rail to top of floor

3'-4"

3'-10½"

8'-6"
5'-8½"

3'-1"

2'-8½' dia wheels.
9" × 4¼' Journals

Scale 0 1 2 3 4 5 6 7 8 9 10 feet

12 TON TRACTION TRUCK

Figure 33

Drawing No. 13/1547

Diagram Book Page 59A

Code: TRK (later coded HYMAC MD by British Rail)
Lot number: 604; Quantity: 10; Built: 1931; Running numbers: 299856—65
Lot number: 605; Quantity: 10; Built: 1931; Running numbers: 299866—75
Lot number: 827; Quantity: 20; Built: 1935; Running numbers: 700400—19
Lot number: 925; Quantity: 10; Built: 1936; Running numbers: 700420—29
Lot number: 1028; Quantity: 25; Built: 1937; Running numbers: 700430—54
Total quantity built: 75
Tare: 6 tons 8 cwt

The minimum curve that the truck will negotiate is 1 chain. All wood floor.
Three pictures have been chosen to illustrate these vehicles in different livery styles.

Plate 42

Plate 43

Plate 44 (above)   This illustrates No. 700426, of the 1937 batch, in bauxite livery, as running, with spoked wheels, in 1940. This picture is most useful inasmuch as it illustrates one way of using these vehicles in traffic and the method of roping a load for transit.

Photograph A. E. West

Plate 42 (bottom left)   No. 299872 of the 1931 lot in grey livery, running with disc wheels.

Photograph British Rail

Plate 43 (top)   No. 700419 of lot 827 seen in grey with a different livery style when compared with that of **Plate 42**.

Photograph British Rail

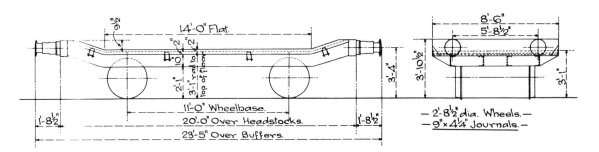

12 TON TRACTION TRUCK

Figure 34

Drawing No. 13/3018

Diagram Book Page 59B

Scale 0 1 2 3 4 5 6 7 8 9 10 Feet.

Code: TRK (later coded HYMAC ME by British Rail)
Lot number: 1202
Quantity: 10
Built: Derby 1939
Running numbers: 706455—64
Tare: 7 tons 3 cwt

The minimum curve that the truck will negotiate is 1 chain. All wood floor. Fully fitted.

Regrettably, no photographs are known to exist which illustrate these vehicles, whose livery condition, when built, would have been similar to that illustrated in **Plate 44.**

Scale 0 1 2 3 4 5 6 7 8 9 10 feet

12 TON DEEP CASE TRUCK

Figure 35

Figure 3

Drawing No. 13/1069

Diagram Book Page 66A

Code: DCK (later coded CASE ME by British Rail)
Tare: 9 tons 9 cwt

The minimum curve that this truck will negotiate is 1½ chains. Wood and metal floor. 'Assent of Southern Railway is required before loading to their line. Consult the Chief Goods Managers Dept. before loading to private sidings on North Stafford Section'.

The history of these vehicles is rather complicated and an attempt to tell the whole story, which starts in the Midland Railway period, is made in an *Illustrated History of Midland Wagons, Volume Two,* Chapter 9, published by O.P.C. However, the LMS obtained four vehicles in 1928 built by Pickering to lot 367 and they carried the running numbers 117288—91. These four vehicles were a continuation of previous Midland Railway practice.

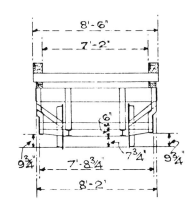

Figure 34

Plate 45 This shows No. 117291 in original condition and livery.
Photograph British Rail

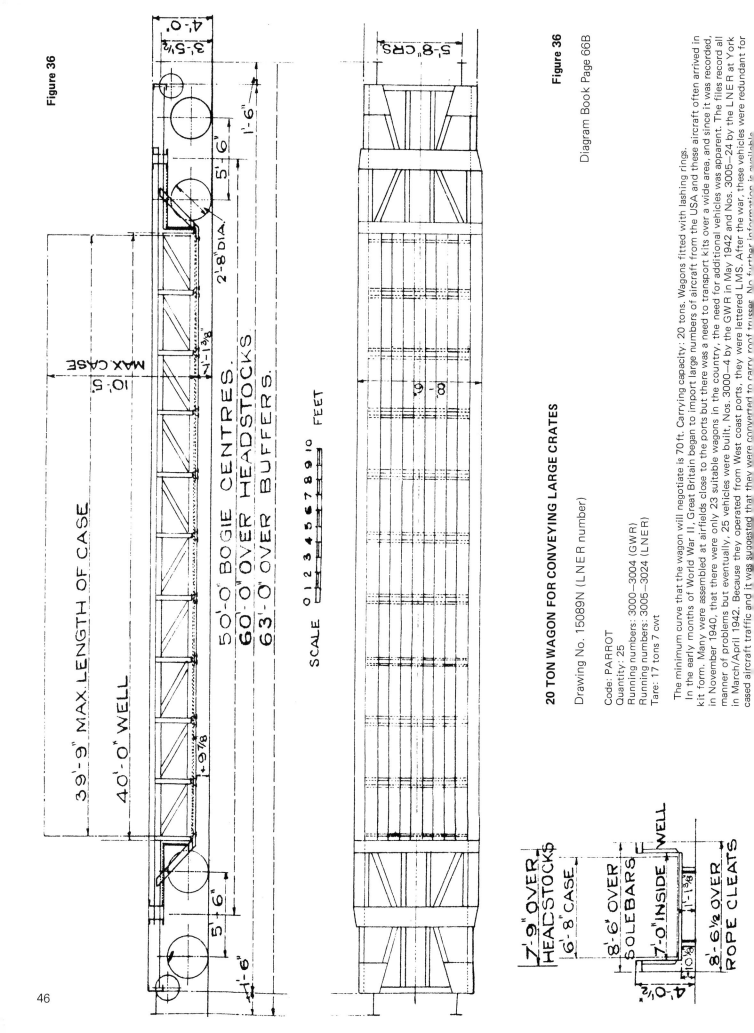

Figure 36

Figure 36

SCALE 0 1 2 3 4 5 6 7 8 9 10 FEET

39'-9" MAX. LENGTH OF CASE

40'-0" WELL

50'-0" BOGIE CENTRES.
60'-0" OVER HEADSTOCKS.
63'-0" OVER BUFFERS.

MAX. CASE 10'-5"

4'-0"

3'-5½"

1'-6"

5'-6"

2'-8" DIA.

1'-1⅜"

5'-6"

1'-6"

1'-⅝"

5'-8" CRS.

8'-6"

7'-9" OVER HEADSTOCKS

6'-8" CASE

8'-6" OVER SOLEBARS

7'-0" INSIDE WELL

1'-1⅜"

10⅝"

4'-0½"

8'-6½" OVER ROPE CLEATS

Diagram Book Page 66B

20 TON WAGON FOR CONVEYING LARGE CRATES

Drawing No. 15089N (LNER number)

Code: PARROT
Quantity: 25
Running numbers: 3000–3004 (GWR)
Running numbers: 3005–3024 (LNER)
Tare: 17 tons 7 cwt

The minimum curve that the wagon will negotiate is 70 ft. Carrying capacity: 20 tons. Wagons fitted with lashing rings.
In the early months of World War II, Great Britain began to import large numbers of aircraft from the USA and these aircraft often arrived in kit form. Many were assembled at airfields close to the ports but there was a need to transport kits over a wide area, and since it was recorded, in November 1940, that there were only 23 suitable wagons in the country, the need for additional vehicles was apparent. The files record all manner of problems but eventually, 25 vehicles were built, Nos. 3000–4 by the GWR in May 1942 and Nos. 3005–24 by the LNER at York in March/April 1942. Because they operated from West coast ports, they were lettered LMS. After the war, these vehicles were redundant for cased aircraft traffic and it was suggested that they were converted to carry roof trusses. No further information is available

46

Plate 46 This illustrates an example of an LNER built vehicle. These were of welded construction, the GWR vehicles were rivetted.

Photograph British Rail

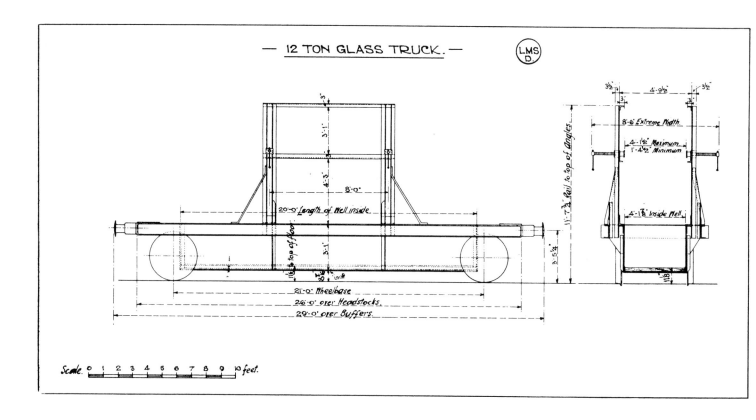

12 TON GLASS TRUCK

Figure 37

Drawing No. 6239

Diagram Book Page 75

Code: GLK (later coded GLASS MD by British Rail)
Lot number: 224; Quantity: 2; Built: Derby 1926; Running numbers: 200064 and 202918
Lot number: 353; Quantity: 8; Built: Derby 1928; Running numbers: 206320, 206935, 212187, 221096, 258391, 268124, 268127 and 355323
Lot number: 409; Quantity: 30; Built: Wolverton 1928; Running numbers: 168876—168905
Lot number: 1017; Quantity: 10; Built: G. R. Turner 1937; Running numbers: 700800—9
Lot number: 1286; Quantity: 10; Built: Derby 1940; Running numbers: 700810—19
Lot number: 1423; Quantity: 6; Built: Derby 1947; Running numbers: 700820—5
Total quantity built: 66
Tare: 8 tons 3 cwt

The minimum curve that the truck will negotiate is 1½ chains. All wood floor in well.
The LMS only issued one diagram for their glass trucks, but fortunately the illustrations enable readers to see the livery changes which took place over the years.

Plate 47 (above right)   This illustrates No. 268127 which was built in 1926, and shows it in original LMS condition.
Photograph British Rail

Plate 48 (below right)   This shows No. 700800 as built by G. R. Turner in 1937. Note the grey body colour, but the livery style is that normally associated with the later bauxite body colour.

Photograph British Rail

Plate 49

Plate 50

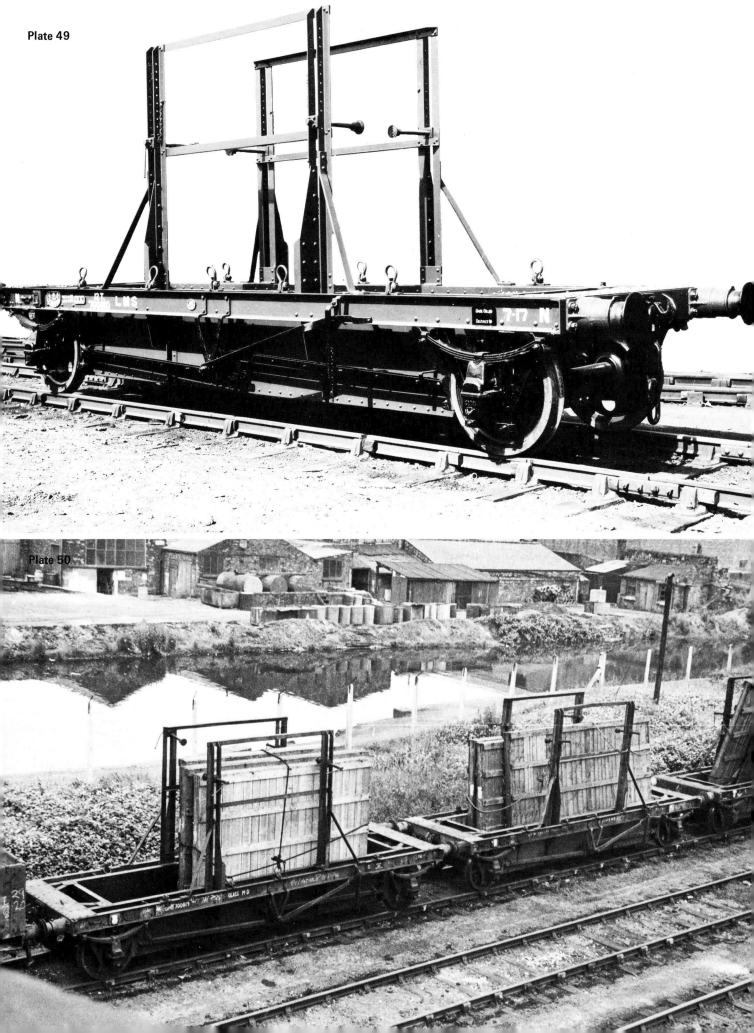

51 This picture of No. M700824 [has b]een included to illustrate the interior [of th]e well. The method of holding the [crat]es steady is clearly visible.

Photograph J. Johnson

12 TON FOUR WHEELED TROLLEY   Figure 38

Drawing No. 13/1070   Diagram Book Page 85A

Code: TYK (later coded FLATROL MA by British Rail)
Lot number: 352
Quantity: 3
Built: Derby 1928
Running numbers: 233925/6 and 266112
Tare: 9 tons 4 cwt (with baulks)
Tare: 7 tons 17 cwt (without baulks)

The minimum curve that the trolley will negotiate is 1½ chains. Wood and metal floor. Binding chains: 2 sets, with screw couplings.

These three vehicles were subtitled 'Chemical Pan' and were the only 12 ton trolleys built by the LMS. **(Photographs are on the next page)**

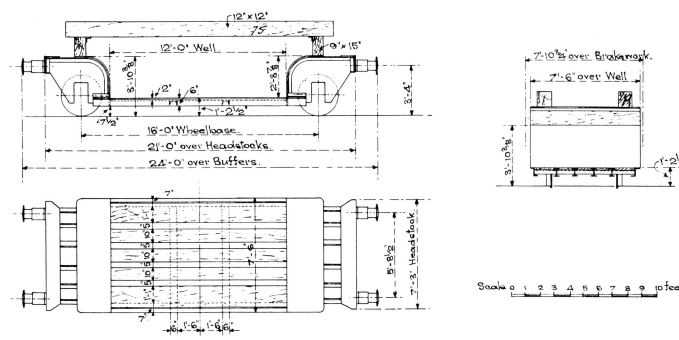

Plate 49 (top left)   No. 700810, showing the final LMS style bauxite livery. The last 16 vehicles built would have entered traffic in this style.

Photograph British Rail

Plate 50 (bottom left)   This picture, taken at St. Helens in 1964, shows three vehicles as part of a train, and clearly illustrates the method of loading the crates. Truck No. M700819 is nearest the camera.

Photograph Author's Collection   51

Plate 52   Vehicle No. 233925, pictured prior to entering traffic, is seen in grey livery.

Photograph British Rail

Plate 53   This illustrates all three vehicles in traffic as part of a special train conveying a load of steelwork. The other vehicles shown are glass wagons, including LMS standard designs. The total train comprised three trolleys and three glass wagons.

Photograph British Rail

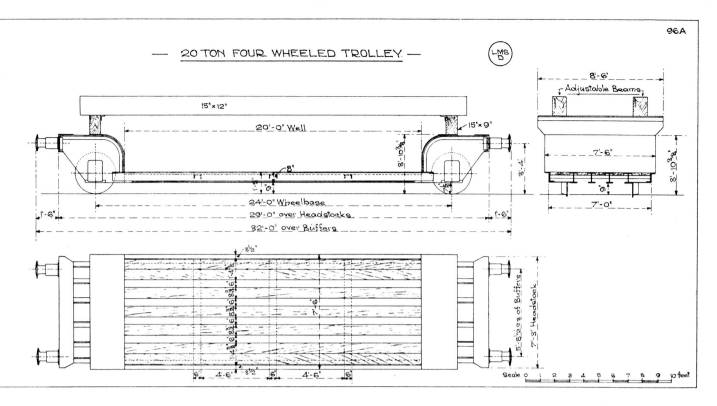

— 20 TON FOUR WHEELED TROLLEY —

20 TON FOUR WHEELED TROLLEY

Figure 39

Drawing No. 11/194

Diagram Book Page 96A

Code: TYO (later coded FLATROL MO by British Rail)
Lot number: 417; Quantity: 9; Built: Derby 1929; Running numbers: 168964—72
Lot number: 828; Quantity: 5; Built: Derby 1935; Running numbers: 700000—4
Lot number: 1213; Quantity: 4; Built: Wolverton 1939; Running numbers: 700010—13
Total quantity built: 18
Tare: 11 tons 15 cwt (with baulks)
Tare: 10 tons 14 cwt (without baulks)

The minimum curve that the trolley will negotiate is 2 chains. Carrying capacity: 20 tons over whole well. Wood and metal floor. Binding chains: 2 sets, with screw couplings.

It should be noted that while the first two lots would have entered traffic in grey livery, the final four vehicles, constructed in 1939, would have entered traffic carrying the bauxite body colour.

Plate 54 (bottom right) This is an unidentified example from lot 417 in original ex-works condition and the layout of the chains are of particular interest. The script on the side of the vehicle gives the tare with and without baulks.

Photograph British Rail

53

Plates 55 & 56 These photographs illustrate No. 168965 in service in 1938. The LMS lettering is now closed up towards the left hand end of the vehicle which is now in bauxite livery. The absence of the baulks and binding chains is also noticeable. **Plate 55** is a general view of the vehicle and **Plate 56** is a close up of the axlebox and end of the trolley.

Photographs A. E. West

Plate 58 No. 700006, as running when first built. While this vehicle is in grey livery, the difference in lettering style from No. 299876 shown in **Plate 57** can clearly be seen.

Photograph British Rail

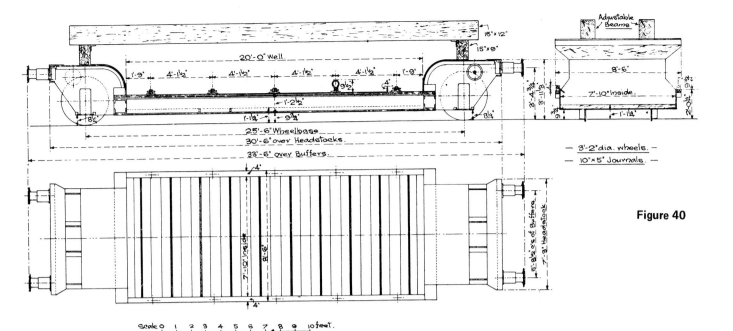

Figure 40

Scale 0 1 2 3 4 5 6 7 8 9 10 feet.

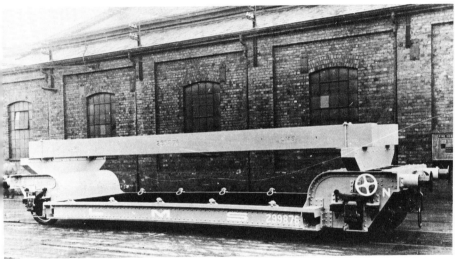

20 TON FOUR WHEELED TROLLEY   Figure 40

Drawing No. 11/229   Diagram Book Page 96B

Code: TYO (later coded WELTROL MA by British Rail)
Lot number: 608; Quantity: 6; Built: Wolverton 1930;
Running numbers: 299876—81
Lot number: 829; Quantity: 4; Built: Wolverton 1935;
Running numbers: 700005—9
Total quantity built: 10
Tare: 14 tons (with baulks)
Tare: 12 tons 10 cwt (without baulks)

The minimum curve which the trolley will negotiate is 2 chains. Carrying capacity: 20 tons over whole well. Wood and metal floor. Screw hand brake.

Prior assent required only to Western section of Southern Region and from Grafton Junction to Andover Junction.

Plate 57   No. 299876, is shown here, in original ex-works condition, and attention is drawn to the style and form of the LMS lettering and number. Letters and numbers are also cut into the timber baulks.

Photograph British Rail

Plate 58

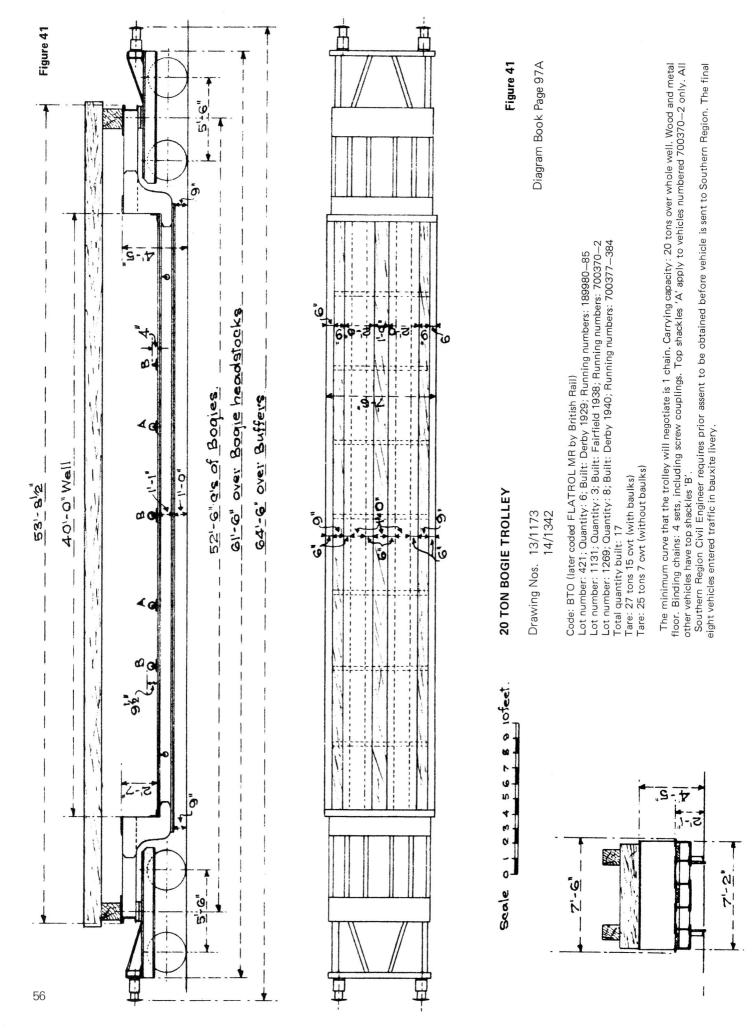

Figure 41

Figure 41

Diagram Book Page 97A

20 TON BOGIE TROLLEY

Drawing Nos. 13/1173
14/1342

Code: BTO (later coded FLATROL MR by British Rail)
Lot number: 421; Quantity: 6; Built: Derby 1929; Running numbers: 189980–85
Lot number: 1131; Quantity: 3; Built: Fairfield 1938; Running numbers: 700370–2
Lot number: 1269; Quantity: 8; Built: Derby 1940; Running numbers: 700377–384
Total quantity built: 17
Tare: 27 tons 15 cwt (with baulks)
Tare: 25 tons 7 cwt (without baulks)

The minimum curve that the trolley will negotiate is 1 chain. Carrying capacity: 20 tons over whole well. Wood and metal floor. Binding chains: 4 sets, including screw couplings. Top shackles 'A' apply to vehicles numbered 700370–2 only. All other vehicles have top shackles 'B'.
   Southern Region Civil Engineer requires prior assent to be obtained before vehicle is sent to Southern Region. The final eight vehicles entered traffic in bauxite livery.

Scale 0 1 2 3 4 5 6 7 8 9 10feet.

53'-8½"

40'-0" Well

52'-6" c/'s of Bogies.

61'-6" over Bogie headstocks.

64'-6" over Buffers

5'-6"

5'-6"

9"

4'-5"

B 4"

A

B

B 1'-1"

1'-0"

9½"

2'-7"

9"

B

6"

6"

9"

6'-0"

7'

0'-0"

6" 9"

6'

9"

6"

6"

9"

7'-6"

7'-2"

4'-5"

2'-1"

56

the tare weight, with and without baulks.

Figure 42

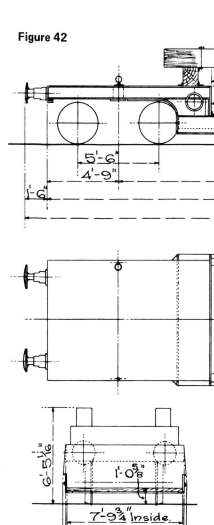

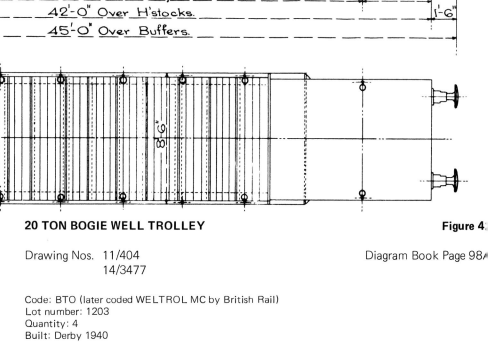

20 TON BOGIE WELL TROLLEY

Figure 4

Drawing Nos.   11/404
               14/3477

Diagram Book Page 98

Code: BTO (later coded WELTROL MC by British Rail)
Lot number: 1203
Quantity: 4
Built: Derby 1940
Running numbers: 700373–6
Tare: 19 tons 14 cwt (with baulks)
Tare: 17 tons 10 cwt (without baulks)

The minimum curve that the truck will negotiate is 1 chain. Carrying capacity: 20 tons. Wood floo
Binding chains: 4 sets, including screw couplings.
'Not to work between Andover Junction and Kimbridge Junction, Lymington Junction an
Lymington. Prior assent required for remainder of Southern Region'
These vehicles entered traffic in bauxite livery but no photographs of them are known to the author.

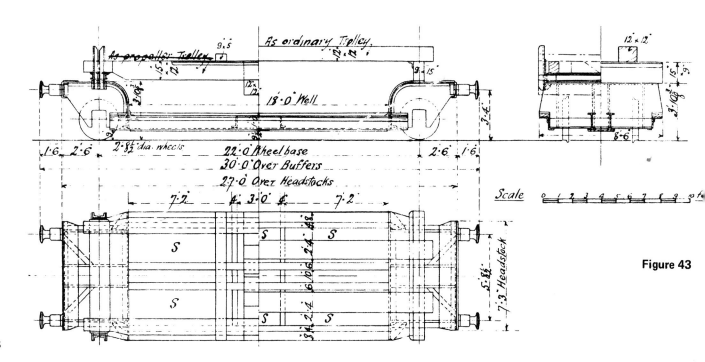

Figure 43

58

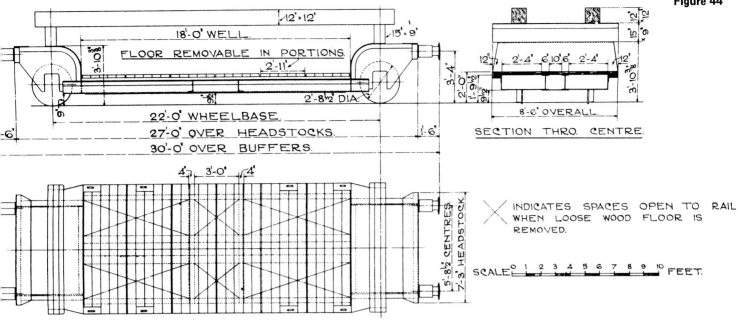

Figure 44

25 TON FOUR WHEELED TROLLEY

Figures 43 & 44

Drawing No. 11/95

Diagram Book Pages 106 & 106 amended

Code: TYR (later coded FLATROL MV by British Rail)
Lot number: 223
Quantity: 6
Built: Birmingham C & W Co. Ltd. 1925
Running numbers: 117577/8, 117580/2/7 and 117591
Tare: 11 tons 12 cwt (with baulks) (Propeller)
Tare: 10 tons (without baulks)
This entry was later deleted and a new entry read:-
Tare: 10 tons 16 cwt (with baulks) (Ordinary)
Tare: 9 tons 12 cwt (without baulks)

The minimum curve that the trolley will negotiate is 1¾ chains. Carrying capacity: 25 tons, (18 tons over 8 ft.) Loose wooden floor on top of metal floor. Binding chains: 2 sets, including screw couplings.

Later, all six vehicles were amended and the full story appears on the diagram which is reproduced as **Figure 44.**

Plate 60   This ex-works picture of No. 117591 is the only illustration known to the author.

Figure 45

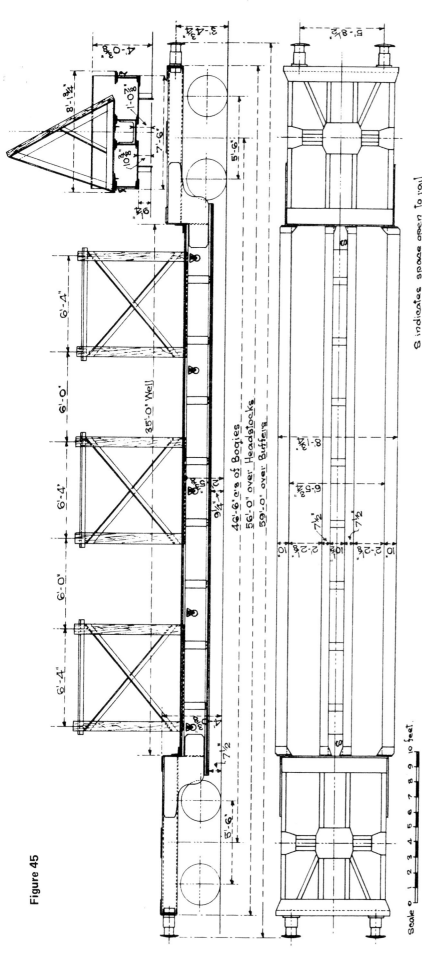

S indicates space open to rail

Scale 0 1 2 3 4 5 6 7 8 9 10 feet

35 TON BOGIE TROLLEY

Figure 45

Drawing No. 12/93   Diagram Book Page 118

Code: BTA (later coded TRESTROL MB by British Rail)
Lot number: 366
Quantity: 3
Built: G. R. Turner 1928
Running numbers: 218857, 249992 and 249998
Tare: 27 tons (with trestles)
Tare: 24 tons 12 cwt (without trestles)

The minimum curve that the trolley will negotiate is 1½ chains. Carrying capacity: 35 tons over whole well (20 tons over 14ft.) All metal floor. Binding chains: 3 sets, including screw couplings.

Plate 61 (above) This shows No. 249992 without trestles. The binding chains across the well should be noted.

Photograph British Rail

Plate 62 (below) This picture of No. 218857 shows the vehicle equipped with a trestle.

Photograph British Rail

L M S

218857

Figure 46

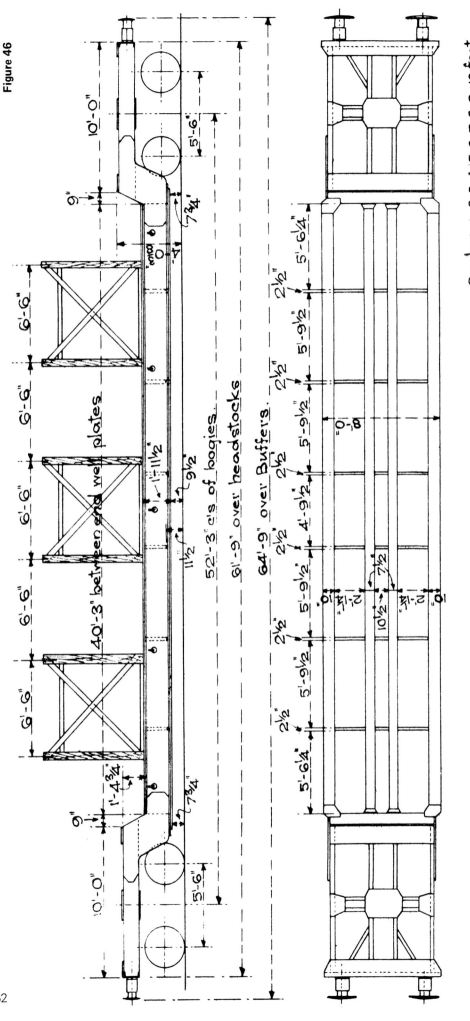

Scale 0 1 2 3 4 5 6 7 8 9 10 feet.

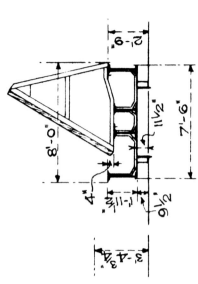

Figure 46

Diagram Book Page 122A

40 TON BOGIE TROLLEY

Drawing No. 13/1207

Code: BTZ (later coded TRESTOL AD by British Rail)
Lot number: 462
Quantity: 4
Built: Derby 1930
Running numbers: 189991—4
Tare: 26 tons 12 cwt (with trestles)
Tare: 24 tons 15 cwt (without trestles)

The minimum curve that the trolley will negotiate is 1½ chains (when uncoupled). Carrying capacity: 40 tons over whole well (30 tons over 10 ft.) All metal floor. Binding chains: 3 sets, including screw couplings. Note: All heights given from rail level are when trolley is unloaded.
'Southern Region Civil Engineer requires prior assent to be obtained before vehicle is sent to Southern Region'.

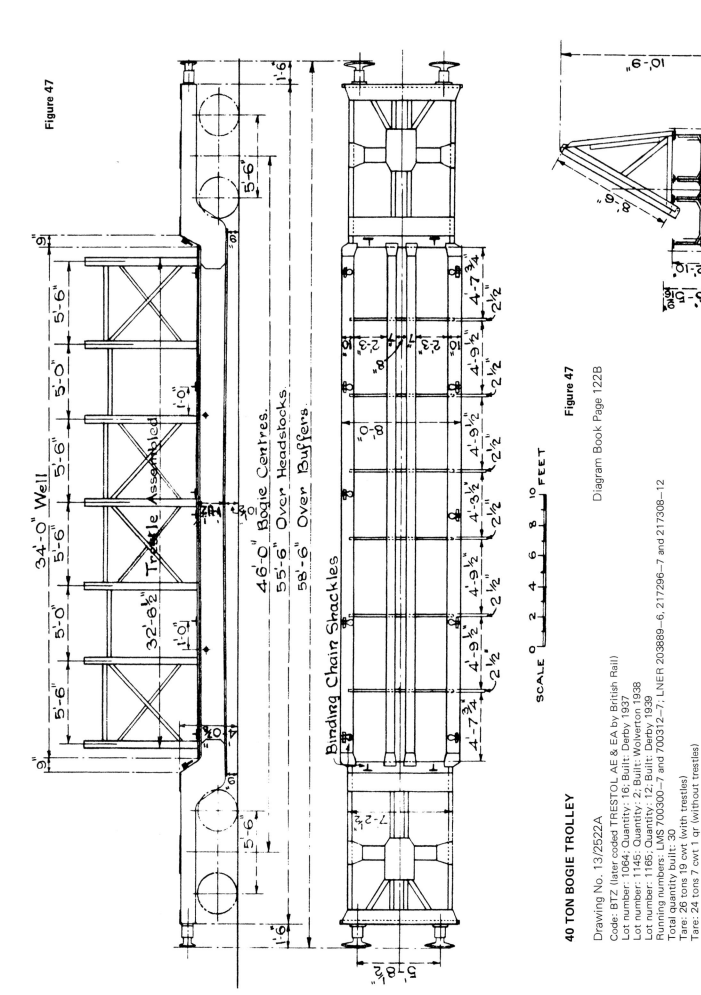

Figure 47

Figure 47

Diagram Book Page 122B

40 TON BOGIE TROLLEY

Drawing No. 13/2522A

Code: BTZ (later coded TRESTOL AE & EA by British Rail)
Lot number: 1064; Quantity: 16; Built: Derby 1937
Lot number: 1145; Quantity: 2; Built: Wolverton 1938
Lot number: 1165; Quantity: 12; Built: Derby 1939
Running numbers: LMS 700300–7 and 700312–7; LNER 203889–6, 217296–7 and 217308–12
*The above running numbers refer to 29 vehicles and No. 217313 (LNER) appears on the diagram but has been deleted.
Other information recorded on the diagram is detailed below.

Total quantity built: 30
Tare: 26 tons 19 cwt (with trestles)
Tare: 24 tons 7 cwt 1 qr (without trestles)

The minimum curve that the trolley will negotiate is 70 ft. if taken round singly. Carrying capacity: 40 tons. All metal

LONDON & NORTH EASTERN RAILWAY

217296

40 TONS

companies was not uncommon, and may have been as a result of some wartime agreement. It should also be noted, that while the construction in the lot book is dated 1938, it is probable that these vehicles entered traffic in the following year or even later.

Photograph British Rail

Plate 65   No. 700305 in original ex-works condition, and the vehicle appears to be in bauxite livery.

Photograph British Rail

Plate 66   This illustration of No. 203890 should be compared with **Plate 64** and the livery style noted. A less bold script has been used.

Photograph British Rail

67 This shows No. 117571 in original con-
. Of particular interest is the girder construction
well behind the headstocks.
Photograph British Rail

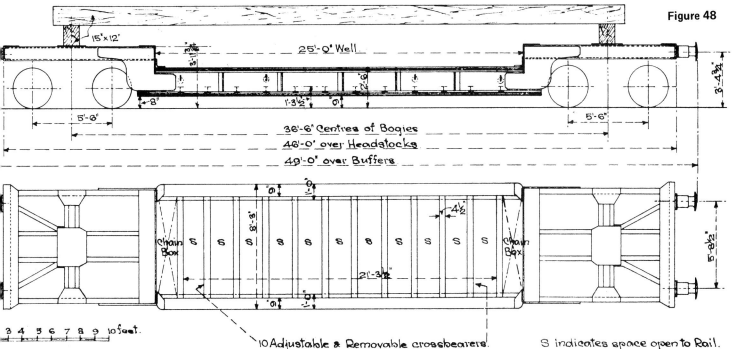

Figure 48

15"×12"

25'-0" Well

3'-1¾"

3'-4¾"

8"

5'-8"

1'-3½"

2'-6"

9"

5'-6"

36'-6" Centres of Bogies
46'-0" over Headstocks
49'-0" over Buffers

Chain Box

8'-3"

4½"

S S S S S S S S S S

21'-3½"

Chain Box

5'-8½"

3 4 5 6 7 8 9 10 feet

10 Adjustable & Removable crossbearers.

S indicates space open to Rail.

0 TON BOGIE TROLLEY   Figure 48

rawing No. 6188   Diagram Book Page 126

ode: BTZ (later coded WELTROL MJ by British Rail)
ot number: 220
uantity: 8
uilt: Birmingham C&W Co. Ltd. 1925
unning numbers: 117556/7/9/62/4/8/71/75
are: 21 tons 17 cwt (with baulks)
are: 20 tons (without baulks)

he minimum curve that the trolley will negotiate is 1
hain. Carrying capacity: 40 tons equally distributed over
ell (30 tons over 12 ft.) All metal floor. Binding chains:
sets, including screw couplings.

'Assent of Southern Railway required before loading to
SWR and SE & CR Sections'. 'Assent of GWR required
efore loading to M & SW Section'. 'Consult the Chief
oods Managers Dept. before loading to the Caledonian
ection

Plate 68 No. 117562 at Crewe in 1962, showing the vehicle in its B R condition.   67
Photograph Author's Collection

Figure 49

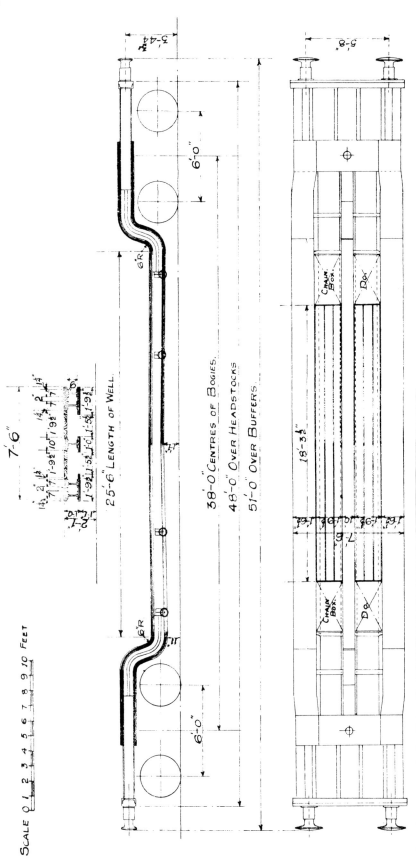

Figure 49

Diagram Book Page 126A

40 TON BOGIE TROLLEY

Drawing No. 11/231

Code: BTZ (later coded FLATROL MBB by British Rail)
Lot number: 609
Quantity: 6
Built: Wolverton 1930
Running numbers: 299882–7
Tare: 26 tons 8 cwt

Trolley to negotiate curves of 1 chain radius when taken round singly. Carrying capacity: 50 tons provided that all loads over 40 tons are individually approved. (The 40 tons load to be distributed over not less than 14 ft. at the centre).

Plate 69 No. 299883 is shown here in ex-works condition. The

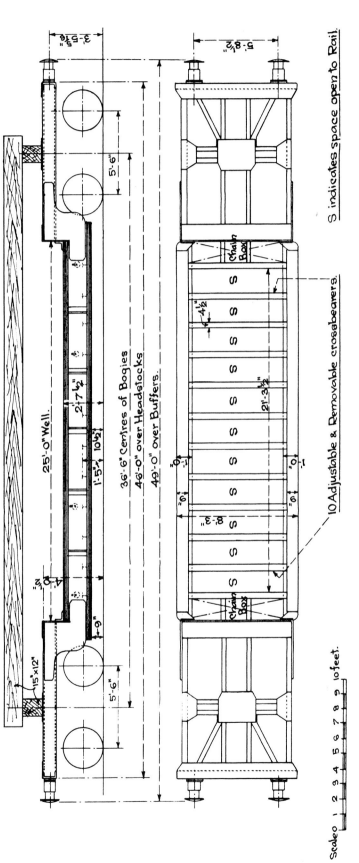

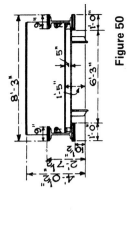

Figure 50

Diagram Book Page 126B

40 TON BOGIE TROLLEY

Drawing No. 13/2570

Code: BTZ (later coded WELTROL MK by British Rail)
Lot number: 1132
Quantity: 4
Built: G. R. Turner 1938
Running numbers: 700308–11
Tare: 22 tons (with baulks)
Tare: 20 tons 5 cwt (without baulks)

The minimum curve that the trolley will negotiate is 1 chain. Carrying capacity: 40 tons equally distributed over well (30 tons over 12 ft.) All metal floor. Binding chains: 4, including screw couplings.

Plate 70   This illustrates a vehicle in original condition carrying the bauxite livery, although it is felt that the tyres had been painted white for photographic purposes only.

Photograph British Rail

Figure 51

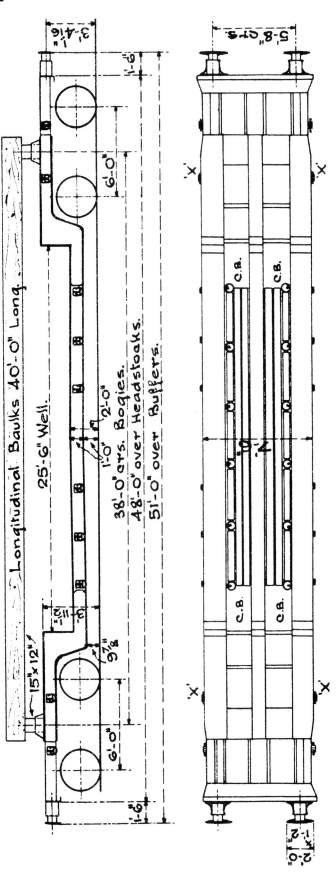

Longitudinal Baulks 40'-0" Long.

25'-6" Well.

38'-0" ctrs. Bogies.
48'-0" over Headstocks.
51'-0" over Buffers.

C.B. = Chain Box.
7'-11" over Brackets marked 'X'.

Scale 0 1 2 3 4 5 6 7 8 9 10 Feet.

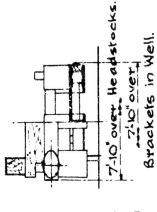

7'-10" over Headstocks.
7'-10" over Brackets in Well.

2'-8½" dia. Wheels.
11"×5½" Journals.

40 TON BOGIE TROLLEY

Figure 51

Drawing No. 11/430   Diagram Book Page 126C

Code: BTZ (later coded FLATROL MCC by British Rail)
Lot number: 1276
Quantity: 4
Built: Wolverton 1940
Running numbers: 700318–21
Tare: 28 tons 17 cwt

The minimum curve that this trolley will negotiate is 1 chain. Carrying capacity: 40 tons over not less than 14 ft. at centre. Steel and wood floor. Binding chains; 4 sets, including screw couplings.

These vehicles entered traffic in bauxite livery during 1941 and no official photographs were taken at the time.

Plate 71 This illustrates No. M700318 as running in 1964.

Photograph Author's Collection

Drawing No. 6248   Diagram Book Page 129

Code: BTZ (later coded WELTROL MC by British Rail)
Lot number: 228
Quantity: 8
Built: Craven 1926
Running numbers: 200185, 202981, 203553, 208381, 211061,
227830 and 245739/40
Tare: 24 tons 19 cwt (with baulks)
Tare: 22 tons (without baulks)

The minimum curve that the trolley will negotiate is 1½ chains.
Carrying capacity: 40 tons equally distributed over well (28 tons
over 14 ft.) All metal floor. Binding chains: 3 sets, including screw
couplings.
'Assent of Southern Railway required before loading to L&SWR'.
'Assent of GWR required before loading to M&SW Section'.
'Consult the Chief Goods Managers Dept. before loading to the
Caledonian Section'.

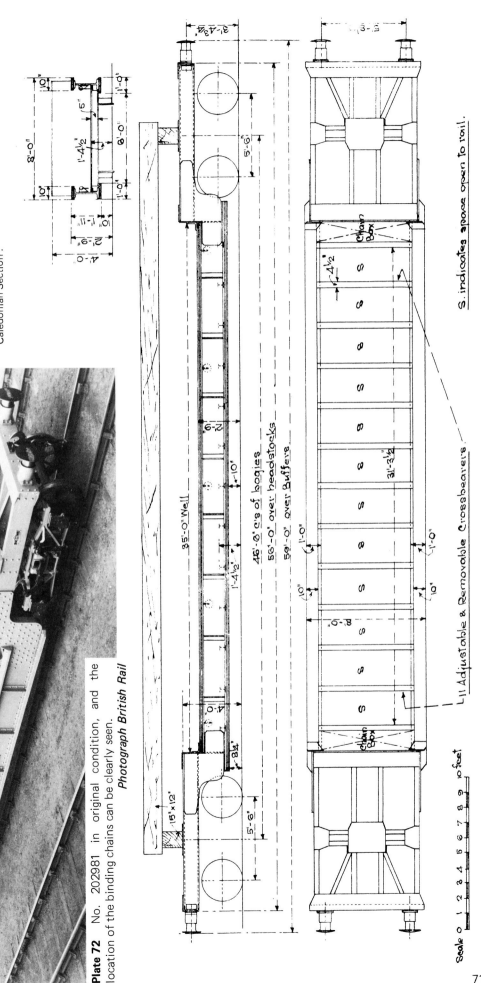

Plate 72 No. 202981 in original condition, and the
location of the binding chains can be clearly seen.
Photograph British Rail

Figure 53

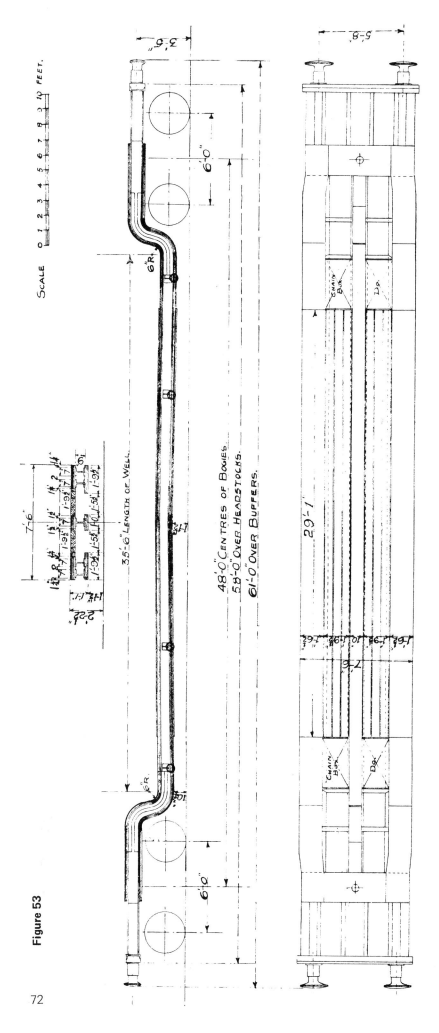

Figure 53

Figure 53

40 TON BOGIE TROLLEY

Drawing No. 11/232   Diagram Book Page 129A

Code: BTZ (later coded MGG by British Rail)
Lot number: 610
Quantity: 6
Built: Wolverton 1930
Running numbers: 299888–93
Tare: 32 tons 8 cwt

Trolley to negotiate curves of 1 chain radius when taken round singly and using buffer plank. Carrying capacity: 50 tons providing that all loads over 40 tons are individually approved. (The 40 tons load to be distributed over not less than 21 ft. at the centre). Wood and steel floor. No binding chains or screw couplings attached.

Plate 73   No. 299888 is shown in original condition, and attention is drawn to the unusual condensed LMS lettering. No doubt, if repainted while still in grey, a more conventional

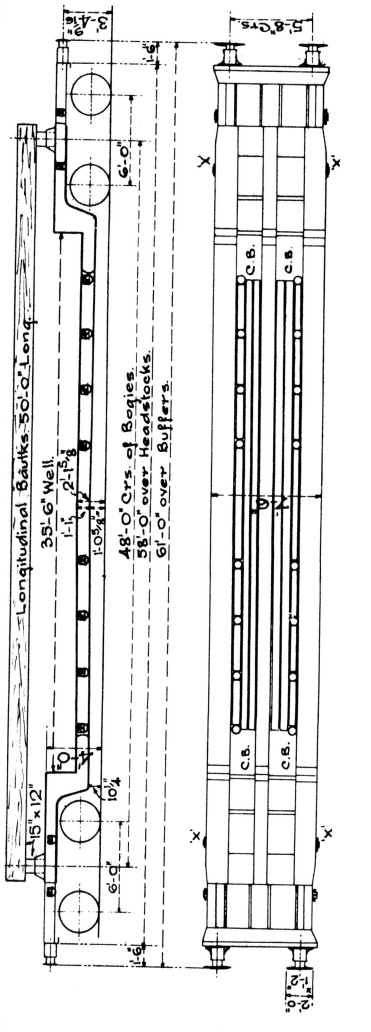

Scale |1 2 3 4 5 6 7 8 9 10| Feet.

C.B. = Chain Box.
7'-11" over Brackets marked 'X'

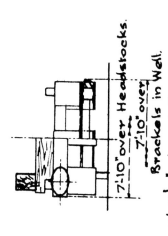

End Section
Elevation. at Centre.

Figure 54

Diagram Book Page 129B

40 TON BOGIE TROLLEY

Drawing No. 11/431

Code: BTZ (later coded MHH by British Rail)
Lot number: 1277
Quantity: 4
Built: Wolverton 1940
Running numbers: 700322–5
Tare: 36 tons

The minimum curve that the trolley will negotiate is 1 chain. Carrying capacity: 40 tons over not less than 21ft. at centre. Steel and wood floor. Binding chains: 4 sets, including screw couplings.

These vehicles entered traffic in bauxite livery in 1941 and, regrettably, no photographs are known to the author.

Figure 55

74

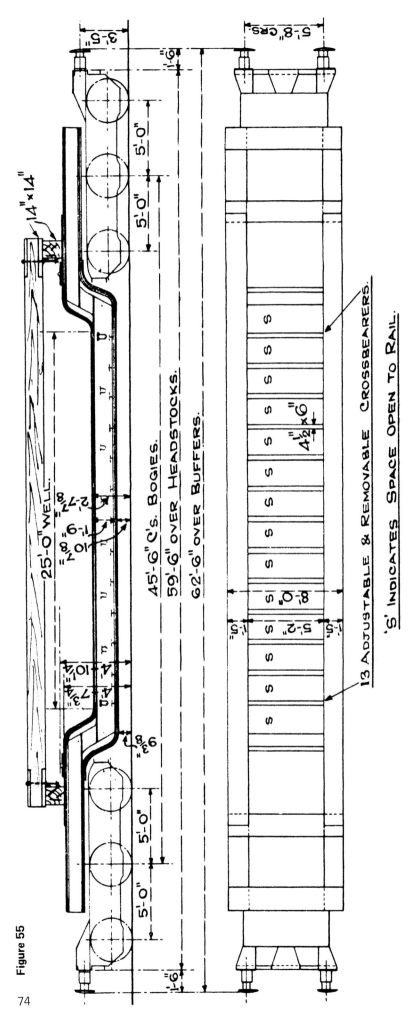

14" × 14"

3'-5" 5'-8" CRS.

1'-6"

5'-0" 5'-0"

25'-0" WELL

45'-6" C's. BOGIES.
59'-6" OVER HEADSTOCKS.
62'-6" OVER BUFFERS.

2'-7⅝"
1'-9⅛"
10'-2⅛"
4'-10¾"
7'-3¾"
9'-3⅜"

5'-0" 5'-0" 5'-0"

1'-6"

8'-0"
5'-2"
4½" × 6"

13 ADJUSTABLE & REMOVABLE CROSSBEARERS.

'S' INDICATES SPACE OPEN TO RAIL.

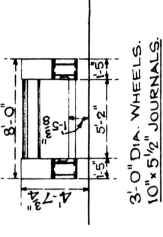

8'-0"
4'-7¾"
1'-5" 5'-2" 1'-5"
8-5⅜" min

3'-0" DIA. WHEELS.
10" × 5½" JOURNALS.

NOTE:- HEIGHTS FROM RAIL ARE UNLOADED.

Plate 74 An illustration of trolley No. 700340 in ex-works condition. Although a poor photograph, it is the only one known to the author.

Photograph British Rail

50 TON BOGIE TROLLEY   Figure 55

Drawing No. 12/427

Diagram Book Page 133A

Code: BTP (later coded WELTROL MR by British Rail)
Lot number: 1072; Quantity: 1; Built: LNER 1937; Running number: 700333
Lot number: 1166; Quantity: 4; Built: LNER 1938; Running numbers: 700337 –40
Total quantity built: 5
Tare: 37 tons 3 cwt (with baulks)
Tare: 33 tons 10 cwt (without baulks)

The minimum curve that the trolley will negotiate is 70 ft. radius. Carrying capacity: 50 tons. This is an example of pre-war co-operation between the LMS and LNER companies and it is regretted that the author has been unable to locate

Figure 56

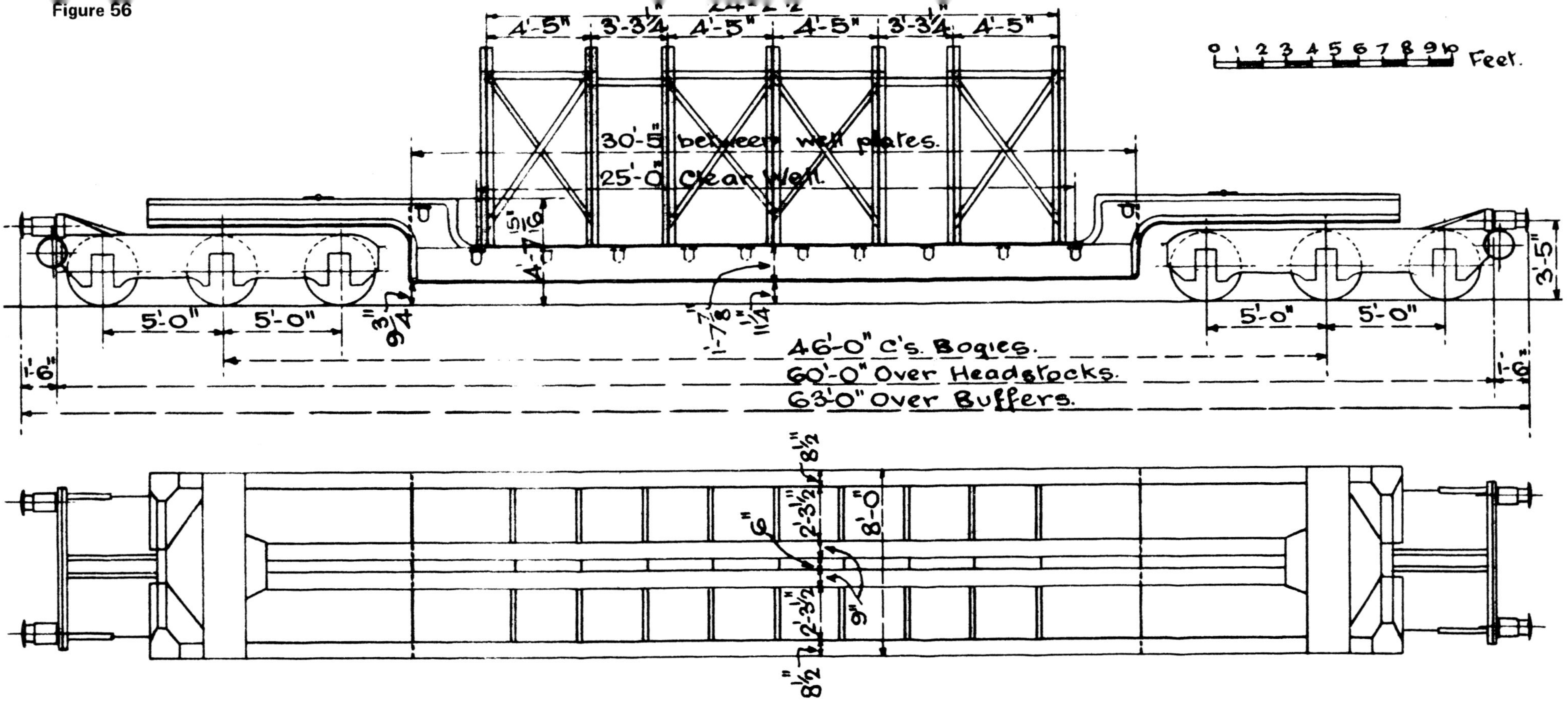

Figure 56

Figure 56

50 TON BOGIE TROLLEY

Drawing No. 11/322   Diagram Book Page 133B

Code: BTP (later coded TRESTROL AF by British Rail)
Lot number: 1071
Quantity: 3
Built: LNER 1938
Running numbers: 700330–2
Tare: 38 tons (with trestles)
Tare: 34 tons 13 cwt (without trestles)

The minimum curve that the trolley will negotiate is 70 ft.
radius. Carrying capacity: 50 tons.
This is a further example of LNER constructions for the
LMSR.

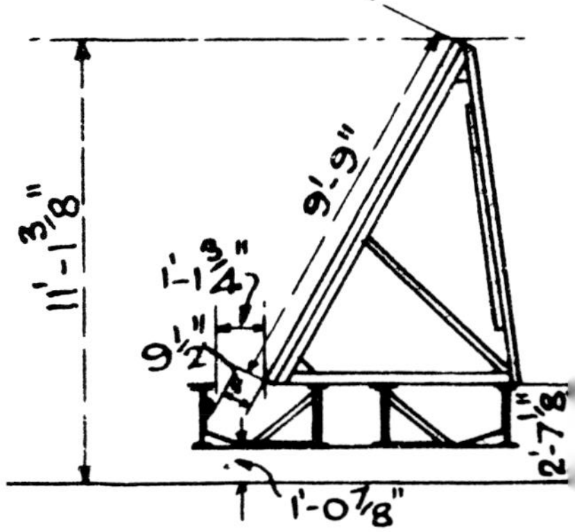

Plate 75   This illustrates No. 700330 in its original
condition.

Photograph British Rail

3'-0" Dia. Wheels
10" × 5½" Journals.

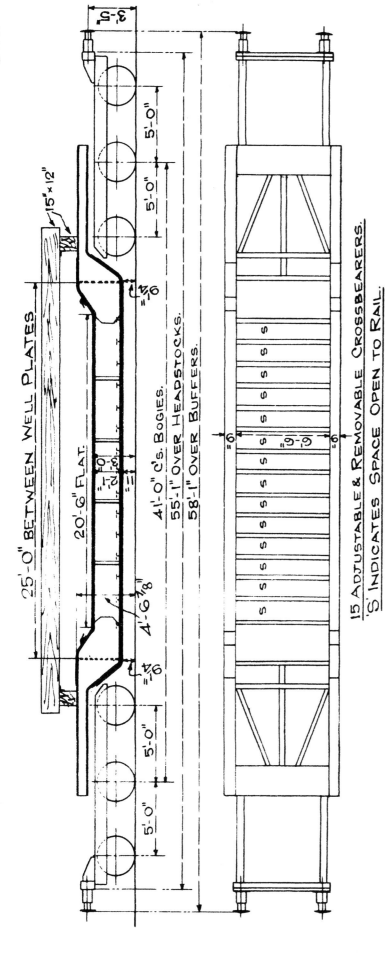

Figure 57

Diagram Book Page 133C

50 TON BOGIE TROLLEY

Drawing No. 12/381

Code: BTP (later coded WELTROL MP by British Rail)
Lot number: 1130
Quantity: 3
Built: Fairfield 1938
Running numbers: 700334—6
Tare: 29 tons 13 cwt (with baulks)
Tare: 28 tons 11 cwt (without baulks)

The minimum curve that the trolley will negotiate is 1½ chains. Carrying capacity: 50 tons over whole of well (40 tons over 12 ft.)
No pictures are known to exist for these vehicles which entered traffic in bauxite livery.

Figure 57

76

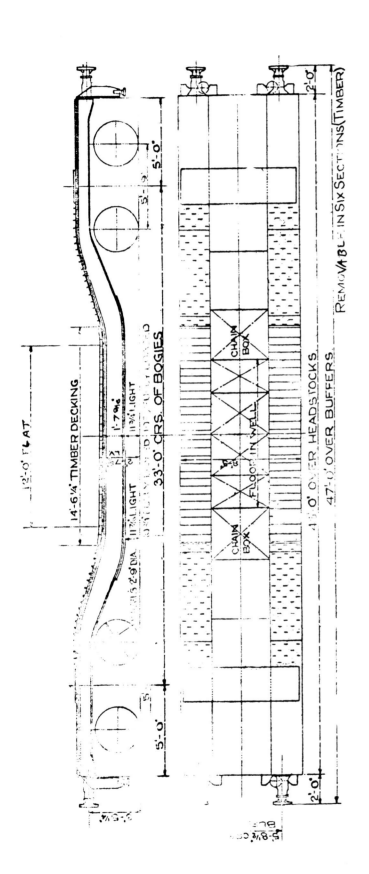

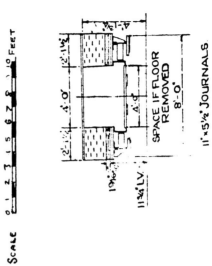

Figure 58

50 TON BOGIE TROLLEY

Diagram Book Page 133D

Quantity: 50
Tare: 26 tons 15 cwt

The minimum curve that the trolley will negotiate is 2 chains. When two or more are coupled together the minimum curve is 3 chains. Carrying capacity: 50 tons. Fitted with screw hand brake and AVB. This diagram illustrates these vehicles in original condition and their later post-1948 condition is depicted in diagram book page 5B **Figure 4**. No photograph or further information is known to the author when running, as shown in **Figure 58**.

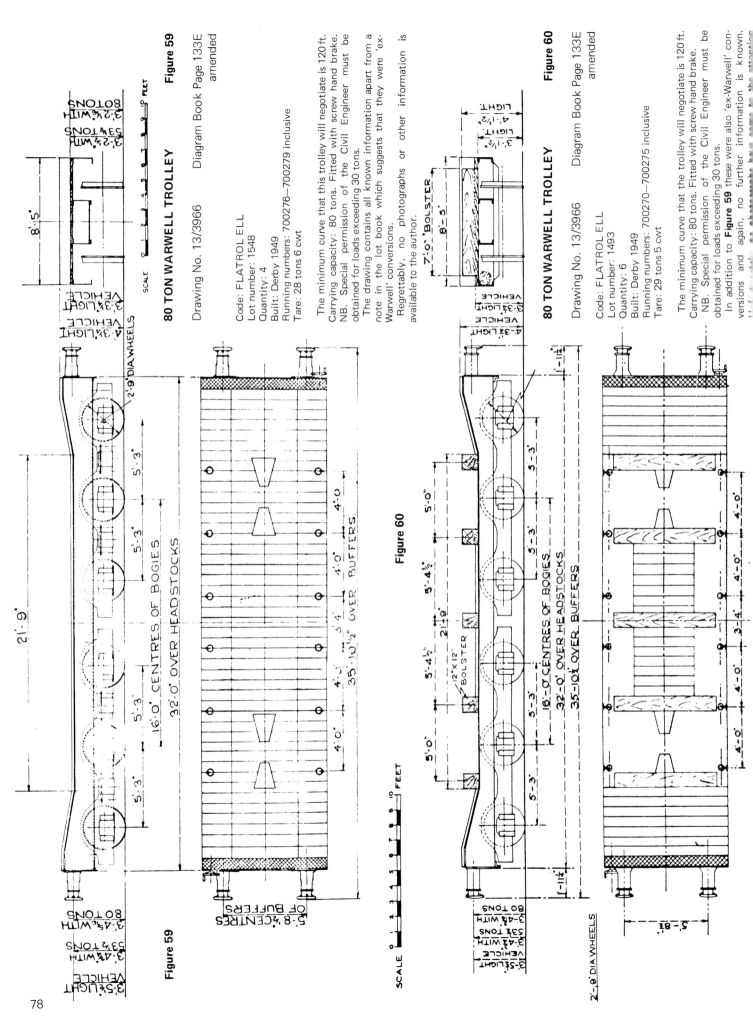

Figure 59

80 TON WARWELL TROLLEY

Diagram Book Page 133E amended

Drawing No. 13/3966

Code: FLATROL ELL
Lot number: 1548
Quantity: 4
Built: Derby 1949
Running numbers: 700276–700279 inclusive
Tare: 28 tons 6 cwt

The minimum curve that this trolley will negotiate is 120 ft. Carrying capacity: 80 tons. Fitted with screw hand brake. NB. Special permission of the Civil Engineer must be obtained for loads exceeding 30 tons. The drawing contains all known information apart from a note in the lot book which suggests that they were 'ex-Warwell' conversions.

Regrettably, no photographs or other information is available to the author.

Figure 60

80 TON WARWELL TROLLEY

Diagram Book Page 133E amended

Drawing No. 13/3966

Code: FLATROL ELL
Lot number: 1493
Quantity: 6
Built: Derby 1949
Running numbers: 700270–700275 inclusive
Tare: 29 tons 5 cwt

The minimum curve that the trolley will negotiate is 120 ft. Carrying capacity: 80 tons. Fitted with screw hand brake. NB. Special permission of the Civil Engineer must be obtained for loads exceeding 30 tons. In addition to **Figure 59** these were also 'ex-Warwell' conversions and again, no further information is known.

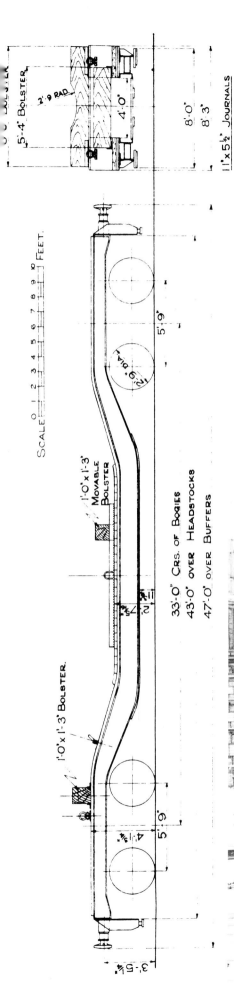

SCALE 0 1 2 3 4 5 6 7 8 9 10 FEET.

5'-4" BOLSTER

2'-9 RAD.

4'-0"

8'-0"

8'-3"

11" x 5½" JOURNALS

2'-9" DIA.

5'-9"

1'-0" x 1'-3" MOVABLE BOLSTER

33'-0" CRS. OF BOGIES

43'-0" OVER HEADSTOCKS

47'-0" OVER BUFFERS

1'-0" x 1'-3" BOLSTER.

5'-9"

4'-1¾"

3'-5¾"

NSU-FISH

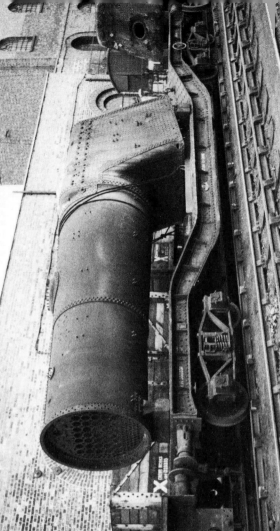

Plate 76 This end view of No. M360334, at Horwich in 1965, gives a good impression of the detail on the top of the vehicle.

Photograph Author's Collection

Plate 77 This shows No. DM360331 at Crewe Works in 1964 and illustrates a vehicle in internal use at the works.

Photograph Author's Collection

Figure 61

Diagram Book Page 133F

50 TON WARWELL TROLLEY

Drawing No. Not known

Code: Not recorded
Quantity: 12
Running numbers: M360329–M360340 inclusive
Tare: 26 tons 15 cwt

The minimum curve that this trolley will negotiate is 2 chains. When two or more are coupled together the minimum curve is 3 chains. Carrying capacity: 50 tons. Fitted with screw hand brake and A.V.B.

Very little is known about these vehicles and the running numbers selected are interesting inasmuch as all post-1934 construction was numbered 400,000 and above. The diagram records all the known information about the vehicles except that, when the author photographed No. M360334 at Horwich in 1965, he recorded a 1942 building plate, which at least gives some clue as to the date of their construction. It is possible that they were built by the Ministry of Supply or the War Department and were not originally railway-owned vehicles, being taken into railway stock prior to nationalization.

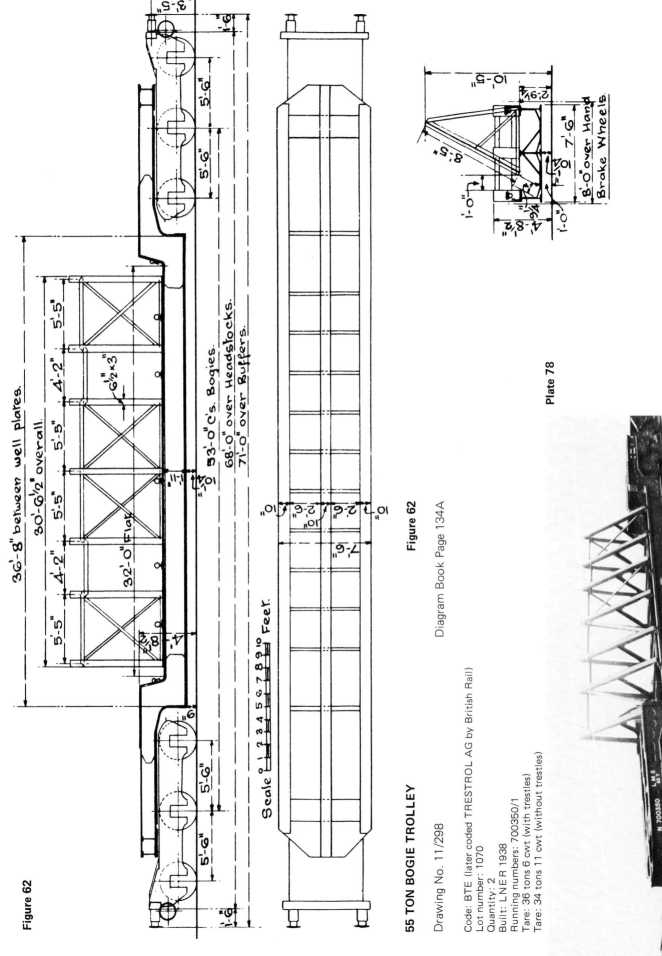

Figure 62

36'-8" between well plates.

30'-0½" overall.

5'-5" 4'-2" 5'-5" 5'-5" 4'-2" 5'-5"

32'-0" Flat.

6½"×3

53'-0" C's. Bogies.

68'-0" over Headstocks.

71'-0" over Buffers.

3'-5"

1'-6"

5'-6" 5'-6" 5'-6"

1'-6"

8'-3"

4'-0"

1'-1"

7'-0"

5'-6" 5'-6" 5'-6"

6"

1'-6"

Scale 0 1 2 3 4 5 6 7 8 9 10 Feet.

Figure 62

Diagram Book Page 134A

10" 2'-6" 2'-6" 10"

7'-6"

10" 10"

55 TON BOGIE TROLLEY

Drawing No. 11/298

Code: BTE (later coded TRESTROL AG by British Rail)
Lot number: 1070
Quantity: 2
Built: LNER 1938
Running numbers: 700350/1
Tare: 36 tons 6 cwt (with trestles)
Tare: 34 tons 11 cwt (without trestles)

10'-5"

2'-9½"

8'-5"

7'-6"

8'-0" over Hand Brake Wheels.

1'-0"

1'-0"

4'-8½"

9¼"

Plate 78

The minimum curve that the trolley will negotiate is 70ft. radius. Carrying capacity: 55 tons over whole of well (45 tons over 16 ft. at centre).

80

Plate 78 No. 700350 in original condition and painted in bauxite livery.
Photograph British Rail

Plate 79 This view of No. M700351, at Horwich in 1964, shows its BR condition during this period of its life.
Photograph Author's Collection

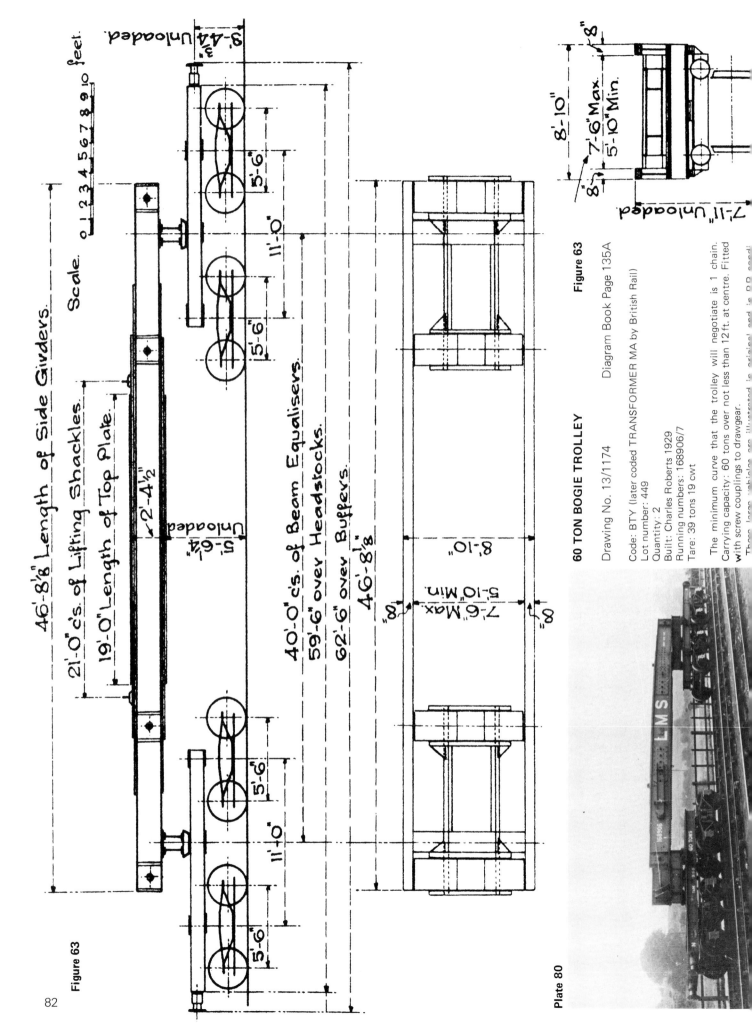

Figure 63

46'-8⅛" Length of Side Girders.
21'-0" c's. of Lifting Shackles.
19'-0" Length of Top Plate.
Scale.
0 1 2 3 4 5 6 7 8 9 10 feet.

3'-4¾" Unloaded.

5'-6"   11'-0"   5'-6"

2'-4½"
5'-6¼" Unloaded.

40'-0" c's. of Beam Equalisers.
59'-6" over Headstocks.
62'-6" over Buffers.
46'-8⅛"

8'-10"
7'-6" Max.
5'-10" Min.
8"   8"

8'-10"
8"
7'-6" Max.
5'-10" Min.
8"

7'-11" Unloaded.

Figure 63

60 TON BOGIE TROLLEY

Drawing No. 13/1174   Diagram Book Page 135A

Code: BTY (later coded TRANSFORMER MA by British Rail)
Lot number: 449
Quantity: 2
Built: Charles Roberts 1929
Running numbers: 168906/7
Tare: 39 tons 19 cwt

The minimum curve that the trolley will negotiate is 1 chain.
Carrying capacity: 60 tons over not less than 12ft. at centre. Fitted
with screw couplings to drawgear.
These large vehicles are illustrated in original red in RR road-

Plate 80

Plate 80 This illustrates No. 168906 pictured as built.
Photograph British Rail

Plate 82 This 1964 view, at Derby, shows the same vehicle in BR ownership, and is taken from the 'other end'. Note the different arrangement together with the 'extra parts' above the main beams.
Photograph Author's Collection

Plate 81 This official photograph shows the top view prior to entering traffic. *Photograph British Rail*

Figure 64

65 TON BOGIE TROLLEY

Diagram Book Page 135B

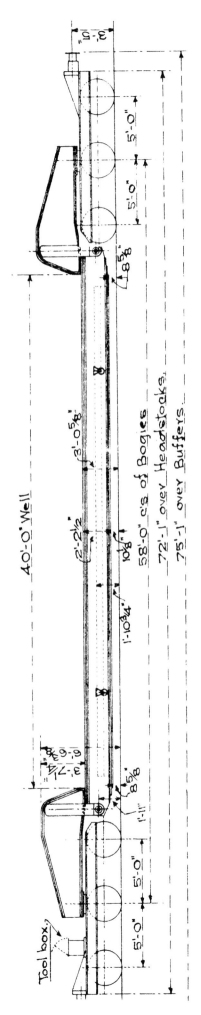

Tool box.

40'-0" Well

3'-7¼"
6'-6⅜"
8⅝"
1'-1"

5'-0"
5'-0"
5'-0"

5'-0"
5'-0"
5'-0"

8⅝"

3'-0⅝"

2'-2½"

1'-10¾"
10⅝"

58'-0" c's of Bogies
72'-1" over Headstocks
75'-1" over Buffers

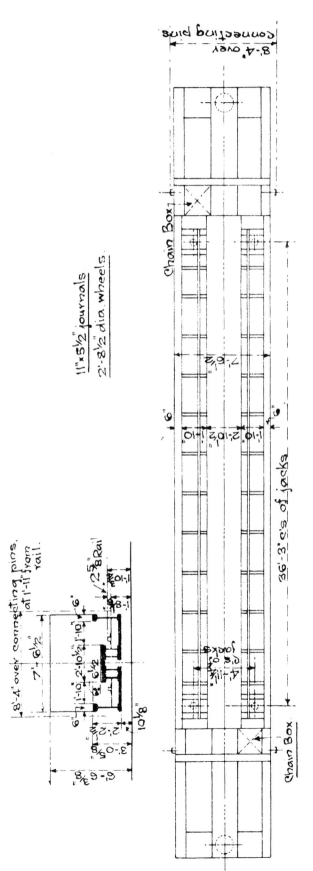

8'-4" over connecting pins, at 1'-1" from rail.

7'-6½"

6"
1'-1"
2'-10½"
1'-10"

6½"
6½"

1'-1"

3'-0⅝"
2'-2½"

6'-6⅜"

2·5⅞" Rail
8'-1"

8¾"

10"

1"×5½" journals
2'-8½" dia. wheels

Chain Box

7'-6½"

6"
2'-10½"
1'-10"
6"

4'-11½"
c's of
jacks

36'-3" c's of jacks

Chain Box

8'-4" over
connecting pins.

Scale. 0 1 2 3 4 5 6 7 8 9 10ft.

Note:- All heights from rail are "light" & will be reduced by ⅞" when trolley fully loaded.

84

65 TON BOGIE TROLLEY

Drawing No. 11/228

Diagram Book Page 135B

Code: BTC (later coded WELTROL ES by British Rail)
Lot number: Part 593
Quantity: 2
Built: Hurst Nelson 1931
Running numbers: 5000 and 5050
Tare: 49 tons 8 cwt

The minimum curve that the trolley will negotiate is 1½ chains. Carrying capacity: 65 tons over not less than 25ft. at the centre. All metal floor. Binding chains: 4 sets, including screw couplings. Weight of each end when detached: 11 tons 12 cwt. 11in. x 5½in. journals. 2ft. 8½in. diameter wheels. Height from rail to underside of trolley when loaded to full capacity: i.e. 65 tons over 18ft. is 7¼in. Note: All heights from rail are 'light'.

This diagram should also be considered with diagram book page 135C inasmuch as the vehicles were built to one lot and by using common parts, two different vehicles could be produced. It would seem that the probable arrangement was to build two of diagram book page 135C or one of each page, but there were insufficient parts to make three vehicles at any time. Transferred to E/NE Region on 3rd February 1958.

Plate 83   This illustrates No. 5000 when first constructed and **Plates 84 & 85** are views of a detached end and well with end.

Photographs British Rail

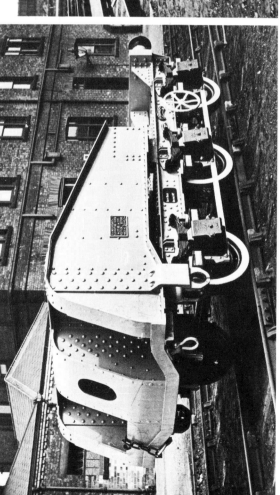

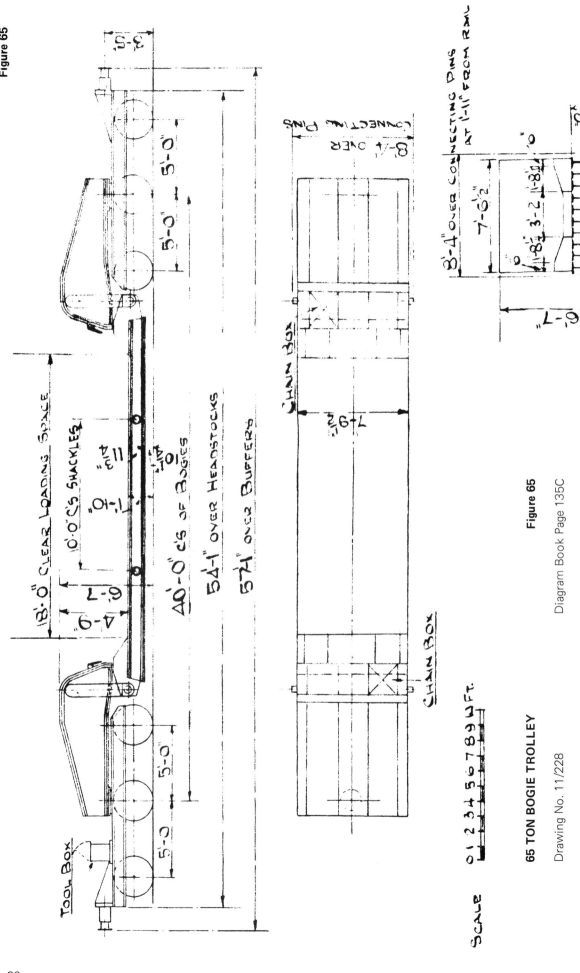

Figure 65

SCALE 0 1 2 3 4 5 6 7 8 9 10 Ft.

65 TON BOGIE TROLLEY

Figure 65

Diagram Book Page 135C

Code: BTC (later coded FLATROL MRR by British Rail)
Lot number: Part 593
Quantity: 1
Built: 1931
Running number: 5000
Tare: 37 tons 7 cwt

The minimum curve that the trolley will negotiate is 1½ chains. Carrying capacity: 65 tons over 18ft. All metal floor. The floor shown fitted here may be replaced by that shown in diagram book page 135B if the need should arise. Binding chains: 4 sets, including screw couplings.

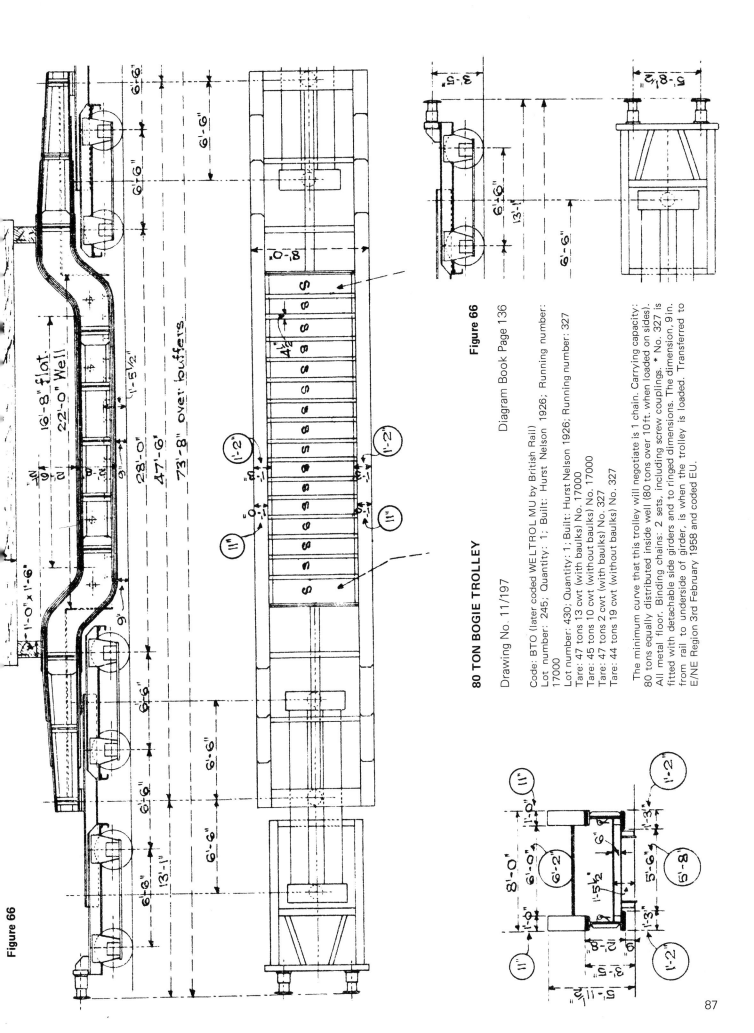

Figure 66

Figure 66

80 TON BOGIE TROLLEY

Diagram Book Page 136

Drawing No. 11/197

Code: BTO (later coded WELTROL MU by British Rail)
Lot number: 245; Quantity: 1; Built: Hurst Nelson 1926; Running number: 17000

Lot number: 430; Quantity: 1; Built: Hurst Nelson 1926; Running number: 327
Tare: 47 tons 13 cwt (with baulks) No. 17000
Tare: 45 tons 10 cwt (without baulks) No. 17000
Tare: 47 tons 2 cwt (with baulks) No. 327
Tare: 44 tons 19 cwt (without baulks) No. 327

The minimum curve that this trolley will negotiate is 1 chain. Carrying capacity: 80 tons equally distributed inside well (80 tons over 10ft. when loaded on sides). All metal floor. Binding chains: 2 sets, including screw couplings. * No. 327 is fitted with detachable side girders and to ringed dimensions. The dimension, 9 in. from rail to underside of girder, is when the trolley is loaded. Transferred to E/NE Region 3rd February 1958 and coded EU.

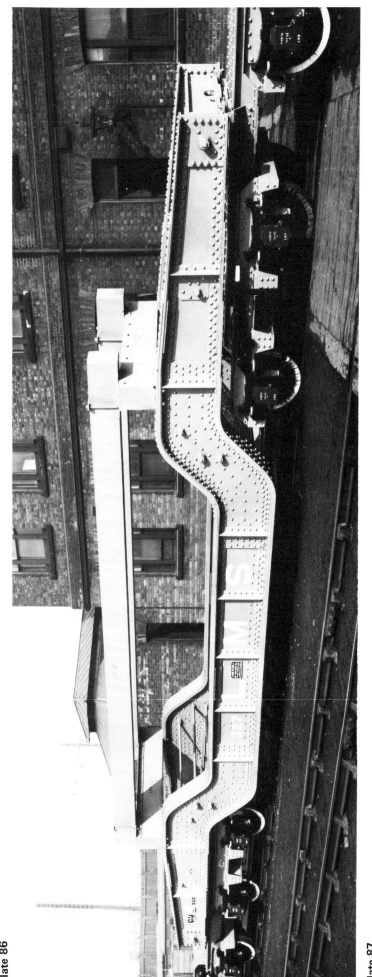

Plate 86

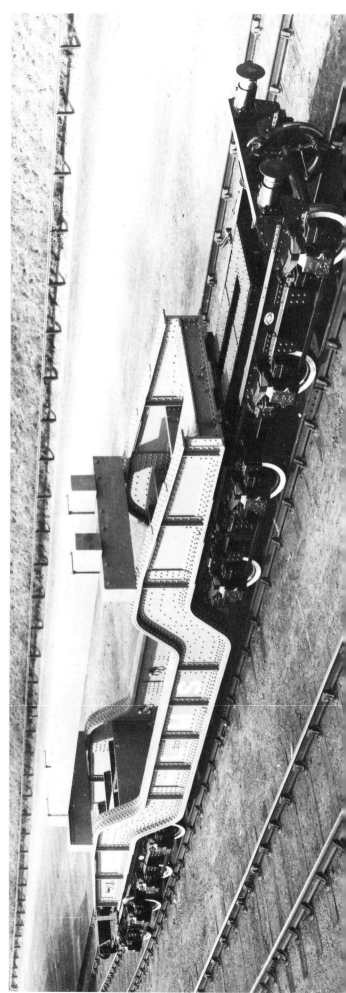

Plate 87

Figure 67

120 TON BOGIE TROLLEY

Diagram Book Page 136A

Drawing No. 15/935

Code: BTW (later coded TRANSFORMER MB by British Rail)
Lot number: 516
Quantity: 1
Built: By the trade 1930
Running number: 300000
Tare: 58 tons 1 cwt

The minimum curve that the trolley will negotiate is 1½ chains. Carrying capacity: 120 tons over 24 ft. (105 tons over 12 ft. at centre). Screw couplings to drawgear.

*The maximum load of 120 tons distributed over 24 ft. is only allowed when the centre of gravity of load lies within 3 in. of the centre line of the trolley. Tools, adjustable legs, packing etc. are carried in separate wagon.

Plate 88 This illustrates the vehicle, the largest built by the LMS, when first constructed and prior to entering traffic.

Photograph British Rail

Plate 87 This picture shows No. 17000 prior to entering traffic.

Photograph British Rail

Photograph British Rail

F.L. = Fully Loaded.

89

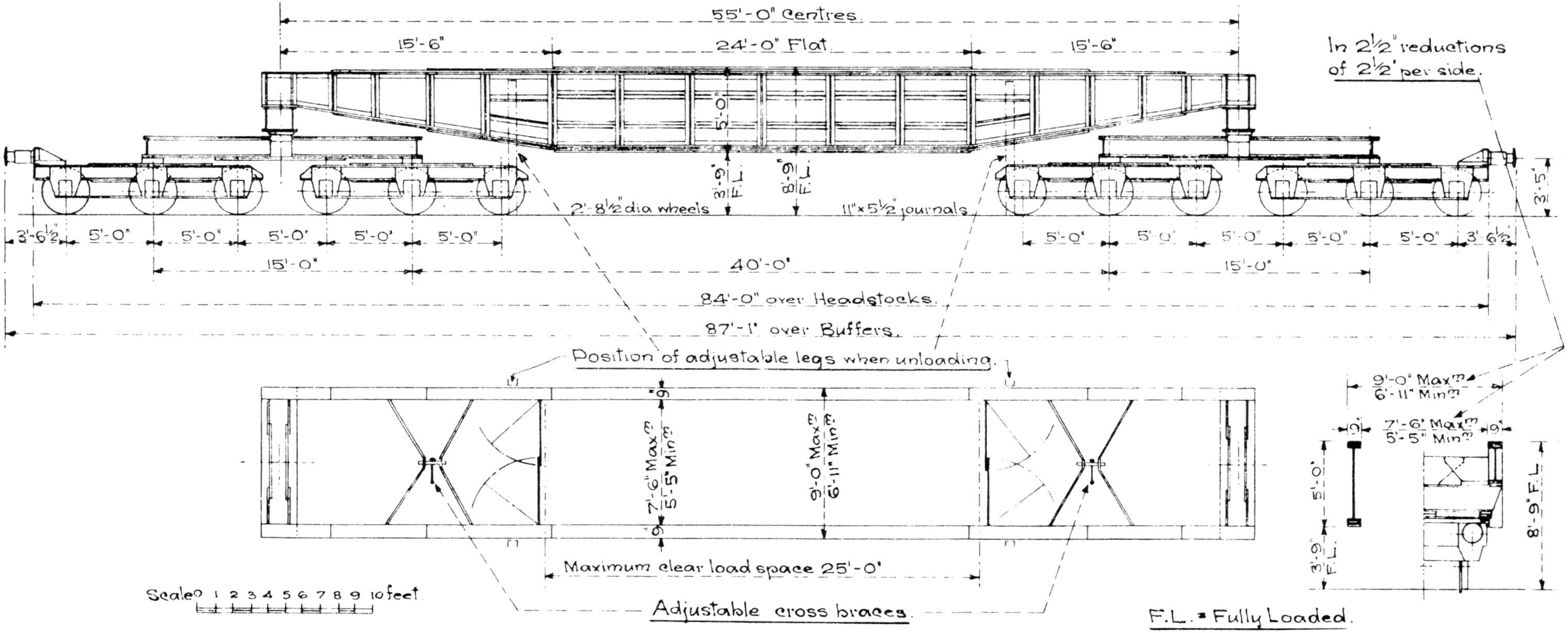

Figure 68

50 TON TWIN GIRDER TRUCK

Diagram Book Page 137

Drawing No. 6515

Code: TGP (later coded GIRDWAG MA by British Rail)
Lot number: 298
Quantity: 2 pairs
Built: Derby 1928
Running numbers: 263369/70 and 269943/4
Tare: 12 tons 6 cwt (per pair)

The minimum curve that the truck will negotiate (as shown)
is 1 chain, and 3 chains when centre of bolster is 57 ft.
Carrying capacity: 50 tons (25 tons per wagon). Binding
chains: 2 sets, including screw coupling (1 set per wagon).
Timber bolster removable.

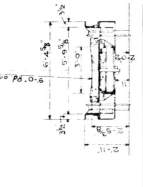

Plate 89 No. 269944 is pictured here in ex-works
condition.

Photograph British Rail

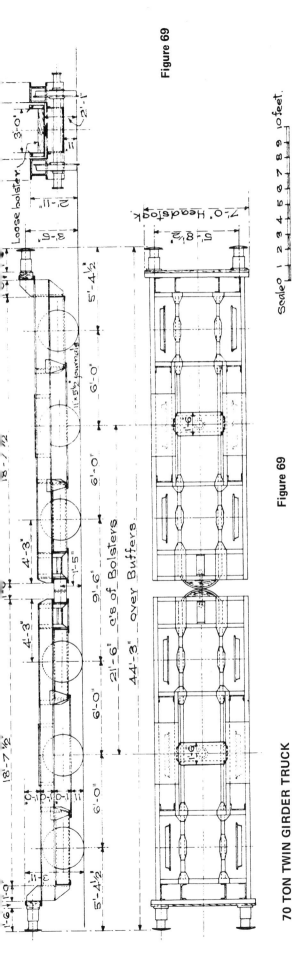

Figure 69

Diagram Book Page 137A

70 TON TWIN GIRDER TRUCK

Drawing No. 13/1545

Code: TGT (later coded GIRDWAG MB by British Rail)
Lot number: 603
Quantity: 1 pair
Built: Derby 1931
Running numbers: 5045/6
Tare: 17 tons 3 cwt (the pair)

The minimum curve that the truck will negotiate (as shown) is 2½ chains. Carrying capacity: 70 tons (35 tons per wagon). Binding chains: 2 sets, including screw couplings (1 set per wagon). Timber bolsters removable.

Plate 90 This depicts these vehicles when first built, and no other photographs are known, by the author, to exist.

Photograph British Rail

Plate 91 (above)   This illustrates No. 168926 and it is believed that this vehicle is part of lot 423, described in the lot book as a '20T chaired sleeper wagon', one of 44 built to drawing 11/189 at Derby. The paint date on the solebar reads 19/12/28 and, while the details of construction should be compared with those of No. 33793 illustrated in **Plate 92**, attention is also drawn to the vehicles in the background. On the extreme left is a 20T ex-Midland goods brake in a very dark body colour as indeed is the refrigerator van in the centre of the picture. The other dark coloured vehicles could well be passenger rated, in which case they are probably painted crimson lake, or, may well be, slate grey. The whole question of livery is further discussed later in this volume in a special chapter dealing with this subject.

Photograph British Rail

Plate 92 (below)   This almost certainly illustrates the single example built to lot 365 in 1928. No further details are contained in the lot book. It is possible that after this vehicle was built an order for a further 44 was placed to lot 423. Unfortunately no other running numbers are known to the author.

Photograph British Rail

In concluding this chapter dealing with Special Wagons, attention is drawn to two illustrations of chaired sleeper trolleys which appear to have been built without being allocated a diagram number.

INDEX OF LMS CONTAINERS

TAKEN FROM THE CONTAINER DIAGRAM BOOK

STEEL CONTAINER TYPE 'A' (VENTILATED)
Page 1

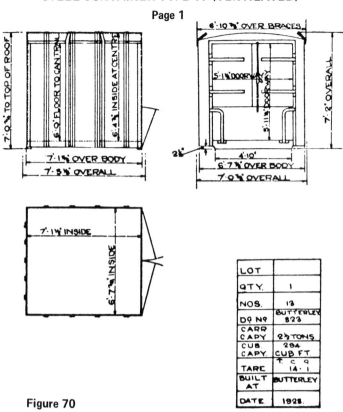

Figure 70

LOT.	
QTY.	1
NOS.	13
Dg Nº	BUTTERLEY 823
CARR CAPY	2½ TONS.
CUB. CAPY.	294 CUB FT.
TARE	T C Q 14·1
BUILT AT	BUTTERLEY
DATE.	1928.

BONMAX PANELLED CONTAINER TYPE 'A'
Page 2

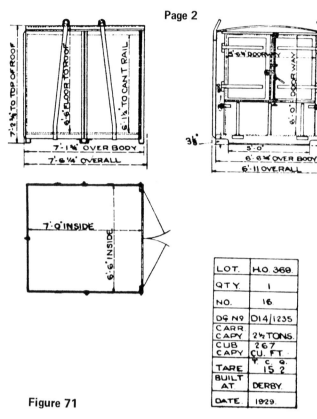

Figure 71

LOT.	H.O. 368.
QTY.	1
NO.	16
Dg Nº	D14/1235
CARR CAPY	2½ TONS.
CUB CAPY	267 CU. FT.
TARE	T. C. Q. 15 2
BUILT AT.	DERBY.
DATE.	1929.

VULCANISED FIBRE PANELLED CONTAINER TYPE 'A'
Page 3

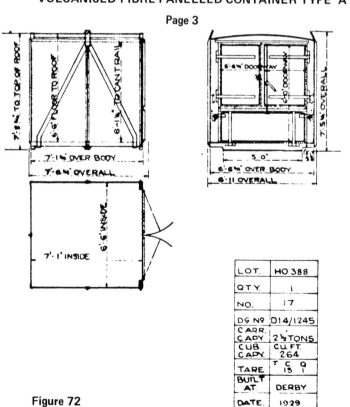

Figure 72

LOT.	HO 388
QTY.	1
NO.	17
Dg Nº	D14/1245
CARR CAPY	2½ TONS
CUB. CAPY.	CU FT. 264
TARE	T C Q 15 1
BUILT AT	DERBY
DATE.	1929

WOOD CONTAINER TYPE 'A'
Page 4

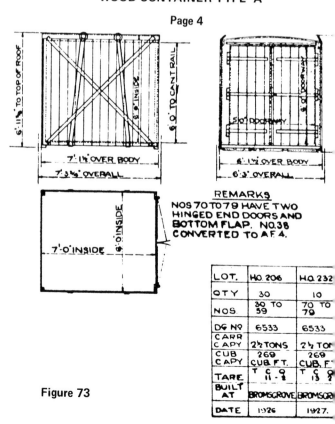

REMARKS
NOS 70 TO 79 HAVE TWO HINGED END DOORS AND BOTTOM FLAP. NO.38 CONVERTED TO A.F.4.

Figure 73

LOT.	HO. 208	H.O. 232
QTY	30	10
NOS	30 TO 59	70 TO 79
Dg Nº	6533	6533
CARR CAPY	2½ TONS	2½ TON
CUB CAPY	269 CUB FT.	269 CUB. F
TARE	T C Q 11·1	T C Q 13 1
BUILT AT	BROMSGROVE	BROMSGRO
DATE.	1926	1927.

Plates 93 & 94   These two pictures illustrate early experimental colours. **Plate 93** shows AEx1 being loaded on to a lorry and no other details are known. **Plate 94** illustrates Ex4 which was built by Charles Roberts and is seen in their works yard. Both appear to be in grey livery but AEx1 has black ironwork while Ex4 is all grey. Neither container appears to have been allocated diagrams in the container diagram book.

Photographs British Rail

WOOD CONTAINER TYPE 'A'

Page 5

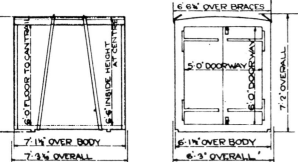

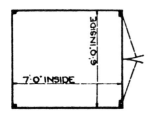

Figure 74

LOT.	HO 220
QTY.	10
NOS.	60 TO 69
DG NO	6590.
CARR. CAPY.	3 TONS
CUB. CAPY	269 CUB FT
TARE	T.C.Q 13·1
BUILT AT.	BROMSGROVE
DATE.	1926.

WOOD CONTAINER TYPE 'A'

Page 6

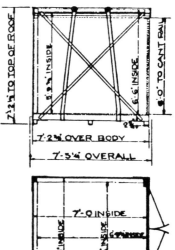

REMARKS

No. 82 INSULATED FOR BANANA TRAFFIC DRG 14/1770A. (INSIDE DIMENSIONS TO CHAIN DOTTED LINES)
NO.91 FITTED WITH SHELVES FOR CONFECTIONERY TRAFFIC TO DRG 14/1461A.

Figure 75

LOT.	H.O 246
QTY.	60
NOS.	80·88 / 80 TO 139
DG NO	6679
CARR. CAPY.	2½ TONS
CUB CAPY.	263 CU. FT
TARE	T.C.Q 16·0
BUILT AT.	BROMSGROVE
DATE.	1927.

WOOD CONTAINER TYPE 'A'

Page 7

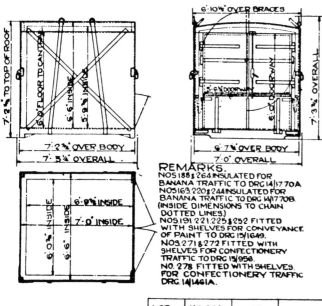

REMARKS.

NOS 188 & 264 INSULATED FOR BANANA TRAFFIC TO DRG 14/1770A
NOS 163,220 & 244 INSULATED FOR BANANA TRAFFIC TO DRG 14/1770B. (INSIDE DIMENSIONS TO CHAIN DOTTED LINES.)
NOS 191, 221,225 & 292 FITTED WITH SHELVES FOR CONVEYANCE OF PAINT TO DRG 15/1649.
NOS.271 & 272 FITTED WITH SHELVES FOR CONFECTIONERY TRAFFIC TO DRG 15/958.
NO. 278 FITTED WITH SHELVES FOR CONFECTIONERY TRAFFIC DRG.14/1461A.

Figure 76

LOT.	HO.349.	HO.370.	H.O 453
QTY.	50	75	60
NOS.	140 TO 189	190 TO 264	265 TO 324
DG NO.	14/1208A.	14/1208A.	14/1208A
CARR. CAPY.	2½ TONS	2½ TONS	2½ TONS
CUB. CAPY.	284 CU. FT	284 CU. FT	284 CU. FT
TARE	T C Q 17 1	T C Q 17 1	T C Q 17 1
BUILT AT.	DERBY	DERBY	BROMSGROVE
DATE	1928	1928	1928-29

BONMAX PANELLED CONTAINER TYPE 'A'

Page 8

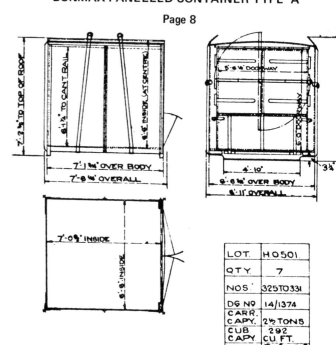

Figure 77

LOT.	H O 501
QTY.	7
NOS.	325 TO 331
DG NO	14/1374
CARR. CAPY.	2½ TONS
CUB CAPY	292 CU. FT
TARE	T C Q 15 2
BUILT AT.	DERBY
DATE.	1929.

Plate 95   This specially posed picture illustrates 2-6-0 'Crab' No. 13119 with five type 'K' containers and a LNWR goods brake. The containers are to be found on page 121 of the diagram book, **Figure 111** and they are loaded on to pre-group low wagons which were used for container traffic.

Photograph British Rail

Plate 96   This interesting picture illustrates the method of loading and carrying two containers into an ex-Midland Railway low goods wagon which is to diagram 305. Before dealing with the containers, this wagon, whose number cannot clearly be seen, has just been repainted grey, and it will be noted that the brakegear has not been altered, it remains on the left of an operator when facing the vehicle. Many pre-group wagons ran in this condition and were never altered before being withdrawn. The containers are from diagram book, page 4, **Figure 73** and were built in 1926. It is difficult to ascertain the colour in which they were painted. It could have been red oxide or slate grey.

Photograph British Rail

Page 9

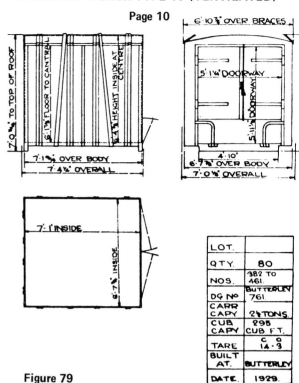

Figure 78

LOT.		
QTY	50	25
NOS.	332 TO 381	462 TO 486
DG No	BIRMINGHAM C&W 14335	BIRMINGHAM C&W 14335
CARR CAPY	2½ TONS	2½ TONS
CUB. CAPY	280 CUB. FT.	280 CUB. FT.
TARE	T. C. Q 17.0	T. C. Q 17.0
BUILT AT	BIRMINGHAM C&W	BIRMINGHAM C&W
DATE	1929.	1929.

Figure 79

LOT.	
QTY.	80
NOS.	382 TO 461
DG No	BUTTERLEY 761
CARR CAPY	2½ TONS
CUB CAPY	295 CUB. FT.
TARE	C. Q 14.3
BUILT AT.	BUTTERLEY
DATE.	1929.

STEEL CONTAINER TYPE 'A' (VENTILATED)

Page 11

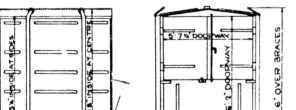
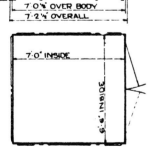
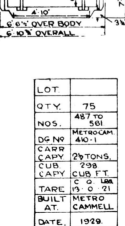

Figure 80

LOT.	
QTY.	75
NOS.	487 TO 561
DG No	METRO-CAM. 410-1
CARR CAPY	2½ TONS.
CUB. CAPY	298 CUB. FT.
TARE	C. Q. Lbs 13.0.21
BUILT AT.	METRO CAMMELL
DATE.	1929.

STEEL CONTAINER TYPE 'A' (VENTILATED)

Page 12

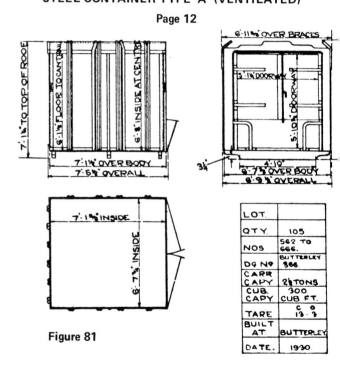

Figure 81

LOT.	
QTY.	105
NOS	562 TO 666.
DG No	BUTTERLEY 866
CARR CAPY	2½ TONS
CUB. CAPY	300 CUB. FT.
TARE	C. Q 13.3
BUILT AT.	BUTTERLEY
DATE.	1930.

Plate 97   This illustrates two type 'A' containers from diagram book, page 6, **Figure 75**, loaded on to the first 'custom bui[lt]' container flat wagon to be built to lot 346 in 1927. Note the method of ensuring that the container did not move whilst transit. It is difficult to ascertain in what colour these containers were painted. It could have been slate grey, red oxide bauxite, and the question of livery is further discussed later in this volume in a special chapter.

Photograph British R[.]

Plate 98   This illustration of A204, on a horse-drawn dray, shows an example of a container to diagram book, page **Figure 76**. The photograph was taken at the Charles Roberts works, and so it is possible that the diagram is in error a[s] the batch 190–264 were built by that company. However, a more likely explanation is that the container has just be[en] repaired and repainted. The finish appears to be in light grey with black ironwork. The use of the 'Barratt' advertiseme[nt] is interesting.

Photograph British R[.]

Plate 99 This illustration of A330, on horse-dray at Derby, shows an item of 19. construction in what appears to be gr livery with black ironwork.

Photograph British R.

Plate 100 A batch of type 'A' ventilated containers which have just been built. The diagram credits the construction to the Butterly Company, and the livery, which is interesting, is believed by the author to be white with black lettering.

Photograph British Rail

STEEL CONTAINER TYPE 'A' (VENTILATED)
Page 13

STEEL CONTAINER TYPE 'A'
Page 14

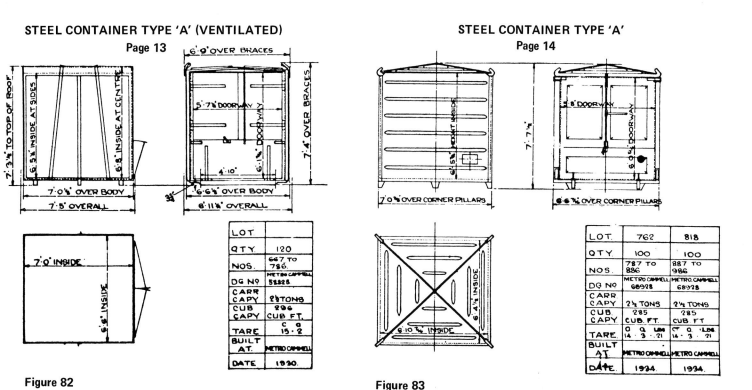

Figure 82

LOT.	
QTY.	120
NOS.	667 TO 786.
DG Nº	METRO CAMMELL 51828
CARR CAPY	2½ TONS
CUB CAPY	296 CUB FT.
TARE	C Q 15 · 2
BUILT AT.	METRO CAMMELL
DATE	1930.

Figure 83

LOT.	762	818
QTY.	100	100
NOS.	787 TO 886	887 TO 986
DG Nº	METRO CAMMELL 68928	METRO CAMMELL 68928
CARR CAPY	2½ TONS	2½ TONS
CUB CAPY	285 CUB. FT.	285 CUB. FT.
TARE	O Q LBS 14 · 3 · 21	C Q LBS 14 · 3 · 21
BUILT AT	METRO CAMMELL	METRO CAMMELL
DATE	1934.	1934.

Plate 101 This illustrates an example of a container on page 14 of diagram book, **Figure 83**, and the details listed on the photograph give considerable information, with the exception of the colour of the paintwork! The author believes it was slate grey, but it could possibly have been red oxide.

Photograph British Rail

WOOD CONTAINER TYPE 'A'
Page 15

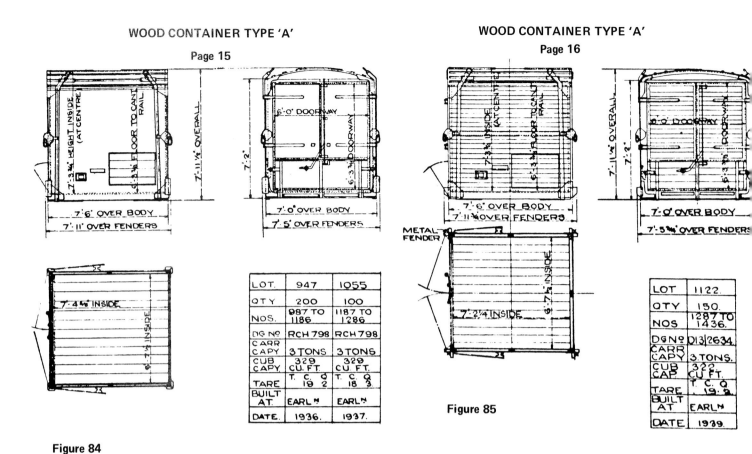

6'-0" DOORWAY
7'-3¾" HEIGHT INSIDE (AT CENTRE)
6'-3½" FLOOR TO CANT RAIL
7'-11½" OVERALL
7'-2"
6'-3½" DOORWAY
7'-6" OVER BODY
7'-11" OVER FENDERS
7'-0" OVER BODY
7'-5" OVER FENDERS
7'-4¾" INSIDE
6'-7½" INSIDE

LOT.	947	1055
QTY	200	100
NOS.	987 TO 1186	1187 TO 1286
DG Nº	RCH 798	RCH 798
CARR CAPY	3 TONS	3 TONS
CUB CAPY	329 CU. FT.	329 CU. FT.
TARE	T. C. Q 19 2	T. C. Q 18 3
BUILT AT.	EARLⁿ	EARLⁿ
DATE.	1936.	1937.

Figure 84

WOOD CONTAINER TYPE 'A'
Page 16

6'-0" DOORWAY
7'-3¼" INSIDE (AT CENTRE)
6'-3½" FLOOR TO CANT RAIL
7'-11½" OVERALL
7'-2"
6'-3½" DOORWAY
7'-6" OVER BODY
7'-11½" OVER FENDERS
7'-0" OVER BODY
7'-5¼" OVER FENDERS
METAL FENDER
7'-2¼" INSIDE
6'-7½" INSIDE

LOT	1122.
QTY	150.
NOS	1287 TO 1436.
DG Nº	D13/2634.
CARR CAPY	3 TONS.
CUB CAP.	322 CU. FT.
TARE	T. C. Q 19 2
BUILT AT	EARLⁿ
DATE	1939.

Figure 85

WOOD CONTAINER TYPE 'A'
Page 17

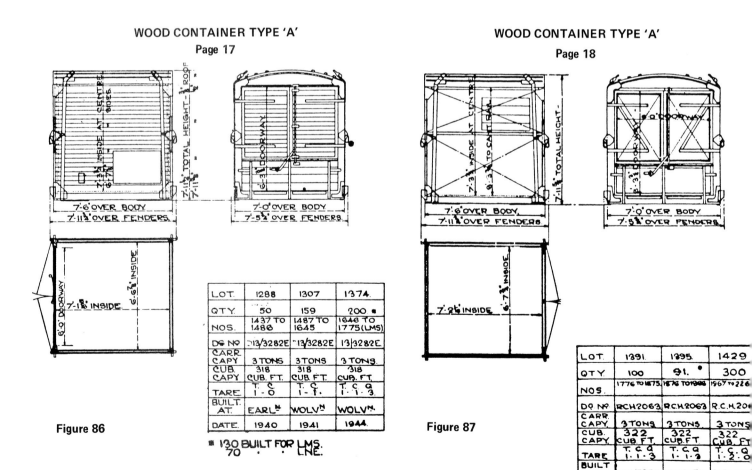

6'-0" DOORWAY
7'-3¾" INSIDE AT CENTRE SIDES
6'-7½"
7'-11½" TOTAL HEIGHT — ROOF
7'-11"
6'-3½" DOORWAY
7'-6" OVER BODY
7'-11½" OVER FENDERS
7'-0" OVER BODY
7'-5¼" OVER FENDERS
6'-6¾" INSIDE
7'-11½" INSIDE
6'-0" DOORWAY

LOT.	1288	1307	1374.
QTY.	50	159	200 ∗
NOS.	1437 TO 1486	1487 TO 1645	1646 TO 1775 (LMS)
DG Nº	D13/3282E	D13/3282E	13/3282E
CARR. CAPY	3 TONS	3 TONS	3 TONS.
CUB. CAPY.	318 CUB. FT.	318 CUB. FT.	318 CUB. FT.
TARE	T. C 1 - 0	T. C 1 - 1.	T. C. Q 1 - 1.
BUILT AT.	EARLⁿ	WOLVⁿ	WOLVⁿ.
DATE.	1940	1941	1944.

Figure 86

∗ 130 BUILT FOR LMS.
70 " " " LNE.

WOOD CONTAINER TYPE 'A'
Page 18

6'-0" DOORWAY
7'-3¾" INSIDE AT CENTRE
6'-7½" TO CANT RAIL
7'-11½" TOTAL HEIGHT
6'-3½" DOORWAY
7'-6" OVER BODY
7'-11" OVER FENDERS
7'-0" OVER BODY
7'-5¾" OVER FENDERS
6'-7¾" INSIDE
7'-2¾" INSIDE

LOT.	1391.	1395.	1429
QTY.	100	91. ∗	300
NOS.	1776 TO 1875	1876 TO 1966	1967 TO 2266
DG Nº	RCH 2063	RCH 2063	R.C.H. 206
CARR. CAPY	3 TONS	3 TONS	3 TONS
CUB. CAPY.	322 CUB FT	322 CUB FT	322 CUB. FT
TARE	T. C. Q 1 . 1 . 3	T. C. Q 1 . 1 . 3	T. C. Q 1 . 2 . 0
BUILT AT.	WOLVERTON	WOLVERTON	EARLSTⁿ
DATE.	1945.	1944.	1946

Figure 87

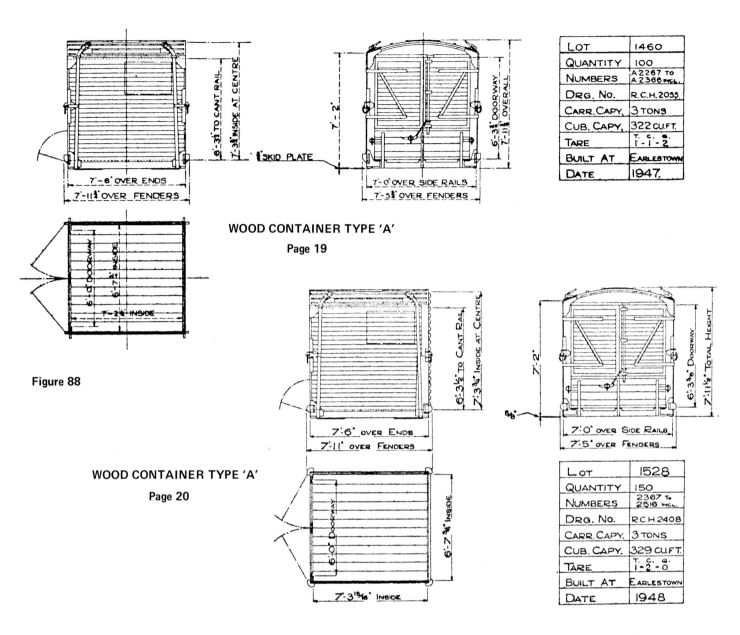

LOT	1460
QUANTITY	100
NUMBERS	A 2267 TO A 2366 INCL.
DRG. No.	R.C.H. 2055
CARR. CAPY.	3 TONS
CUB. CAPY.	322 CU.FT.
TARE	T. C. Q. 1 - 1 - 2
BUILT AT	EARLESTOWN
DATE	1947.

WOOD CONTAINER TYPE 'A'

Page 19

Figure 88

WOOD CONTAINER TYPE 'A'

Page 20

LOT	1528
QUANTITY	150
NUMBERS	2367 TO 2516 INCL.
DRG. No.	R.C.H. 2408
CARR. CAPY.	3 TONS
CUB. CAPY.	329 CU.FT.
TARE	T. C. Q. 1 - 2 - 0
BUILT AT	EARLESTOWN
DATE	1948

Figure 89

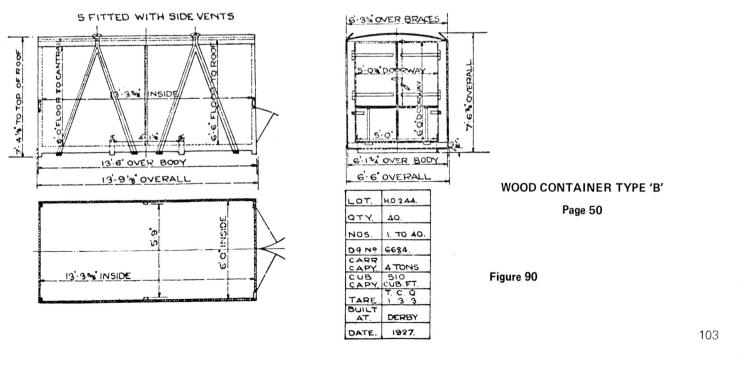

WOOD CONTAINER TYPE 'B'

Page 50

LOT.	H.O.244.
QTY.	40.
NOS.	1. TO 40.
DG No	6684.
CARR CAPY.	4 TONS
CUB CAPY.	510 CUB.FT.
TARE	T. C. Q. 1 3 3
BUILT AT.	DERBY
DATE.	1927.

Figure 90

Plate 104 (above) This illustrates a well-used container in service. The number is not clear but it does appear to be BX443 and coincides with diagram book, page 54, **Figure 94**. The 'X' does not appear on the diagram, so it would seem that the rating was altered at some date. It is difficult to be sure about the colour, but it is possible that it was freight stock grey with white lettering.

Photograph A. E. West

Plate 102 (left) The diagram suggests this container was built in 1936 and, if A988 was constructed after the livery change, its body colour could be bauxite with black ironwork or crimson lake.

Photograph British Rail

Plate 103 Container B31 was photographed on the experimental 'one off' container flat truck built in 1927 to lot 346 also illustrated in **Plate 97**. The question of the container livery is confusing. Is it slate grey or bauxite grey? The date of construction of page 50 containers was 1927 **(Figure 90)**.

Photograph British Rail

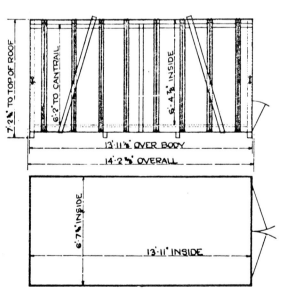

REMARKS.

NOS. 67 & 78, FITTED WITH SHELVES ETC. FOR BISCUIT TRAFFIC DG. 14/1665. NO. 123, FITTED WITH SHELVES FOR CONFECTIONERY TRAFFIC DG. 14/1461A. NO. 125, FITTED WITH SIDE DOORS ETC. DG. 14/1956. AS A 'BD' TYPE. (SEE CHAIN DOTTED LINES)

Figure 91

LOT	H.O.351	H.O.371	H.O.452	H.O.491
QTY	50	75	80	20
NOS.	41 TO 79 92 TO 102	80 TO 91 103 TO 165	166 TO 245	246 TO 265
DG No	14/1211	14/1211	14/1211A	14/1211A
CARR CAPY.	4 TONS	4 TONS	4 TONS	4 TONS
CUB CAPY.	574 CU. FT.	574 CU. FT.	574 CU. FT.	574 CU. FT.
TARE. T.C.Q	1 7 2	1 7 2	1 7 2	1 7 2
BUILT AT.	DERBY.	DERBY.	DERBY.	DERBY
DATE.	1928	1928	1928	1929

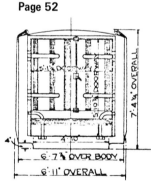

Figure 92

LOT	
QTY	100
NOS	266 TO 385
DG No	752 BUTTERLEY
CARR CAPY	4 TONS
CUB CAPY	577 CUB FT
TARE T.C.Q	1 3 0
BUILT AT.	BUTTERLEY
DATE.	1929

REMARKS
NOS. 274, 275, 301, 305, 333, 345. & 352 FITTED UP FOR FURNITURE TRAFFIC TO DRG 16/885 PAINTED LMS. LAKE & RE-LETTERED KX. (H.O.765.)

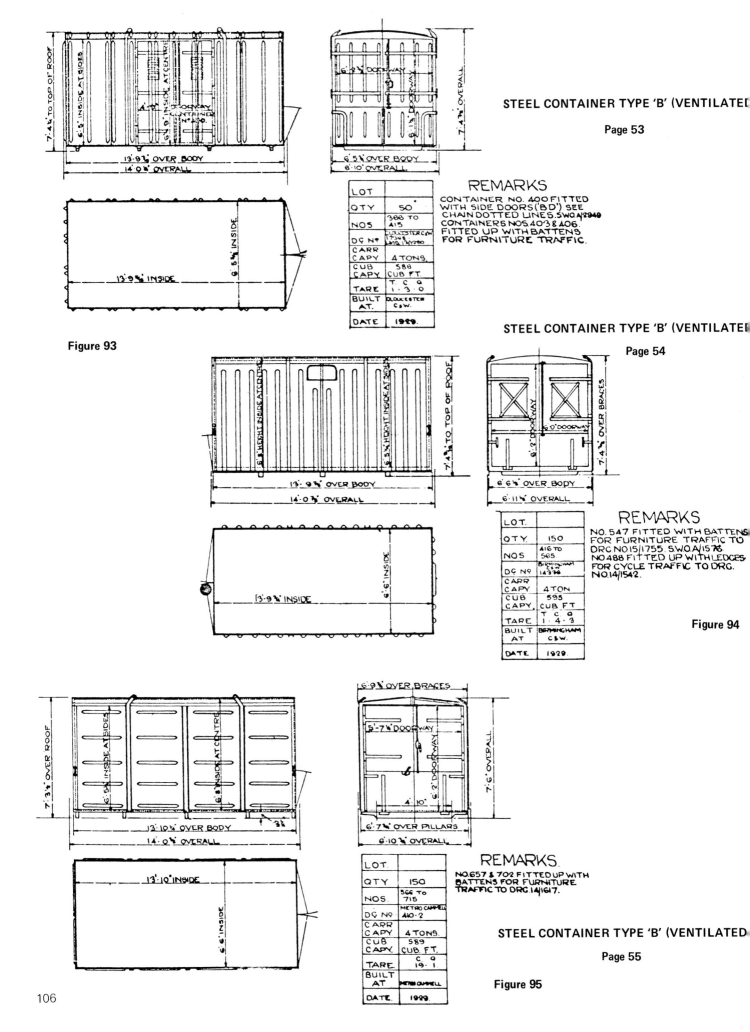

STEEL CONTAINER TYPE 'B' (VENTILATED)

Page 53

7'4½" TO TOP OF ROOF
6'5¼" INSIDE AT SIDES
6'8⅛" INSIDE AT CENTRE
DOORWAY CONTAINER Nº 400
6'2¾" DOORWAY
6'3" DOORWAY
7'4½" OVERALL
13'9⅛" OVER BODY
14'0⅛" OVERALL
6'5¼" OVER BODY
8'10" OVERALL

13'9⅝" INSIDE
6'5¼" INSIDE

REMARKS

CONTAINER NO. 400 FITTED WITH SIDE DOORS ('BD') SEE CHAIN DOTTED LINES. S.W.O.A/2949 CONTAINERS NOS 403 & 406 FITTED UP WITH BATTENS FOR FURNITURE TRAFFIC.

LOT	
QTY	50
NOS	366 TO 415
DG Nº	GLOUCESTER C&W 1753 & 1712. 1.N/280
CARR CAPY	4 TONS
CUB CAPY	588 CUB FT
TARE	T C Q 1·3·0
BUILT AT	GLOUCESTER C&W.
DATE	1929.

Figure 93

STEEL CONTAINER TYPE 'B' (VENTILATED)

Page 54

6'5⅛" HEIGHT INSIDE AT CENTRE
6'5⅜" HEIGHT INSIDE AT SIDES
7'4½" TO TOP OF ROOF
13'9¾" OVER BODY
14'0⅜" OVERALL
6'2" DOORWAY
6'0" DOORWAY
7'4½" OVER BRACES
6'6½" OVER BODY
6'11¾" OVERALL

13'9¾" INSIDE
6'6" INSIDE

REMARKS

NO. 547 FITTED WITH BATTENS FOR FURNITURE TRAFFIC TO DRG NO 15/1755. S.W.O.A/1575. NO 488 FITTED UP WITH LEDGES FOR CYCLE TRAFFIC TO DRG. NO.14/1542.

LOT.	
QTY.	150
NOS	416 TO 565.
DG Nº	BIRMINGHAM C&W 14379
CARR CAPY	4 TON
CUB CAPY.	595 CUB FT
TARE	T C Q 1·4·3
BUILT AT	BIRMINGHAM C&W.
DATE	1929.

Figure 94

6'9½" OVER BRACES
7'3½" OVER ROOF
6'5¼" INSIDE AT SIDES
6'8" INSIDE AT CENTRE
5'7¾" DOORWAY
6'2" DOORWAY
7'6" OVERALL
4'10"
13'10¼" OVER BODY
14'0¼" OVERALL
3¼"
6'7¾" OVER PILLARS
6'10¾" OVERALL

13'10" INSIDE
6'6" INSIDE

REMARKS.

NO.657 & 702 FITTED UP WITH BATTENS FOR FURNITURE TRAFFIC TO DRG.14/1617.

STEEL CONTAINER TYPE 'B' (VENTILATED)

Page 55

LOT.	
QTY	150
NOS.	566 TO 715
DG Nº	METRO CAMPBELL A10·2
CARR CAPY	4 TONS
CUB CAPY.	589 CUB. FT.
TARE	T C Q ·19·1
BUILT AT	METRO CAMPBELL
DATE	1929.

Figure 95

106

Plate 105   No. BX566, pictured on a horse dray, is an example of diagram book, page 55, **Figure 95** and was built in 1929. The livery appears to be wagon grey with black hinges.

Photograph British Rail

Plate 106   This photograph of B716, taken when loaded on to an ex-LNWR low goods wagon, which is branded For container traffic 'X', shows the single example, built by the Butterley Company for Banana traffic. The body colour is lighter than the light grey of the wagon, but darker than the white of the lettering. It could be cream or light stone, with black lettering.

Photograph British Rail

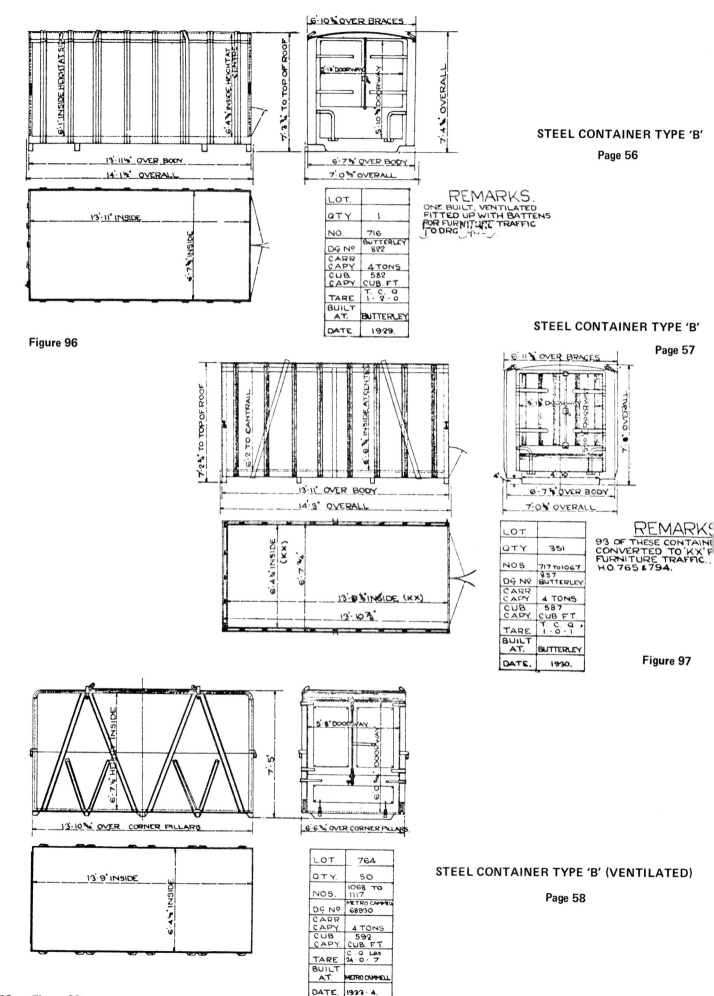

STEEL CONTAINER TYPE 'B'

Page 56

LOT.	
QTY	1
NO.	716
DG Nº	BUTTERLEY 822
CARR CAPY	4 TONS
CUB CAPY	582 CUB. FT.
TARE	T. C. Q 1 · 2 · 0
BUILT AT.	BUTTERLEY
DATE.	1929.

REMARKS.
ONE BUILT, VENTILATED
FITTED UP WITH BATTENS
FOR FURNITURE TRAFFIC
TO DRG

Figure 96

STEEL CONTAINER TYPE 'B'

Page 57

LOT.	
QTY	351
NOS.	717 to 1067
DG Nº	857 BUTTERLEY
CARR CAPY	4 TONS
CUB CAPY.	587 CUB FT.
TARE	T. C. Q. 1 · 0 · 1
BUILT AT.	BUTTERLEY
DATE.	1930.

REMARKS
93 OF THESE CONTAINE
CONVERTED TO 'KX' F
FURNITURE TRAFFIC.
H.O. 765 & 794.

Figure 97

STEEL CONTAINER TYPE 'B' (VENTILATED)

Page 58

LOT.	764
QTY.	50
NOS.	1068 TO 1117
DG Nº	METRO CAMMELL 68830
CARR CAPY	4 TONS
CUB CAPY	592 CUB. FT.
TARE	C. Q. LBS 24 · 0 · 7
BUILT AT.	METRO CAMMELL
DATE.	1933. 4.

Figure 98

Plate 107 (left) As with **Plate 101**, this picture of container B1117, diagram book, page 58, **Figure 98**, is informative except that it does not give the body colour, which could be either red oxide or slate grey.

Photograph British Rail

Plate 108 (below) No. BY1071 is seen in traffic, loaded on an ex-LNWR low goods wagon branded for container traffic. Wagon No. 217157 has been fitted with LMS axleboxes.

Photograph British Rail

Plate 109 (bottom) This illustration of B1118 should be compared with that in **Plate 107**. Reference to **Figures 98 & 99** will show that two different designs were being tried out. The livery comments in **Plate 107** are also applicable to this container.

Photograph British Rail

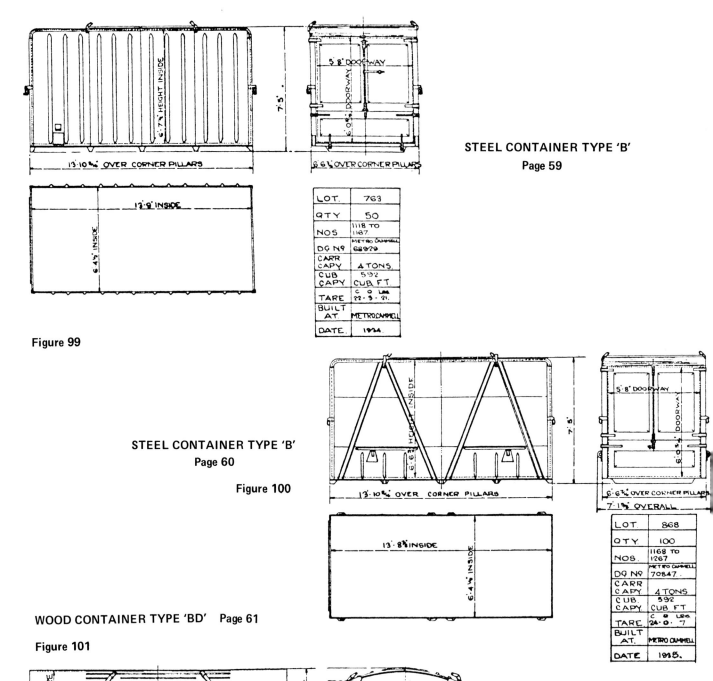

STEEL CONTAINER TYPE 'B'
Page 59

Figure 99

LOT.	763
QTY	50
NOS	1118 TO 1187
DG Nº	METRO CAMMELL 68979
CARR CAPY	4 TONS
CUB CAPY	592 CUB. FT.
TARE	C Q LBS 22-3-21.
BUILT AT.	METRO CAMMELL
DATE.	1924.

STEEL CONTAINER TYPE 'B'
Page 60

Figure 100

LOT	868
QTY	100
NOS.	1168 TO 1267
DG Nº	METRO CAMMELL 70847
CARR CAPY	4 TONS
CUB. CAPY	592 CUB FT
TARE.	C Q LBS 24-0-7
BUILT AT.	METRO CAMMELL
DATE.	1925.

WOOD CONTAINER TYPE 'BD'   Page 61

Figure 101

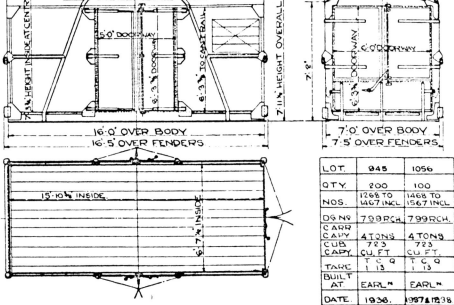

	LOT.	945	1056
	QTY.	200	100
	NOS.	1268 TO 1467 INCL	1468 TO 1567 INCL
	DG Nº	799 RCH.	799 RCH.
	CARR CAPY	4 TONS	4 TONS
	CUB CAPY	723 CU. FT.	723 CU. FT.
	TARE	T C Q 1 13	T C Q 1 13
	BUILT AT.	EARLⁿ	EARLⁿ
	DATE.	1936.	1937 & 1938.

Plate 110 (top right)   This illustrates c
tainer No. B1279 which, according
Figure 101, was to become 'type E
The livery was almost certainly bauxite v
black ironwork, but there is a possibl
that it was crimson lake.

Photograph British .

Plate 111 (bottom right)   BD container
1643, pictured on a rail mounted trol
appears to be in dark grey livery with b
ironwork. This is surprising, in view of
date of construction, and no explanation
be given.

Photograph British

For Traders adhesive Labels only

To carry 4 Tons
Tare 1. 15.0
Capacity 723 cb.ft.

LONDON MIDLAND & SCOTTISH
RAILWAY

L M S
B 1279

B 1279   DOOR TO DOOR CONTAINER TRANSPORT

To carry 4 Tons
Capacity 709 cb.ft.
Tare 1. 14.0

L M S
BD 1643

LONDON MIDLAND
RAILWAY

BD 1643   DOOR TO DOOR CONTAINER TRANSPORT

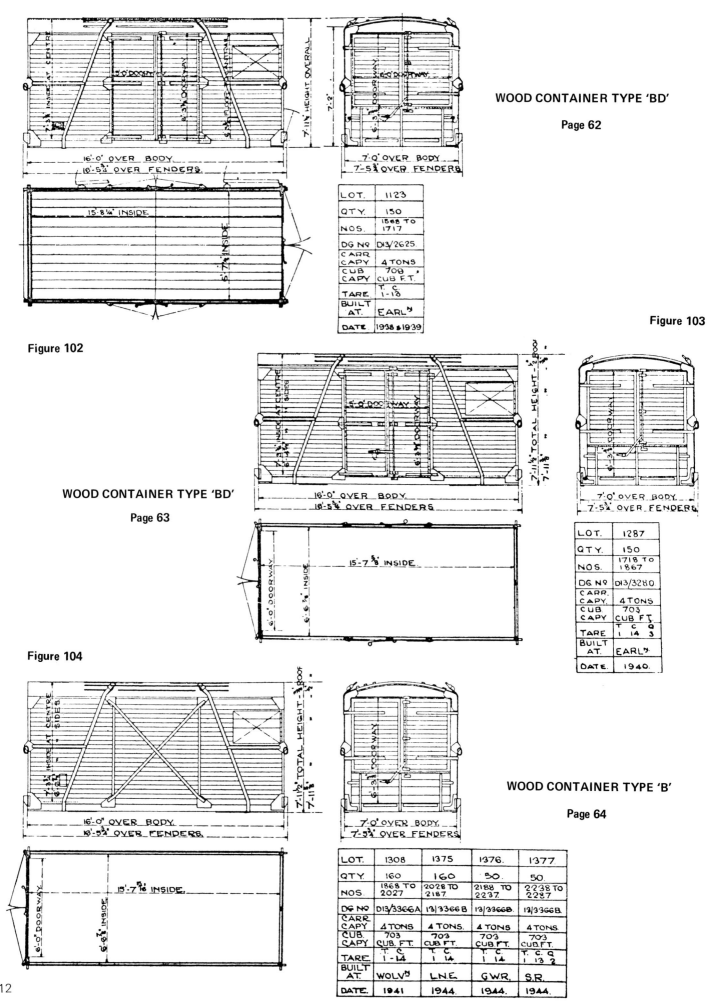

WOOD CONTAINER TYPE 'BD'

Page 62

Figure 103

Figure 102

LOT.	1123
QTY.	150
NOS.	1568 TO 1717
DG Nº	D13/2625.
CARR CAPY	4 TONS
CUB CAPY	709 CUB F.T.
TARE	T. C. 1-18
BUILT AT.	EARLᴺ
DATE.	1938 & 1939

WOOD CONTAINER TYPE 'BD'

Page 63

LOT.	1287
QTY.	150
NOS.	1718 TO 1867
DG Nº	D13/3280
CARR. CAPY.	4 TONS
CUB. CAPY	703 CUB FT.
TARE	T C Q 1 14 3
BUILT AT.	EARLᴺ
DATE.	1940.

Figure 104

WOOD CONTAINER TYPE 'B'

Page 64

LOT.	1308	1375	1376.	1377.
QTY.	160	160	50.	50.
NOS.	1868 TO 2027	2028 TO 2187	2188 TO 2237	2238 TO 2287
DG Nº	D13/3366A	13/3366B	13/3366B.	13/3366B.
CARR CAPY	4 TONS	4 TONS	4 TONS	4 TONS
CUB. CAPY	703 CUB. FT.	703 CUB FT.	703 CUB.FT.	703 CUB.FT.
TARE	T. C. 1-14	T. C. 1 14	T. C. 1 14	T. C. Q 1 13 2
BUILT AT.	WOLVᴺ	L.N.E.	G.W.R.	S.R.
DATE.	1941	1944.	1944.	1944.

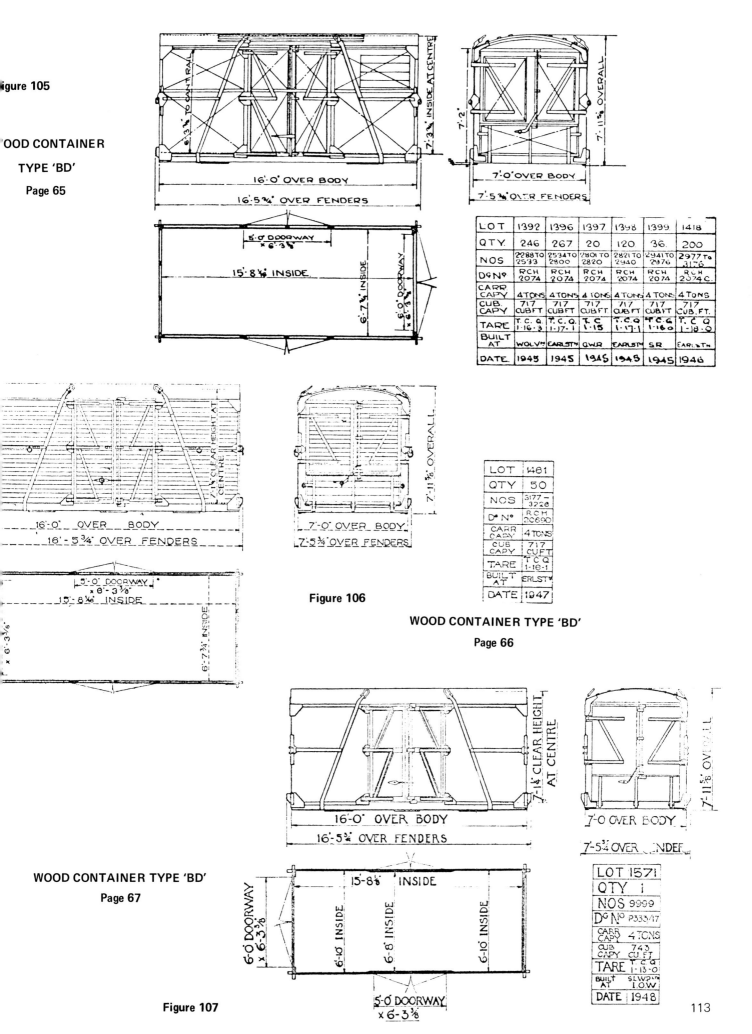

Figure 105

WOOD CONTAINER
TYPE 'BD'
Page 65

16'-0" OVER BODY
16'-5¾" OVER FENDERS
5'-0" DOORWAY × 6'-3⅜"
15'-8⅛" INSIDE
6'-7¾" INSIDE
6'-0" DOORWAY × 6'-3⅜"
6'-3¼" TO CENTRAL
7'-3¼" INSIDE AT CENTRE
7'-2"
7'-5¾" OVERALL
7'-0" OVER BODY
7'-5¾" OVER FENDERS

LOT	1392	1396	1397	1398	1399	1418
QTY.	246	267	20	120	36	200
NOS	2288 TO 2533	2534 TO 2800	2801 TO 2820	2821 TO 2940	2941 TO 2976	2977 TO 3176
D⁰ Nº	RCH 2074	RCH 2074	RCH 2074	RCH 2074	RCH 2074	RCH 2074C.
CARR CAPY	4 TONS	4 TONS	4 TONS	4 TONS	4 TONS	4 TONS
CUB CAPY	717 CUB FT	717 CUB FT	717 CUB FT	717 CUB FT	717 CUB FT	717 CUB. FT.
TARE	T.C.Q. 1-16-3	T.C.Q. 1-17-1	T.C. 1-15	T.C.Q 1-17-1	T.C.Q 1-16-0	T.C.Q 1-18-0
BUILT AT	WOLV'N	EARLST'N	GWR	EARLST'N	S.R.	EARLST'N
DATE	1945	1945	1945	1945	1945	1946

16'-0" OVER BODY
16'-5¾" OVER FENDERS
5'-0" DOORWAY × 6'-3⅜"
15'-8⅛" INSIDE
6'-7¾" INSIDE
6'-3⅜"
7'-1¼" CLEAR HEIGHT AT CENTRE
7'-11⅞" OVERALL
7'-0" OVER BODY
7'-5¾" OVER FENDERS

LOT	1461
QTY	50
NOS	3177 – 3226
D⁰ Nº	RCH 2069D
CARR CAPY	4 TONS
CUB CAPY	717 CU FT
TARE	T.C.Q 1-16-1
BUILT AT	ERLST'N
DATE	1947

Figure 106

WOOD CONTAINER TYPE 'BD'
Page 66

WOOD CONTAINER TYPE 'BD'
Page 67

16'-0" OVER BODY
16'-5¾" OVER FENDERS
15'-8⅛" INSIDE
6'-0" DOORWAY × 6'-3⅜"
6'-10" INSIDE
6'-8" INSIDE
6'-10" INSIDE
5'-0" DOORWAY × 6'-3⅜"
7'-1¼" CLEAR HEIGHT AT CENTRE
7'-11⅞" OVERALL
7'-0" OVER BODY
7'-5¾" OVER FENDER

LOT	1571
QTY	1
NOS	9999
D⁰ Nº	P333/47
CARR CAPY	4 TONS
CUB CAPY	743 CU FT
TARE	T.C.Q 1-13-0
BUILT AT	S.I.W⁰'N I.O.W
DATE	1948

Figure 107

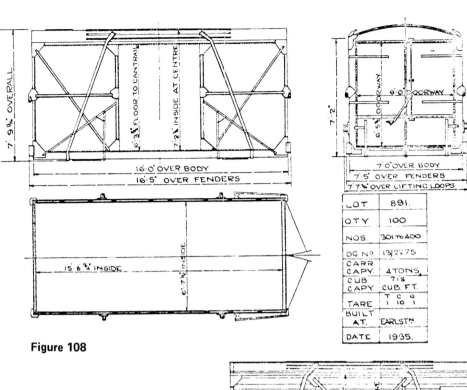

Figure 108

LOT	891.
QTY	100
NOS.	301 TO 400
DG Nº	13/2275
CARR CAPY.	4 TONS.
CUB CAPY	713 CUB. FT.
TARE	T. C. Q 1 · 10 · 1
BUILT AT.	EARLSTN
DATE	1935.

WOOD CONTAINER TYPE 'BK'
Page 100

Plate 112 (top right) This picture of No B2253, loaded on a Southern Railway low fit, was taken in August 1944. The Souther Railway built 50 containers for the LM which is, of course, why the container wa photographed on a Southern vehicle, No 39154. The livery appears to be bauxite wit white lettering.

Photograph British Ra

Plate 113 (bottom right) This illustratio of container K1 shows the single exampl built at Derby in 1932. The livery wa crimson lake with yellow lettering whic appears to be shaded to the right and belo in black. The 'lifting ironwork' has bee picked out in black.

Photograph British Ra

WOOD CONTAINER TYPE 'BK'
Page 101

Figure 109

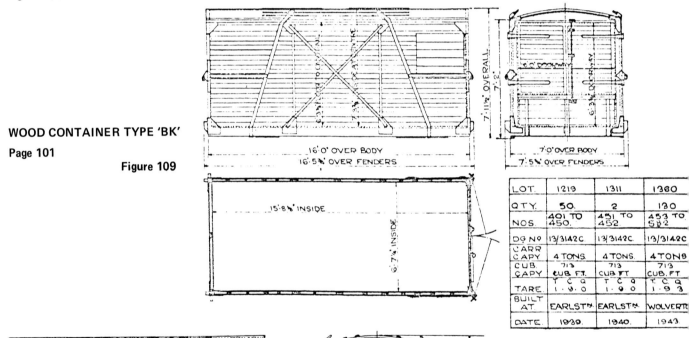

LOT.	1219	1311	1360
QTY.	50.	2	130
NOS.	401 TO 450.	451 TO 452	453 TO 582
DG Nº	13/3142C.	13/3142C.	13/3142C.
CARR CAPY	4 TONS.	4 TONS.	4 TONS
CUB CAPY	713 CUB. FT.	713 CUB FT	713 CUB. FT.
TARE	T. C. Q 1 · 8 · 0	T. C Q 1 · 9 · 0	T. C. Q 1 · 9 · 3
BUILT AT.	EARLSTN.	EARLSTN.	WOLVERTN
DATE.	1939.	1940.	1943.

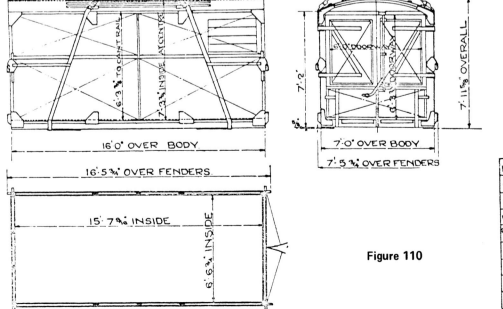

Figure 110

WOOD CONTAINER TYPE 'BK
Page 102

LOT	1393
QTY.	64.
NOS	583 TO 646
DG Nº	RCH. 2108.
CARR. CAPY	4 TONS.
CUB CAPY	708 CUB. FT.
TARE	T. C. Q 1 · 12 · 0
BUILT AT.	WOLVERTON
DATE	1945

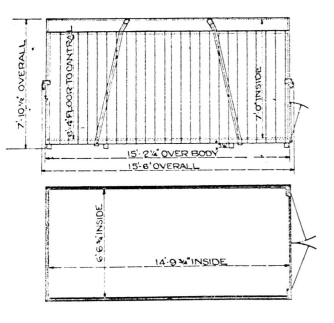

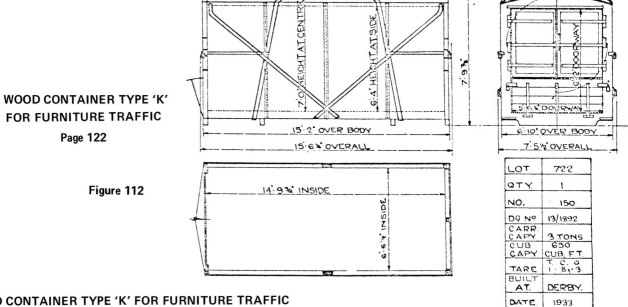

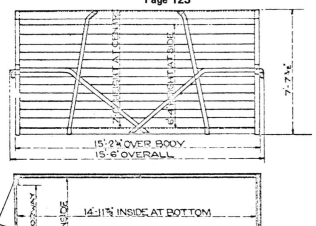

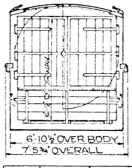

WOOD CONTAINER TYPE
FOR FURNITURE TRAFFI[C]
Page 121

Figure 111

LOT.	637	638	680	708
QTY	99	1	40	9
NOS.	2-100	1	101-140	141-149
DG Nº	13/1633F	13/1633F	13/1633F	13/1633F
CARR CAPY	3 TONS	3 TONS	3 TONS	3 TONS
CUB CAPY	650 CU.FT.	650 CU.FT.	650 CU.FT.	650 CU.FT.
TARE	T.C.Q 1 9 2	T.C.Q 1 9 2	T.C.Q 1 9 2	T.C.Q 1 9 2
BUILT AT	EARLSTN	DERBY	DERBY	DERBY
DATE	1932	1932	1933	1933

WOOD CONTAINER TYPE 'K'
FOR FURNITURE TRAFFIC
Page 122

Figure 112

LOT.	722
QTY	1
NO.	150
DG Nº	13/1892
CARR CAPY	3 TONS
CUB CAPY	650 CUB.FT.
TARE	T.C.Q 1-8-3
BUILT AT	DERBY
DATE	1933

WOOD CONTAINER TYPE 'K' FOR FURNITURE TRAFFIC
Page 123

LOT.	753	813
QTY	50	100
NOS.	151 TO 200	201 TO 300
DG Nº	13/1954B	13/1954B
CARR CAPY	3 TONS	3 TONS
CUB CAPY	650 CUB.FT.	650 CUB.FT.
TARE	T.C.Q 1-12-0	T.C.Q 1-12-0
BUILT AT	EARLSTN	EARLSTN
DATE	1933&1934	1934

Plate 114 (top right) This illustrates [container] K112, which was built at Derby in 1[933?]. As with No. K1, this container was [also] allocated to diagram book, page [122]. **Figure 111**, but it will be noted that t[here] are both livery and detail differences. [The] containers are loaded on ex-LNWR [low] goods wagons as converted for conta[iner] traffic.

Photograph British [Railways]

Plates 115 & 116 (overleaf) Container [No.] K203 was constructed in 1934 and is [illu]strated in crimson lake livery with ye[llow] lettering. The container is loaded on an [ex-] LNWR low goods wagon converted [for] container traffic. Note the end lett[ering] arrangement which differs when comp[ared] with containers of earlier construction.

Photographs British [Railways]

Plate 116

STEEL CONTAINER TYPE 'KX'

Page 124

Figure 114

6' 11¼" OVER BRACES

6' 7¾" OVER BODY

7' 0¾" OVERALL

7' 2' OVERALL

7' 1¼" TO TOP OF ROOF

6' 1¼" TO CANTRAIL

6' 6¼" INSIDE

13' 11" OVER BODY

14' 3' OVERALL

6' 6¼" INSIDE

13' 8" INSIDE

LOT	
Q.T.Y.	93.
NOS.	1, 3 -13, 15, 17, 18, 20, 22, 29, 31 - 42, 44 - 100.
DG N°	857 BUTTERLEY
CARR CAPY	3 TONS
CUB CAPY	555 CUB. FT.
TARE	T. C. Q. 1 . 4 . 0
BUILT AT.	BUTTERLEY &c
DATE	1929·1930.

REMARKS.
CONVERTED FROM 'B' TY
DIA. PAGE 218
43 CONVERTED ON HO 76.
50 · · · 79

Plate 117 This picture, of container No.
KX82, when loaded on an ex-LNWR, 10'
low goods wagon, was taken in November
1938 and shows one of the B type con
versions. The details are recorded in the
diagram book, page 124, **Figure 114**. The
livery of No. KX82 was crimson lake with
yellow lettering, as previously noted. See
Plate 111.

Photograph A. E. West

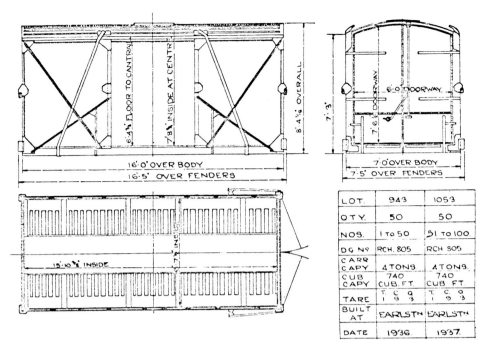

Figure 115

WOOD CONTAINER TYPE 'BC'

Page 125

LOT.	943	1053
QTY.	50	50
NOS.	1 TO 50	51 TO 100
DG Nº	RCH. 805	RCH 805
CARR CAPY	4 TONS	4 TONS
CUB CAPY	740 CUB. FT.	740 CUB FT.
TARE	T C Q 1 9 3	T C Q 1 9 3
BUILT AT	EARLSTN	EARLSTN
DATE	1936	1937

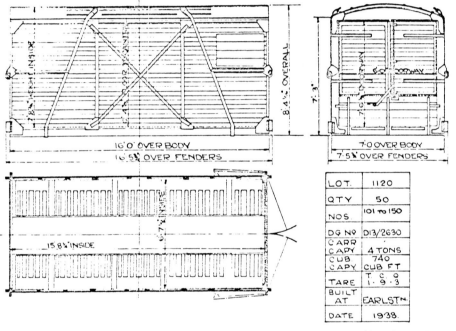

WOOD CONTAINER TYPE 'BC'

Page 126

LOT.	1120
QTY	50
NOS.	101 TO 150
DG Nº	D13/2630
CARR CAPY	4 TONS
CUB CAPY	740 CUB FT
TARE	T C Q 1 · 9 · 3
BUILT AT	EARLSTN
DATE	1938

Figure 116

Plate 118 This picture of No. BC70 was taken in 1937 and shows an example of a container designed to carry bicycles. The livery appears to be bauxite with some black ironwork, but there is a possibility it could be crimson lake.

Photograph British Rail

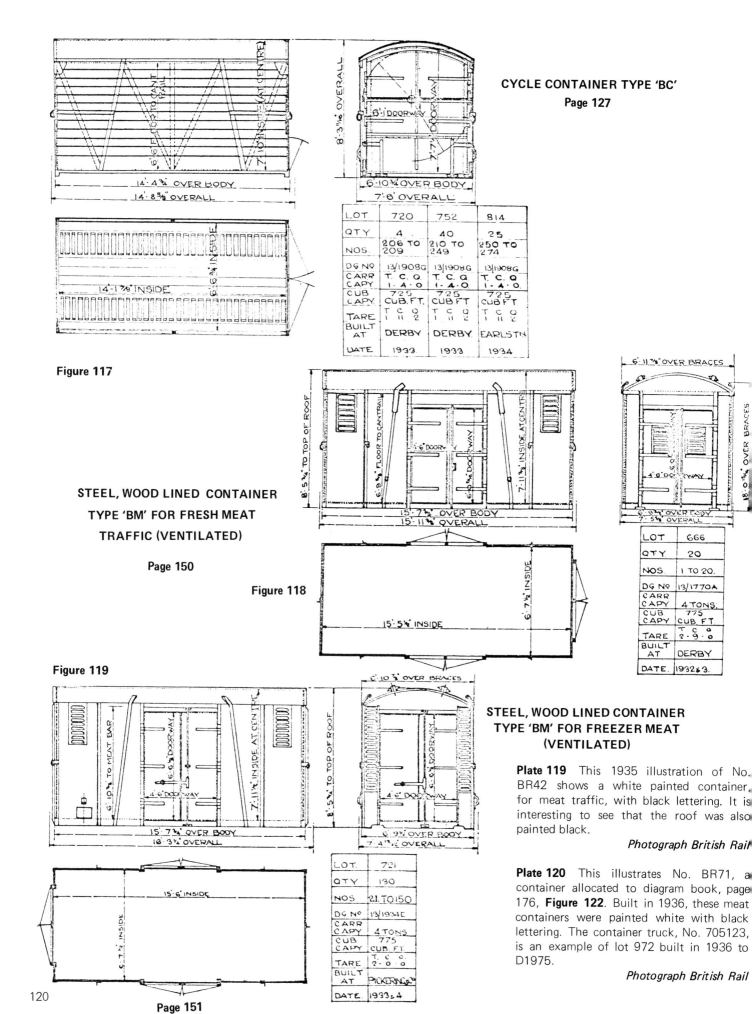

CYCLE CONTAINER TYPE 'BC'
Page 127

Figure 117

LOT	720	752	814
QTY	4	40	25
NOS.	206 TO 209	210 TO 249	250 TO 274
DG No	13/1908G	13/1908G	13/1908G
CARR CAPY	T.C.Q 1.4.0	T.C.Q 1.4.0	T.C.Q 1.4.0
CUB CAPY	725 CUB.FT.	725 CUB FT	725 CUB FT
TARE	T C Q 1.11.2	T C Q 1.11.2	T C Q 1.11.2
BUILT AT	DERBY	DERBY	EARLSTN
DATE	1933	1933	1934

STEEL, WOOD LINED CONTAINER TYPE 'BM' FOR FRESH MEAT TRAFFIC (VENTILATED)

Page 150

Figure 118

LOT	666
QTY	20
NOS.	1 TO 20
DG No	13/1770A
CARR CAPY	4 TONS
CUB CAPY	775 CUB FT
TARE	T C Q 2.9.0
BUILT AT	DERBY
DATE	1932&3

Figure 119

STEEL, WOOD LINED CONTAINER TYPE 'BM' FOR FREEZER MEAT (VENTILATED)

Plate 119 This 1935 illustration of No. BR42 shows a white painted container, for meat traffic, with black lettering. It is interesting to see that the roof was also painted black.

Photograph British Rail

Plate 120 This illustrates No. BR71, a container allocated to diagram book, page 176, **Figure 122**. Built in 1936, these meat containers were painted white with black lettering. The container truck, No. 705123, is an example of lot 972 built in 1936 to D1975.

Photograph British Rail

LOT	721
QTY	130
NOS.	21 TO 150
DG No	13/19?ME
CARR CAPY	4 TONS
CUB CAPY	775 CUB FT
TARE	T C Q 2.0.0
BUILT AT	PICKERING
DATE	1933&4

Page 151

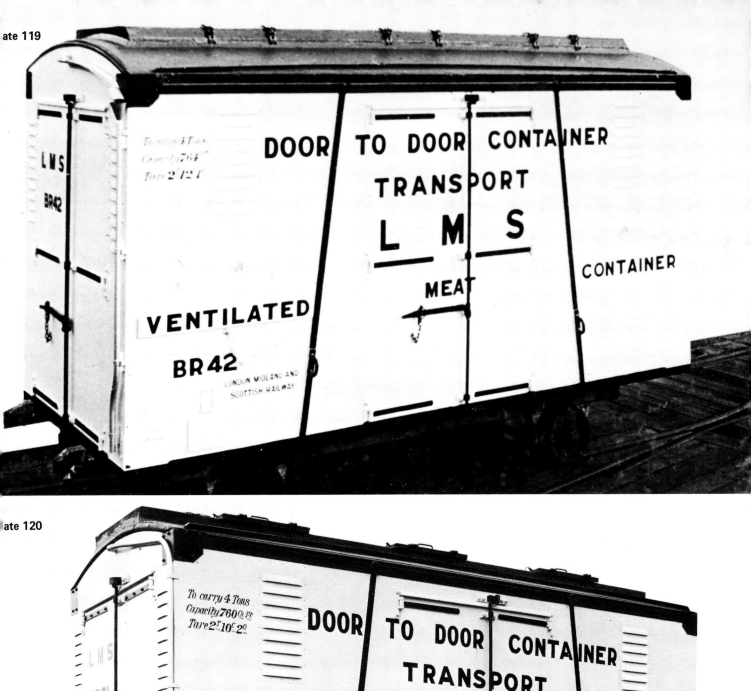

LMS
BR42

Transport 4 Tons
Capacity 764 Cu Ft
Tare 2ᵀ 12ᶜ

DOOR TO DOOR CONTAINER
TRANSPORT
L M S
MEAT   CONTAINER

VENTILATED
BR 42
LONDON MIDLAND AND
SCOTTISH RAILWAY

L M S
BR71

To carry 4 Tons
Capacity 760 Cu Ft
Tare 2ᵀ 10ᶜ 2ᑫ

DOOR TO DOOR CONTAINER
TRANSPORT
L M S
MEAT   CONTAINER

INSULATED
BR71
LONDON MIDLAND AND
SCOTTISH RAILWAY

55
5/6/36

N   LMS
705123   TO CARRY BR
CONTAINER ONLY   5-14-1 P.17-36 N

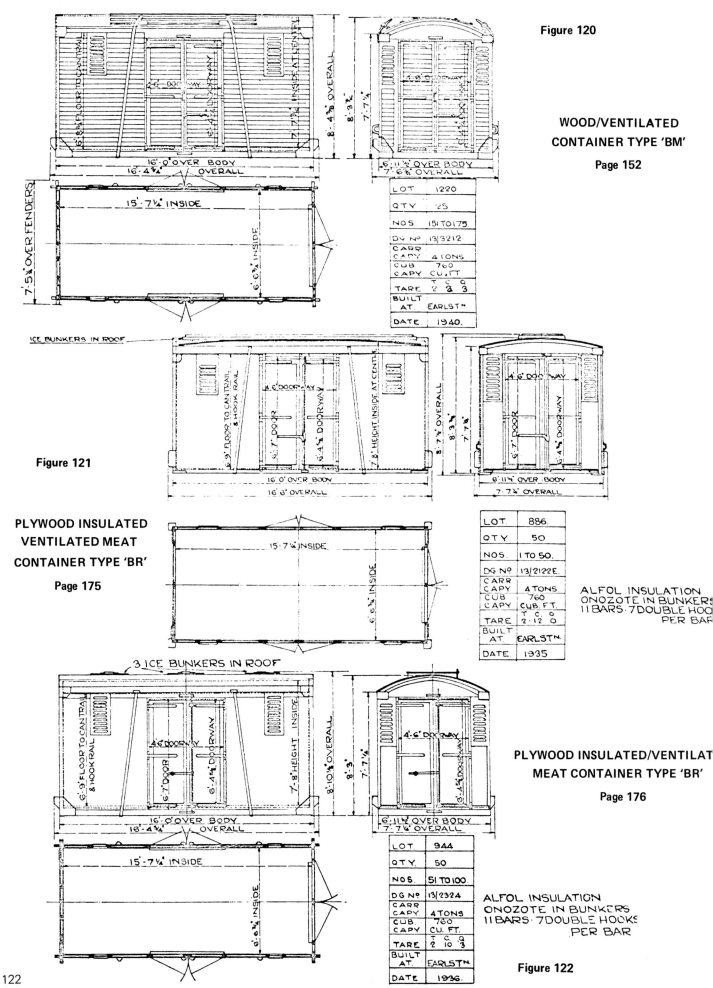

WOOD/VENTILATED CONTAINER TYPE 'BM'

Page 152

Figure 120

LOT	1220
QTY	25
NOS	151 TO 175
DG N°	13/3212
CARR CAPY	4 TONS
CUB CAPY	760 CU. FT.
TARE	T C Q 2 8 3
BUILT AT	EARLSTN
DATE	1940

PLYWOOD INSULATED VENTILATED MEAT CONTAINER TYPE 'BR'

Page 175

Figure 121

LOT	886
QTY	50
NOS	1 TO 50
DG N°	13/2122E
CARR CAPY	4 TONS
CUB CAPY	760 CUB. FT.
TARE	T. C. Q 2 12 0
BUILT AT	EARLSTN
DATE	1935

ALFOL INSULATION
ONOZOTE IN BUNKERS
11 BARS 7 DOUBLE HOOKS
PER BAR

PLYWOOD INSULATED/VENTILATED MEAT CONTAINER TYPE 'BR'

Page 176

LOT	944
QTY	50
NOS	51 TO 100
DG N°	13/2324
CARR CAPY	4 TONS
CUB CAPY	760 CU. FT.
TARE	T C Q 2 10 3
BUILT AT	EARLSTN
DATE	1936

ALFOL INSULATION
ONOZOTE IN BUNKERS
11 BARS 7 DOUBLE HOOKS
PER BAR

Figure 122

122

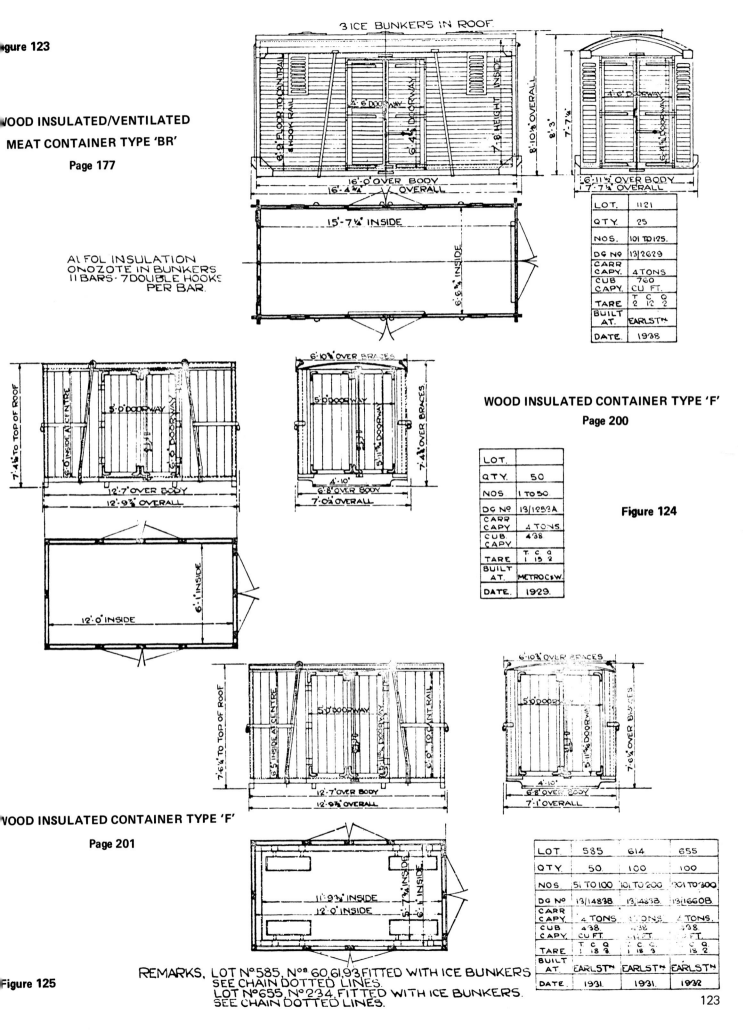

Figure 123

WOOD INSULATED/VENTILATED

MEAT CONTAINER TYPE 'BR'

Page 177

3 ICE BUNKERS IN ROOF.

4'.6' DOORWAY

6'.9' FLOOR TO CONTA
& HOOK RAIL

6'.4½' DOORWAY

7'.8' HEIGHT INSIDE

8'.10½' OVERALL

8'.3'

7'.7½'

4'.6' DOORWAY

6'.4½' DOORWAY

6'.11½' OVER BODY
7'.7½' OVERALL

16'.0' OVER BODY
16'.4¾' OVERALL

15'.7¼' INSIDE

6'.6½' INSIDE

AI FOL INSULATION
ONOZOTE IN BUNKERS
11 BARS · 7 DOUBLE HOOKS
PER BAR.

LOT.	1121
QTY.	25
NOS.	101 TO 125.
DG Nº	13/2629
CARR CAPY.	4 TONS
CUB CAPY.	760 CU FT.
TARE	T C Q 2 12 2
BUILT AT.	EARLSTN
DATE.	1938

WOOD INSULATED CONTAINER TYPE 'F'

Page 200

7'.4½' TO TOP OF ROOF

6'.0' INSIDE A CENTRE

5'.0' DOORWAY

12'.7' OVER BODY
12'.9¾' OVERALL

6'.1' INSIDE

12'.0' INSIDE

6'.10¾' OVER BRACES

5'.0' DOORWAY

5'.11½' DOORWAY

7'.4' OVER BRACES

4'.10'
6'.8' OVER BODY
7'.0½' OVERALL

LOT.	
QTY.	50
NOS.	1 TO 50.
DG Nº	13/1253A
CARR CAPY	4 TONS.
CUB. CAPY	438
TARE	T. C Q 1 15 2
BUILT AT.	METROC&W.
DATE.	1929.

Figure 124

WOOD INSULATED CONTAINER TYPE 'F'

Page 201

7'.6¼' TO TOP OF ROOF

6'.5' INSIDE A CENTRE

5'.0' DOORWAY

6'.0' TO CANT RAIL

12'.7' OVER BODY
12'.9¾' OVERALL

6'.10¾' OVER BRACES

5'.0' DOORS

5'.11½' DOORWAY

7'.6¼' OVER BRACES

4'.10'
6'.8' OVER BODY
7'.1' OVERALL

11'.9¾' INSIDE
12'.0' INSIDE

5'.7¾' INSIDE
6'.0'

Figure 125

REMARKS. LOT Nº 585. Nºs 60,61,93 FITTED WITH ICE BUNKERS
SEE CHAIN DOTTED LINES.
LOT Nº 655. Nº 234 FITTED WITH ICE BUNKERS.
SEE CHAIN DOTTED LINES.

LOT.	585	614	655
QTY.	50	100	100
NOS.	51 TO 100	101 TO 200	201 TO 300
DG Nº	13/1483B	13/1483B	13/1660B
CARR CAPY	4 TONS	4 TONS	4 TONS.
CUB CAPY	438 CU FT.	438 CU FT.	438 CU FT.
TARE	T. C Q 1 18 2	T C Q 1 18 3	T C Q 1 18 2
BUILT AT	EARLSTN	EARLSTN	EARLSTN
DATE	1931.	1931.	1932.

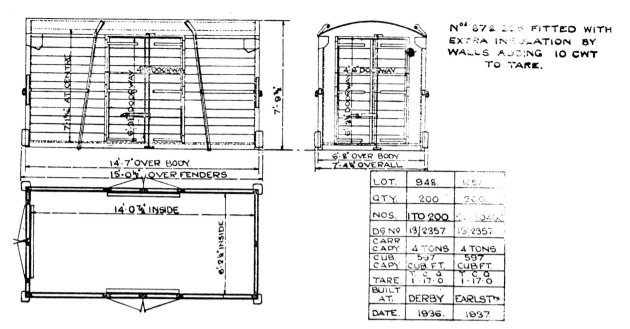

N°s. 872-200 FITTED WITH
EXTRA INSULATION BY
WALLS ADDING 10 CWT
TO TARE.

LOT.	948.	1087
QTY.	200	200
NOS.	1 TO 200	201 TO 400
DG Nº	13/2357	13/2357
CARR CAPY.	4 TONS	4 TONS
CUB. CAPY	597 CUB FT.	597 CUB FT.
TARE.	T. C. Q 1·17·0	T. C. Q 1·17·0
BUILT AT.	DERBY	EARLST^N
DATE.	1936.	1937.

Figure 126   WOOD CONTAINER INSULATED TYPE 'FM' FOR IMPORTED MEAT TRAFFIC

Page 202

Figure 127

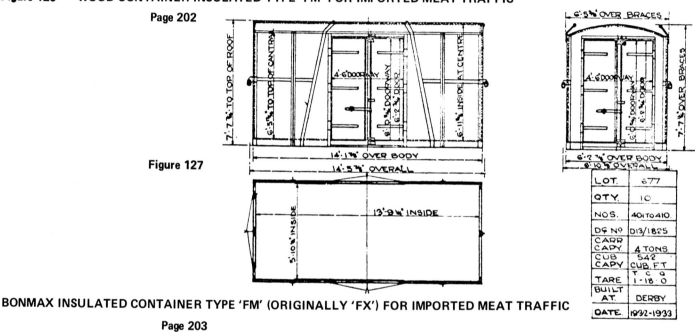

LOT.	677
QTY.	10
NOS.	401 TO 410.
DG Nº	D13/1825
CARR CAPY.	4 TONS
CUB CAPY	542 CUB FT.
TARE	T.C.Q 1·18·0
BUILT AT.	DERBY
DATE.	1932-1933

BONMAX INSULATED CONTAINER TYPE 'FM' (ORIGINALLY 'FX') FOR IMPORTED MEAT TRAFFIC

Page 203

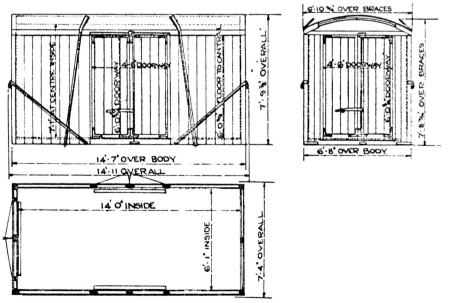

LOT.	678
QTY.	10
NOS.	411 TO 420
DG Nº	13/1784
CARR CAPY.	4 TONS
CUB CAPY	582 CUB FT.
TARE	T. C. Q 2·4·0.
BUILT AT.	DERBY
DATE.	1933.

Figure 128

124   **WOOD INSULATED CONTAINER TYPE 'FM' (ORIGINALLY 'FX') FOR IMPORTED MEAT TRAFFIC**   Page 204

Plate 121 This picture shows a batch of containers, built to diagram book, page 200, **Figure 124**, which are in ex-works condition. Painted white, with black roofs and lettering, with some black ironwork, they are seen on ex-LNWR low goods wagons which have been converted for container traffic.

Photograph British Rail

Plates 122 & 123 These photographs illustrate containers FM194 and FM209 of diagram book, page 202, **Figure 126** and demonstrate the problem of being specific about livery details. When first built, one lot may have had white roofs and the other lot, black roofs. The layout of the 'LMS Container Service' wording is also interesting. It should, however, be pointed out that No. FM194 was built at Derby and No. FM209 was built at Earlestown, which helps to explain their variations.

Photographs British Rail

Plate 124

Plate 125

Plate 124 (top left) The drawing in diagram book, page 203 was originally classified 'FX' and this original livery style depicted, shows black lettering and black roof. On reclassification, a renumbering took place as recorded in **Figure 127**. The container truck, No. 199984, is from D1838 to be found in An *Illustrated History of LMS Wagons, Volume One,* page 148.

Photograph British Rail

Plates 125 (bottom left) & 126 (right) These photographs show two examples of 'FM' containers before renumbering from the 'FX' series, when painted in white livery with black lettering. Fortunately, both ends are shown and the livery appears to be identical. The containers, Nos. 199997 and 199981, are both examples of D1838 vehicles.

Photographs British Rail

Plate 127 A further example of a white painted container with black lettering, prior to renumbering and reclassifying from 'FR' to 'FX', is illustrated in this picture. It is interesting to compare how the livery is set out on the side of the container.

Photograph British Rail

Plate 128 This picture of No. FM606 illustrates an example from diagram book, page 207, **Figure 131**, but again underlines the impossibility of being able to accurately describe the livery of LMS containers, without the use of many pictures.

Photograph British Rail

WOOD CONTAINER INSULATED TYPE 'FM' (ORIGINALLY 'FX') FOR IMPORTED MEAT TRAFFIC

Page 205

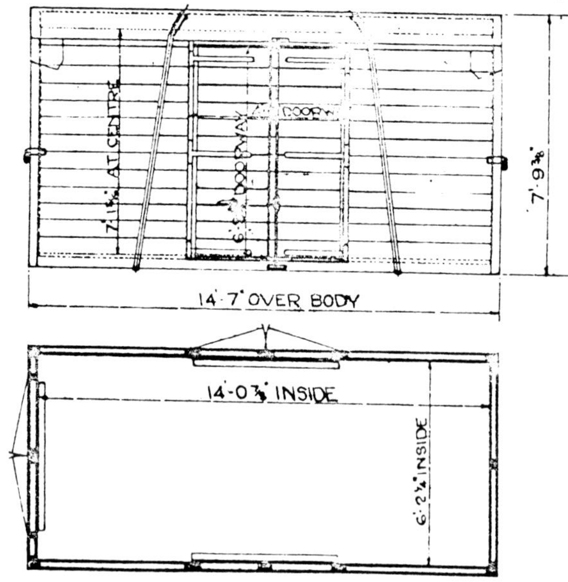

7'-1¾" AT CENTRE
6'-5½" DOORWAY
4'-0" DOORWAY
7'-9⅜"
14'-7" OVER BODY
14'-0⅞" INSIDE
6'-2¼" INSIDE

DOORWAY
6'-8" OVER BODY

LOT.	717
QTY.	130
NOS.	421 TO 550.
DG Nº	D13/1939
CARR CAPY	4 TONS.
CUB. CAPY.	597 CUB. FT.
TARE	T. C. Q. 1-16-0
BUILT AT.	EARLSTN.
DATE.	1933

8 MEAT BARS
6 SINGLE HOOKS
PER BAR

Figure 129

WOOD CONTAINER INSULATED TYPE 'FM' (ORIGINALLY 'FX') FOR IMPORTED MEAT TRAFFIC

Page 206

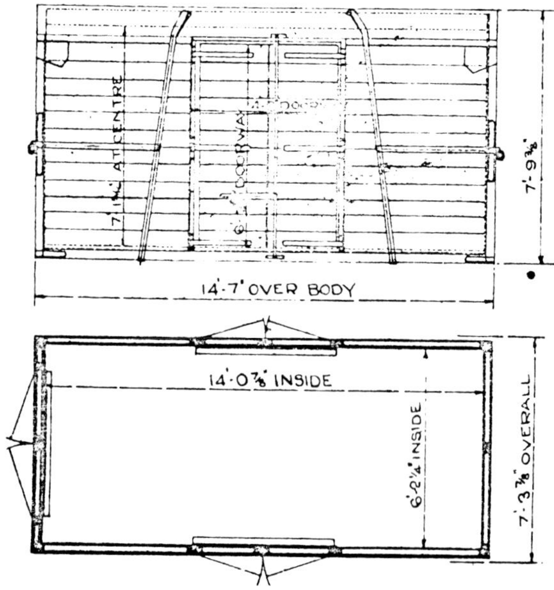

7'-1¾" AT CENTRE
6'-5½" DOORWAY
4'-0" DOORWAY
7'-9⅜"
14'-7" OVER BODY
14'-0⅞" INSIDE
6'-2¼" INSIDE
7'-3⅞" OVERALL

4'-0" DOORWAY
6'-3½" DOORWAY
6'-8" OVER BODY

Nos. 5[illegible] & 594 FITTED WITH EXTRA INSULA BY WALLS ADDING 10 TO TARE.

Figure 130

LOT.	885
QTY.	50.
NOS.	551 TO 600.
DG Nº	D13/2199
CARR. CAPY.	4 TONS
CUB. CAPY.	597. CUB. FT.
TARE.	T. C. Q. 1-19-2
BUILT AT.	EARLSTN
DATE.	1935.

8 MEAT BARS
6 SINGLE HOOKS
PER BAR

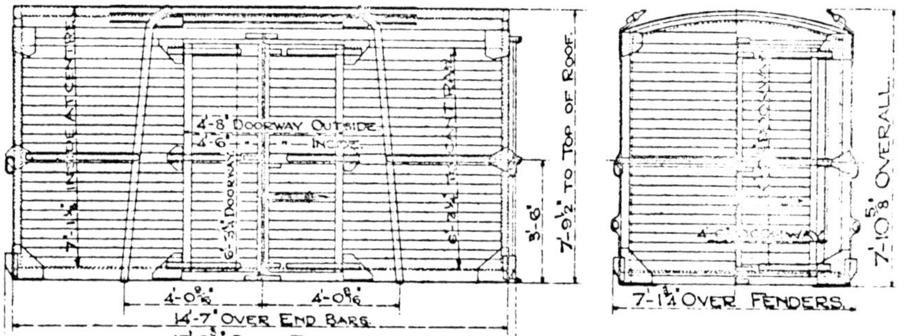

4'-8" DOORWAY OUTSIDE
4'-6" INSIDE
6'-3½" DOORWAY
7'-9½" TO TOP OF ROOF.
3'-6"
4'-0 9/16"
4'-0 9/16"
14'-7" OVER END BARS.
15'-0½" OVER FENDERS.
7'-10⅝" OVERALL
4'-DOORWAY
7'-1¼" OVER FENDERS.

INSULATED MEAT CONTAINER TYPE 'FM' (WOOD)

Page 207

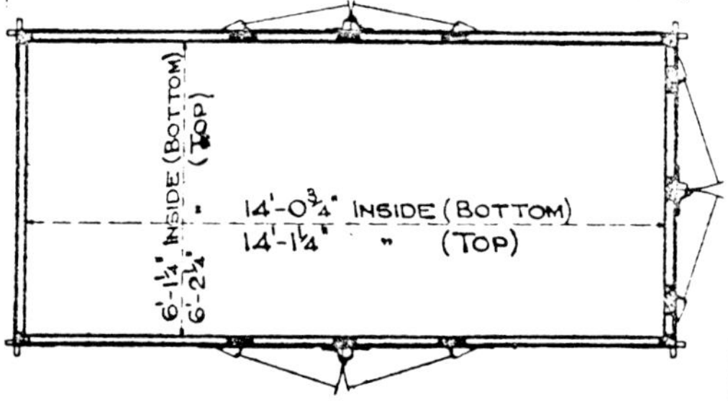

14'-0¾" INSIDE (BOTTOM)
14'-1¼" " (TOP)
6'-1¼" INSIDE (BOTTOM)
6'-2¼" (TOP)

LOT	1300	1462	1531
QTY.	101	130	125
NOS.	601-701	702-831	832-956
DG Nº	D13/3347	13/3856	13/3856
CARR. CAPY	4 TONS	4 TONS	4 TONS
CUB CAPY	600 CU. FT.	600 CU. FT.	600 CU. FT.
TARE.	T. C. 2-1	T. C. Q. 2.5.0	T. C. Q. 2.5.0
BUILT AT.	DERBY & WOLVERTON.	EARLSTN.	EARLSTN
DATE.	1941	1947	1948

Figure 131

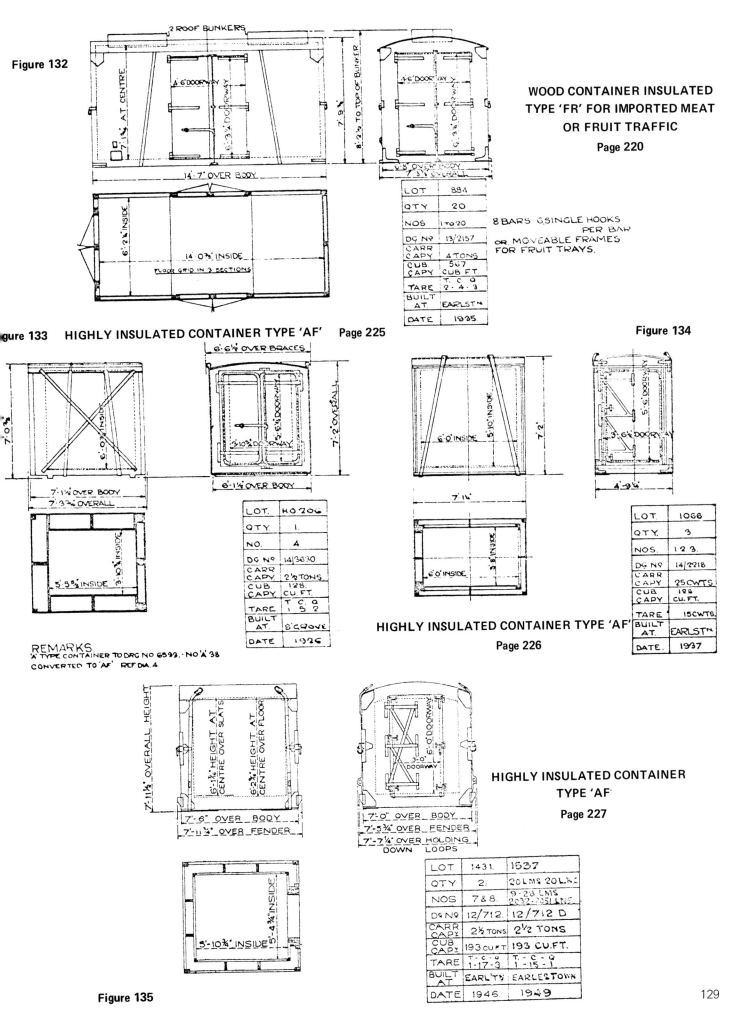

Figure 132

WOOD CONTAINER INSULATED TYPE 'FR' FOR IMPORTED MEAT OR FRUIT TRAFFIC

Page 220

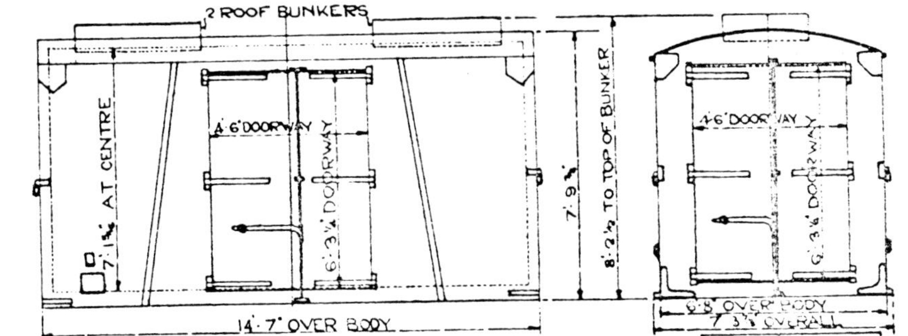
2 ROOF BUNKERS
4'6" DOORWAY
7'1¾" AT CENTRE
6'3¼" DOORWAY
7'9¾"
8'2½" TO TOP OF BUNKER
14'7" OVER BODY
4'6" DOORWAY
6'3¼" DOORWAY
6'8" OVER BODY
7'3½" OVERALL

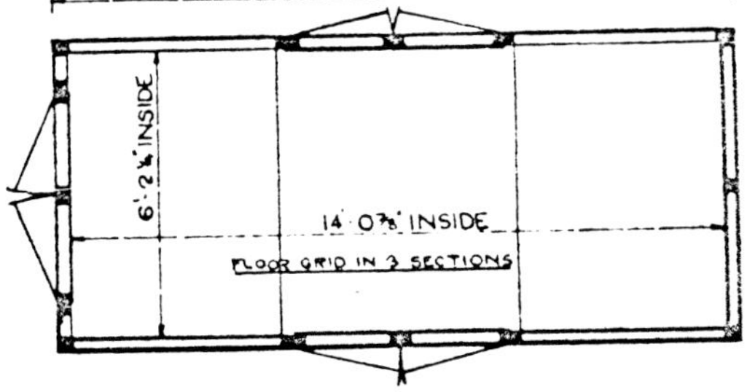
6'2⅞" INSIDE
14'0⅞" INSIDE
FLOOR GRID IN 3 SECTIONS

LOT	884
QTY	20
NOS	1 TO 20
DG No	13/2157
CARR CAPY	4 TONS
CUB CAPY	567 CUB FT
TARE	T C Q 2 - 4 - 3
BUILT AT	EARLSTN
DATE	1935

8 BARS 6 SINGLE HOOKS PER BAR
OR MOVEABLE FRAMES FOR FRUIT TRAYS.

Figure 133 HIGHLY INSULATED CONTAINER TYPE 'AF' Page 225

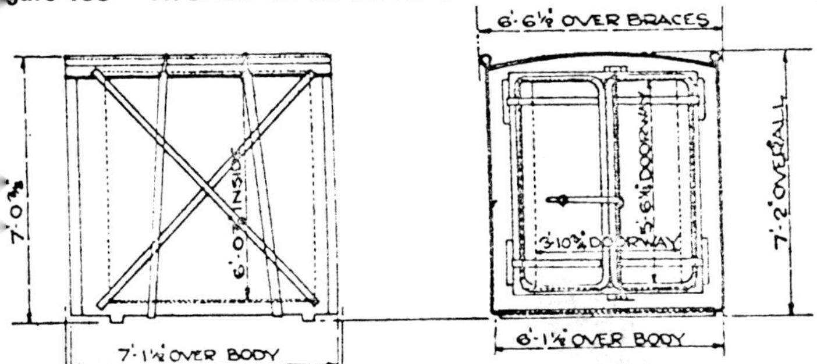
6'6½" OVER BRACES
7'0⅜"
6'0" INSIDE
5'6¾" DOORWAY
3'10¾" DOORWAY
7'2" OVERALL
7'1¼" OVER BODY
7'3¾" OVERALL
6'1¼" OVER BODY

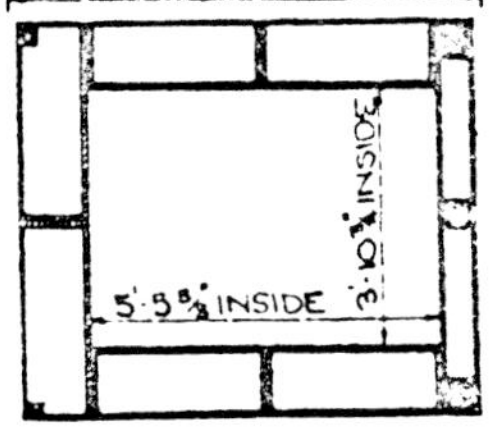
3'10⅞" INSIDE
5'5⅝" INSIDE

LOT.	HO 206
QTY	1.
NO.	4.
DG No	14/3630
CARR CAPY	2½ TONS
CUB. CAPY.	128. CU. FT.
TARE	T C Q 1 5 2
BUILT AT	S'GROVE
DATE	1926

REMARKS
'A' TYPE CONTAINER TO DRG NO 6593. - NO 'A' 38
CONVERTED TO 'AF' REF DIA. 4

Figure 134

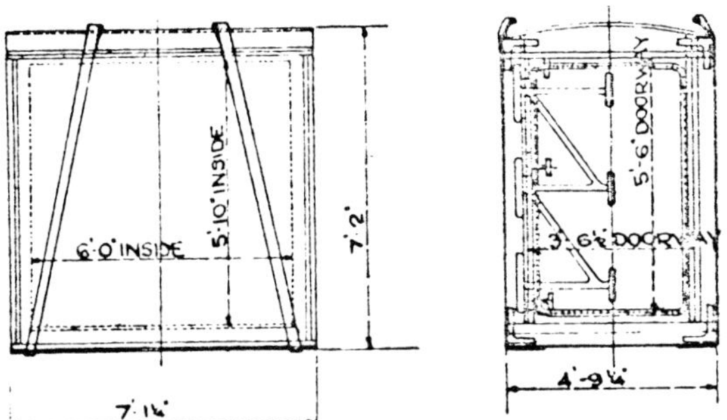
5'10" INSIDE
6'0" INSIDE
7'2"
5'6" DOORWAY
3'6½" DOORWAY
7'1½"
4'9¼"

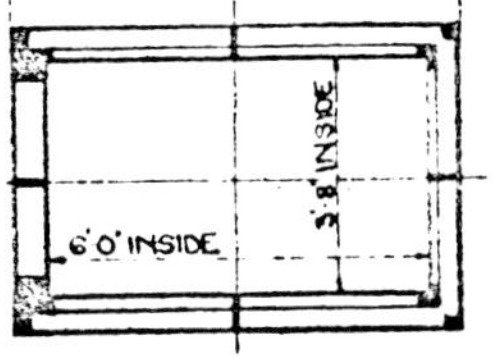
3'8" INSIDE
6'0" INSIDE

LOT.	1066
QTY.	3
NOS.	1 2 3.
DG No	14/2218
CARR CAPY	25 CWTS
CUB CAPY	188 CU. FT.
TARE	15 CWTS.
BUILT AT.	EARLSTN
DATE.	1937

HIGHLY INSULATED CONTAINER TYPE 'AF'

Page 226

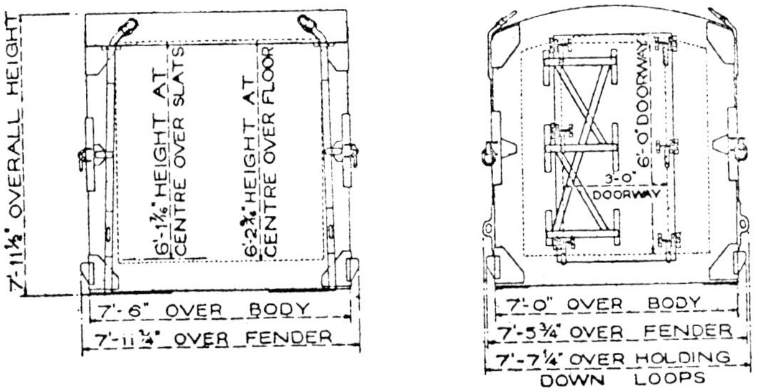
7'11½" OVERALL HEIGHT
6'1⅛" HEIGHT AT CENTRE OVER SLATS
6'2¾" HEIGHT AT CENTRE OVER FLOOR
7'-6" OVER BODY
7'-11¼" OVER FENDER
6'-0" DOORWAY
3'-0" DOORWAY
7'-0" OVER BODY
7'-5¾" OVER FENDER
7'-7¼" OVER HOLDING DOWN LOOPS

HIGHLY INSULATED CONTAINER TYPE 'AF'

Page 227

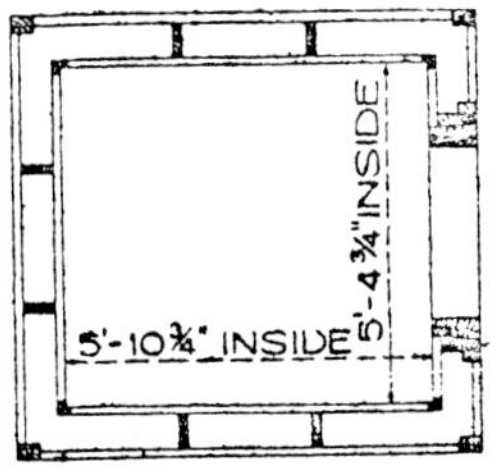
5'-4¾" INSIDE
5'-10¾" INSIDE

LOT	1431.	1537
QTY	2.	20 LMS 20 L.N.E
NOS	7 & 8.	9-28 LMS 2032-2051 LNE
DG No	12/712.	12/712 D
CARR CAPY	2½ TONS	2½ TONS
CUB CAPY	193 CU FT	193 CU.FT.
TARE	T - C - Q 1-17-3	T. - C - Q 1 - 15 - 1
BUILT AT	EARL'TN	EARLESTOWN
DATE	1946	1949

Figure 135

Plate 129 This illustrates container No. FR6 loaded on to truck No. 232196, an example of a container truck built to D1813 as shown in an *Illustrated History of LMS Wagons, Volume One*, page 148. The body colour is white with black ironwork. The roof and lettering are also in black.

Photograph British Rail

Plate 130 Although the drawing in diagram book, page 226, **Figure 134**, states that the only examples were numbered 1, 2 and 3. No. E5 is clearly to this diagram and is painted white with black lettering. Whether it was renumbered as above after construction, or if further examples were built, is not known to the author.

Photograph British Rail

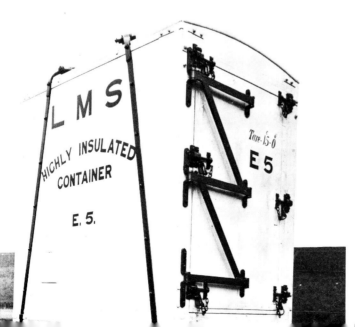

Plate 1

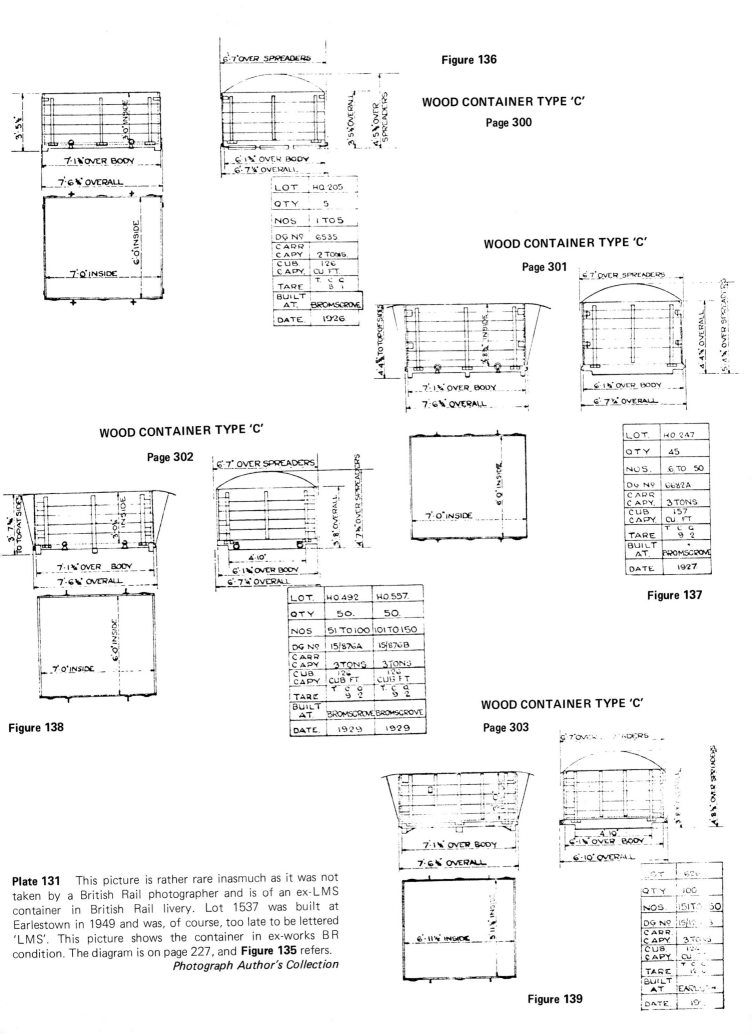

Figure 136

WOOD CONTAINER TYPE 'C'

Page 300

6' 7" OVER SPREADERS

3'·5½" OVERALL — 4'·5½" OVER SPREADERS

3'·5½"

3'·0" INSIDE

7'·1½" OVER BODY

7'·6½" OVERALL

6'·1½" OVER BODY
6'·7½" OVERALL

6'·0" INSIDE

7'·0" INSIDE

LOT	HO 205
QTY	5
NOS	1 TO 5
DG NO	6535
CARR CAPY	2 TONS
CUB CAPY.	126 CU. FT.
TARE	T C Q 8 1
BUILT AT.	BROMSGROVE
DATE.	1926

WOOD CONTAINER TYPE 'C'

Page 301

6' 7" OVER SPREADERS

4'·4½" TO TOP OF SIDE

3'·8½" INSIDE

4'·4½" OVERALL — 5'·4½" OVER SPREADERS

7'·1½" OVER BODY

7'·6½" OVERALL

6'·1½" OVER BODY

6'·7½" OVERALL

6'·0" INSIDE

7'·0" INSIDE

LOT.	HO 247
QTY	45
NOS.	6 TO 50
DG NO	6682A
CARR CAPY	3 TONS
CUB CAPY.	157 CU. FT.
TARE	T C Q 9 2
BUILT AT.	BROMSGROVE
DATE	1927

Figure 137

WOOD CONTAINER TYPE 'C'

Page 302

6' 7" OVER SPREADERS

3'·7½" TO TOP AT SIDE

3'·0" INSIDE

3'·8" OVERALL — 4'·7½" OVER SPREADERS

7'·1½" OVER BODY

7'·6½" OVERALL

4'·10"

6'·1½" OVER BODY

6'·7½" OVERALL

6'·0" INSIDE

7'·0" INSIDE

LOT.	HO 492	HO 557.
QTY	50.	50.
NOS	51 TO 100	101 TO 150
DG NO	15/876A	15/876B
CARR CAPY	3 TONS	3 TONS
CUB CAPY	126 CUB FT	126 CUB FT
TARE	T C Q 9 2	T C Q 9 2
BUILT AT.	BROMSGROVE	BROMSGROVE
DATE.	1929	1929

Figure 138

WOOD CONTAINER TYPE 'C'

Page 303

6' 7" OVER SPREADERS

4'·8½" OVER SPREADERS

7'·1½" OVER BODY

7'·6½" OVERALL

4'·10"

6'·1½" OVER BODY

6'·10" OVERALL

5'·11½" INSIDE

6'·11½" INSIDE

LOT	625
QTY	100
NOS.	151 TO 250
DG NO	15/1003
CARR CAPY	3 TONS
CUB CAPY	126 CU
TARE	T C Q 12 2
BUILT AT	EARLESTOWN
DATE.	19..

Figure 139

Plate 131   This picture is rather rare inasmuch as it was not taken by a British Rail photographer and is of an ex-LMS container in British Rail livery. Lot 1537 was built at Earlestown in 1949 and was, of course, too late to be lettered 'LMS'. This picture shows the container in ex-works BR condition. The diagram is on page 227, and **Figure 135** refers.
Photograph Author's Collection

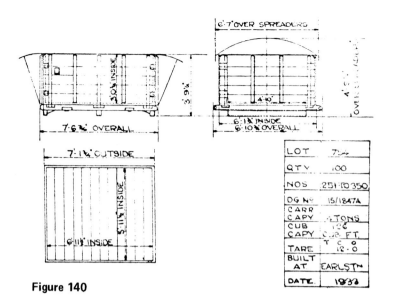

WOOD CONTAINER TYPE 'C'

Page 304

Figure 140

LOT	714
QTY	100
NOS	251 TO 350
DG Nº	15/1847A
CARR CAPY	4 TONS
CUB CAPY	126 CUB. FT.
TARE	T C Q 12 · 0
BUILT AT	EARLSTN
DATE	1932

Figure 141

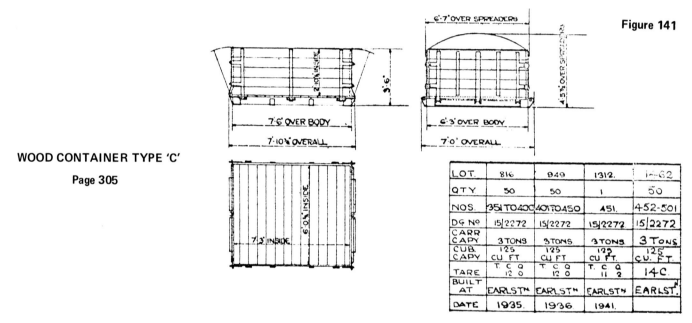

WOOD CONTAINER TYPE 'C'

Page 305

LOT.	816	949	1312.	1462
QTY	50	50	1	50
NOS.	351 TO 400	401 TO 450	451.	452-501
DG Nº	15/2272	15/2272	15/2272	15/2272
CARR CAPY	3 TONS	3 TONS	3 TONS	3 TONS
CUB. CAPY	125 CU FT	125 CU FT	125 CU. FT.	125 CU. FT.
TARE	T. C. Q 12 0	T. C. Q 12 0	T. C. Q 11 2	14C.
BUILT AT	EARLSTN	EARLSTN	EARLSTN	EARLST.
DATE	1935.	1936	1941	

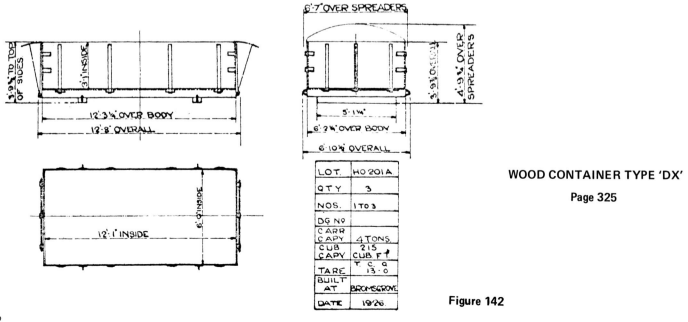

WOOD CONTAINER TYPE 'DX'

Page 325

LOT.	HO 201A
QTY	3
NOS.	1 TO 3
DG Nº	
CARR CAPY	4 TONS.
CUB CAPY	215 CUB FT
TARE	T. C. Q 13 · 0
BUILT AT	BROMSGROVE
DATE	1926

Figure 142

Plate 132 This 'C' type container, built at Bromsgrove in 1929, is pictured on a horse dray and shows how these containers were painted. The lettering was white, wagon grey for the outside, unpainted inside, with all ironwork inside and outside painted black.

Photograph British Rail

Plate 133 Container No. C370, built in 1935, appears to be painted in wagon grey with black ironwork. It is rather remarkable that the ironwork should be treated in this manner rather than the whole container being finished in a grey colour, as was the practice for all goods stock.

Photograph British Rail

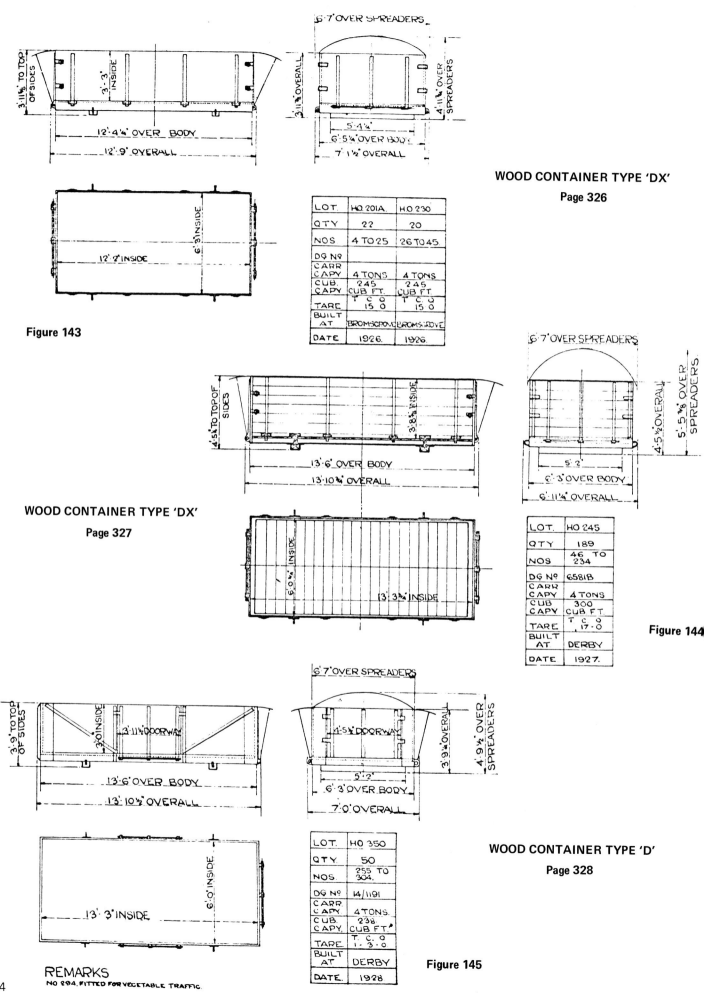

WOOD CONTAINER TYPE 'DX'

Page 326

Figure 143

LOT.	H.O.201A.	H.O.230
QTY	22	20
NOS	4 TO 25	26 TO 45
DG Nº		
CARR CAPY	4 TONS	4 TONS
CUB. CAPY	245 CUB FT.	245 CUB FT.
TARE	T. C. Q 15 0	T. C. Q 15 0
BUILT AT	BROMSGROVE	BROMSGROVE
DATE	1926.	1926.

WOOD CONTAINER TYPE 'DX'

Page 327

LOT.	HO 245
QTY	189
NOS	46 TO 234
DG Nº	6581B
CARR CAPY	4 TONS
CUB CAPY	300 CUB FT.
TARE	T. C. Q 17 0
BUILT AT	DERBY
DATE	1927.

Figure 144

WOOD CONTAINER TYPE 'D'

Page 328

LOT.	HO 350
QTY	50
NOS	255 TO 304.
DG Nº	14/1191
CARR CAPY	4 TONS.
CUB. CAPY	238 CUB FT.
TARE	T. C. Q 1. 3. 0
BUILT AT	DERBY
DATE.	1928

Figure 145

REMARKS
NO 294. FITTED FOR VEGETABLE TRAFFIC.

Plates 134 & 135 These illustrations, are examples of containers from diagram book, page 326, **Figure 143**, and have been selected to show the interior of open containers. **Plate 135** shows the exterior livery and **Plate 134** shows No. D27 loaded on to an ex-MR long low wagon No. 78693, and this wagon is in dirty grey livery. The container appears to be even darker, but whether it is slate grey or bauxite cannot be ascertained.

Photographs British Rail

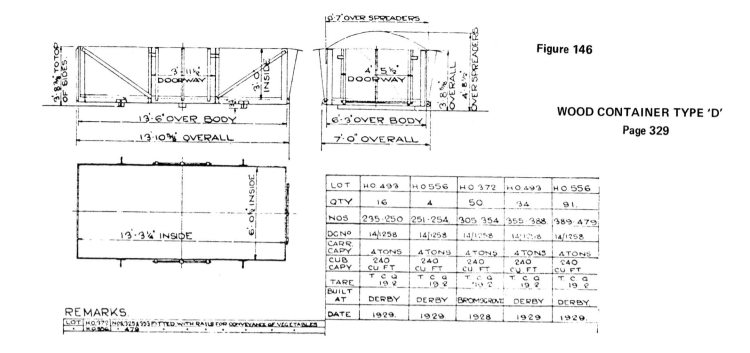

Figure 146

WOOD CONTAINER TYPE 'D'
Page 329

LOT	HO.493	HO.556	HO.372	HO.493	HO.556
QTY	16	4	50	34	91
NOS	235-250	251-254	305-354	355-388	389-479
DG No	14/1258	14/1258	14/1258	14/1258	14/1258
CARR CAPY	4 TONS	4 TONS	4 TONS	4 TONS	4 TONS
CUB CAPY	240 CU FT	240 CU FT	240 CU FT	240 CU FT	240 CU FT
TARE	T C Q 19 2	T C Q 19 2	T C Q 19 2	T C Q 19 2	T C Q 19 2
BUILT AT	DERBY	DERBY	BROMSGROVE	DERBY	DERBY
DATE	1929.	1929	1928	1929	1929.

REMARKS.
LOT HO.372 NOS 325 & 353 FITTED WITH RAILS FOR CONVEYANCE OF VEGETABLES
HO.556 479

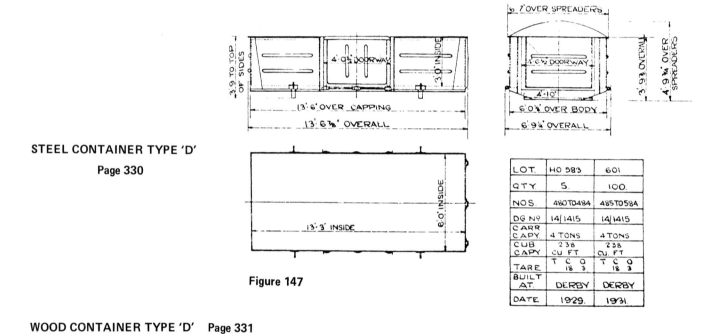

STEEL CONTAINER TYPE 'D'
Page 330

Figure 147

LOT	HO 583	601
QTY	5.	100.
NOS	480 TO 484	485 TO 584
DG No	14/1415	14/1415
CARR CAPY	4 TONS	4 TONS
CUB CAPY	238 CU FT	238 CU FT
TARE	T C Q 18 3	T C Q 18 3
BUILT AT	DERBY	DERBY
DATE	1929.	1931

WOOD CONTAINER TYPE 'D'   Page 331

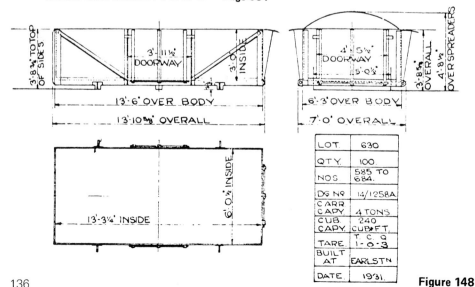

LOT	630
QTY	100
NOS	585 TO 684
DG No	14/1258A
CARR CAPY	4 TONS
CUB CAPY	240 CUB FT
TARE	T C Q 1-0-3
BUILT AT	EARLSTN
DATE	1931

Figure 148

Plate 136 (top right) No. D214 is pictured being unloaded at Salford. The livery is wagon grey.

Photograph British Rail

Plate 137 (bottom right) This picture of a 'D' type container to diagram book, page 329, **Figure 146** shows a wagon grey container with black ironwork and white lettering. Note the black ironwork and unpainted wood on the inside.

Photograph British Rail

Plate 136

Plate 137

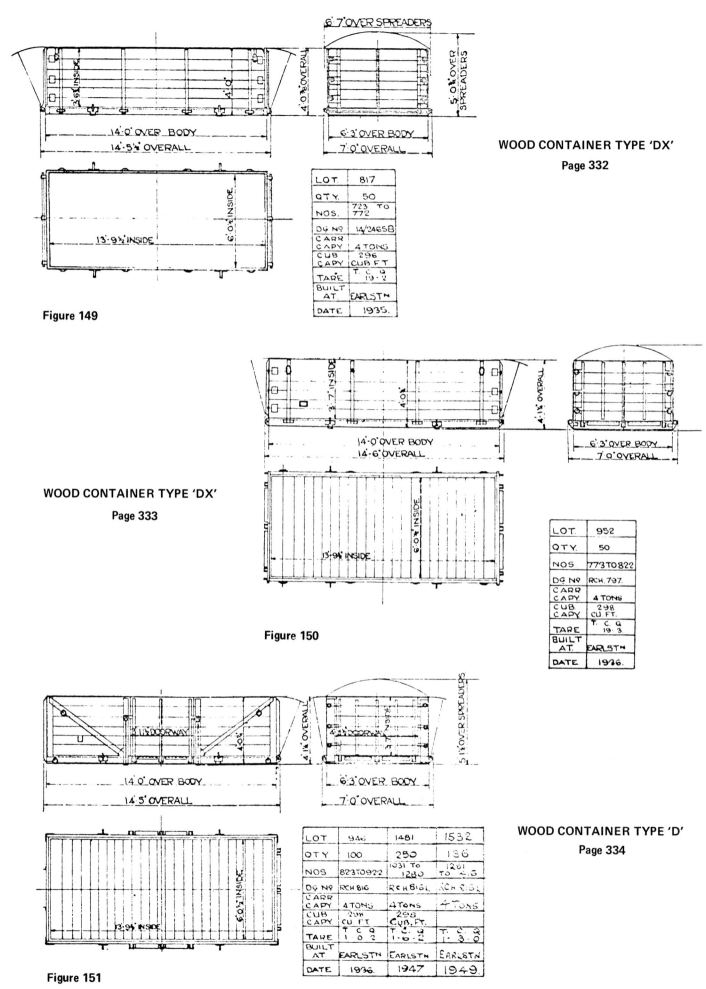

WOOD CONTAINER TYPE 'DX'

Page 332

Figure 149

LOT.	817
Q.T.Y.	50
NOS.	723 TO 772
DG N⁰	14/2465B
CARR CAPY	4 TONS
CUB CAPY	296 CUB FT.
TARE	T. C. Q. 19·2
BUILT AT.	EARLSTN
DATE	1935.

WOOD CONTAINER TYPE 'DX'

Page 333

Figure 150

LOT.	952
Q.T.Y.	50
NOS.	773 TO 822
DG N⁰	RCH. 797.
CARR CAPY	4 TONS
CUB CAPY	298 CU. FT.
TARE	T. C. Q. 19·3
BUILT AT.	EARLSTN
DATE	1936.

WOOD CONTAINER TYPE 'D'

Page 334

Figure 151

LOT.	946	1481	1532
Q.T.Y.	100	250	186
NOS.	823 TO 922	1031 TO 1280	1281 TO 465
DG N⁰	RCH 816	RCH 816L	RCH 816L
CARR CAPY	4 TONS	4 TONS	4 TONS
CUB CAPY	298 CU FT.	298 CU. FT.	
TARE	T. C. Q. 1·0·2	T. C. Q. 1·0·2	T. C. Q. 1·3·0
BUILT AT	EARLSTN	EARLSTN	EARLSTN
DATE	1936.	1947	1949

Plate 138 This picture of No. D757 is an example of a container from diagram book, page 332, **Figure 149** and it appears to be in grey livery with black ironwork and white lettering.

Photograph British Rail

Plate 139 This picture of No. D882 shows a container in grey livery with black ironwork, and while no photographs are known to exist for vehicles built to lots 1481 and 1532, no doubt they would have entered traffic in bauxite livery. The ex-Highland Railway twin bolsters, in the background, are of particular interest. No. 460531 is in bauxite livery.

Photograph British Rail

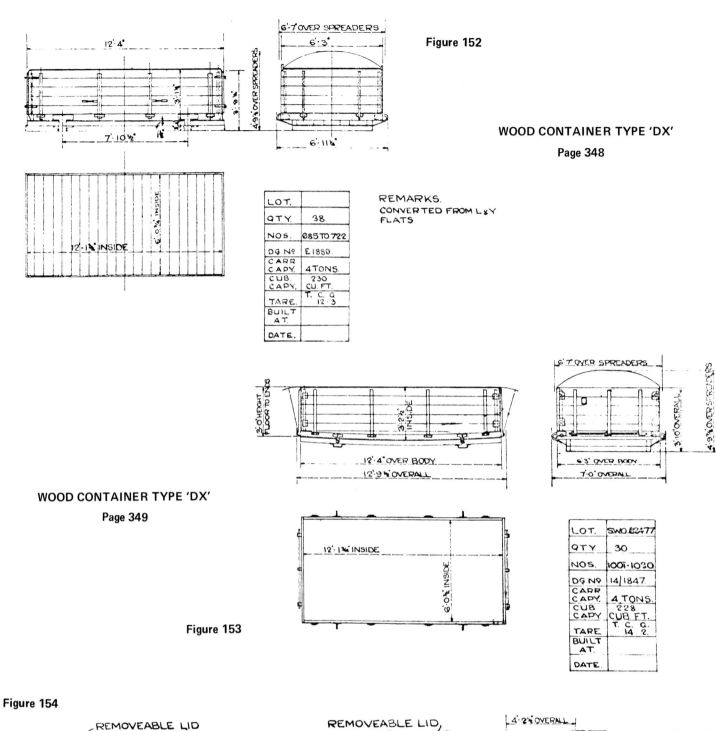

Figure 152

WOOD CONTAINER TYPE 'DX'

Page 348

REMARKS.
CONVERTED FROM L&Y
FLATS

LOT.	
QTY.	38.
NOS.	685 TO 722
DG Nº	E1889.
CARR CAPY.	4 TONS.
CUB. CAPY.	230 CU. FT.
TARE.	T. C. Q. 12 · 3
BUILT AT.	
DATE.	

WOOD CONTAINER TYPE 'DX'

Page 349

Figure 153

LOT.	SWO 62477
QTY	30
NOS.	1001-1030
DG Nº	14/1847
CARR CAPY.	4 TONS.
CUB CAPY	228 CUB. FT.
TARE	T. C. Q. 14 · 2.
BUILT AT.	
DATE.	

Figure 154

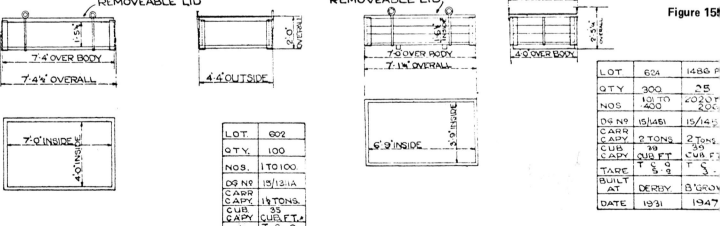

Figure 155

LOT.	602
QTY.	100
NOS.	1 TO 100.
DG Nº	15/1311A
CARR CAPY.	1½ TONS.
CUB. CAPY.	35 CUB. FT.
TARE.	T. C. Q. 6 · 2
BUILT AT.	DERBY.
DATE.	1931.

LOT.	624	1486 P
QTY	300	25
NOS.	101 TO 400	2020 TO 206
DG Nº	15/1451	15/145
CARR CAPY	2 TONS	2 TONS
CUB CAPY	39 CUB. FT.	39 CUB. FT
TARE	T. C. Q. 5 · 2	T. C 5 ·
BUILT AT	DERBY	B'GROV
DATE	1931	1947

WOOD CONTAINER TYPE 'H'

Page 350

WOOD CONTAINER TYPE 'H'

Page 351

WOOD CONTAINER TYPE 'H'

Page 352

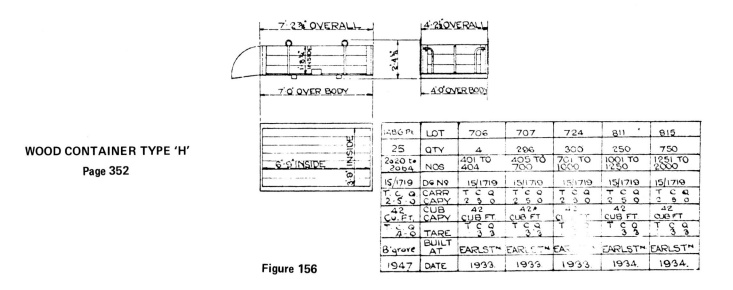

		LOT	706	707	724	811	815
1486 Pt	LOT		706	707	724	811	815
25	QTY		4	296	300	250	750
2020 to 2064	NOS		401 TO 404	405 TO 700	701 TO 1000	1001 TO 1250	1251 TO 2000
15/1719	DG Nº		15/1719	15/1719	15/1719	15/1719	15/1719
T C Q 2·5·0	CARR CAPY		T C Q 2 5 0	T C Q 2 5 0	T C Q 2 5 0	T C Q 2 5 0	T C Q 2 5 0
42 CU.FT.	CUB CAPY		42 CUB FT	42 CUB FT	42	42 CUB FT	42 CUB FT
T C Q 4·0	TARE		T C Q 3 3	T C Q 3 3	T	T C Q 3 3	T C Q 3 3
B'grove	BUILT AT		EARLSTN	EARLSTN	EAR	EARLSTN	EARLSTN
1947	DATE		1933	1933	1933	1934	1934

Figure 156

Plate 140   This undated and unusual picture of No. H315, hanging high over London, with St. Paul's Cathedral in the background, clearly shows how 'H' type containers were used to convey building material direct to the site. These containers, to diagram book, page 351, **Figure 155**, appear to be painted grey and the picture clearly shows the lettering used on the sides and ends of the container.

Photograph Real Photographs

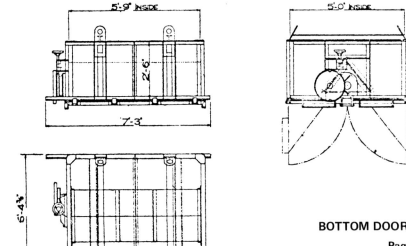

Figure 157

LOT	1552
QUANTITY	3
NOS.	BULK DROP 1 TO 3
DRG.Nº.	
CARR CAPACITY	3 TONS
CUBIC CAPACITY	63 CU.FT.
TARE	19 CWTS
BUILT AT	Brompton & Edwards
DATE	1948

BOTTOM DOOR CONTAINER

Page 380

WOOD COLLAPSIBLE CONTAINER TYPE 'PF' FOR FISH TRAFFIC — FLEETWOOD TO BELFAST   Page 400

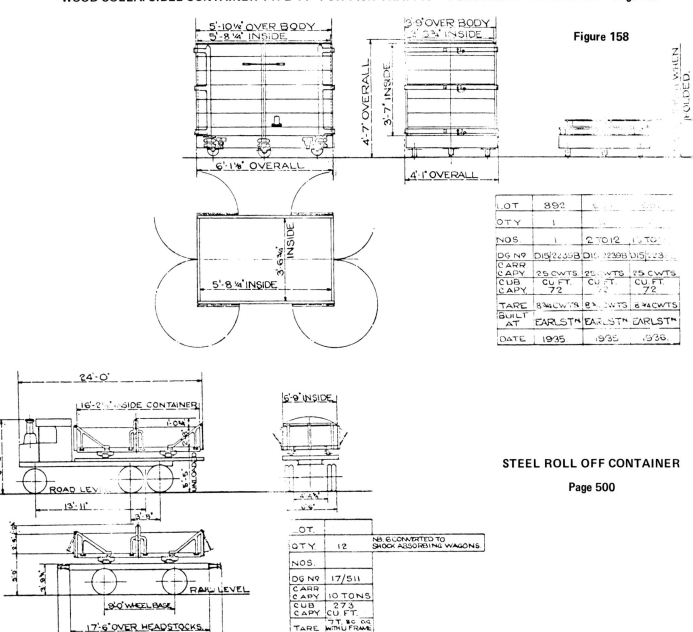

Figure 158

LOT	892		
QTY	1		
NOS.	1	2 TO 12	13 TO 1?
DG Nº	D15/2239B	D15/2239B	D15/223?
CARR CAPY	25 CWTS	25 CWTS	25 CWTS
CUB CAPY	CU.FT. 72	CU.FT. 72	CU.FT. 72
TARE	8¾ CWTS	8¾ CWTS	8¾ CWTS
BUILT AT	EARLSTⁿ	EARLSTⁿ	EARLSTⁿ
DATE	1935	1935	1936

STEEL ROLL OFF CONTAINER

Page 500

LOT		
QTY	12	NB. 6 CONVERTED TO SHOCK ABSORBING WAGONS.
NOS.		
DG Nº	17/511	
CARR CAPY	10 TONS	
CUB CAPY	273 CU.FT.	
TARE	7T. 8C ○○ WITH U FRAME	
BUILT AT		
DATE	1931	

Figure 159

Plate 141 This picture of No. H1664 shows an example of the final lot built to diagram book, page 352, **Figure 156**. It appears to be in grey livery with black ironwork.

Photograph British Rail

Plate 142 This picture of No. 3 shows an example of P400 **Figure 158** in light grey livery, with black ironwork and white lettering.

Photograph British Rail

Plates 143 to 145 illustrate examples of P500 **Figure 159**.

Plate 143 Chassis No. 323364 has a 6.8.31 paint date and shows the original condition of these chassis and containers.

Photograph British Rail

Plate 144 This illustration of No. SAW when mounted on chassis No. 285560 with 4.6.35 paint date, should be compared w **Plate 143**.

Photograph British R

Plate 145 No. ROC 8 seen in service wi chassis No. 139974. This picture, taken 1939, again shows a grey livery, almc identical, when new, to that displayed the vehicles illustrated in **Plate 144**.

Photograph A. E. W

INDEX

Type	Page	Nos.	Type	Page	Nos.
F	200	1-50	A	5	60-69
F	201	51-300	A	6	80-139
FM	202	1-400	A	7	140-324
FM	203	401-410	A	8	325-331
FM	204	411-420	A	9	332-381
FM	205	421-550			462-486
FM	206	551-600	A	10	382-461
FM	207	601-701	A	11	487-561
FM	207	702-831	A	12	562-666
FM	207	832-956	A	13	667-786
			A	14	787-986
FR	220	1-20	A	15	987-1286
			A	16	1287-1436
AF	225	4	A	17	1437-1775
AF	226	1, 2, 3	A	18	1776-1966
AF	227	7, 8	A	18	1967-2266
AF	227	9-28	A	19	2267-2366
AF	227	LNE	A	20	2367-2516
		2032-2051			
			B	50	1-40
C	300	1-5	B	51	41-265
C	301	6-50	B	52	266-365
C	302	51-150	B	53	366-415
C	303	151-250	B	54	416-565
C	304	251-350	B	55	566-715
C	305	351-451	B	56	716
C	305	452-501	B	57	717-1067
			B	58	1068-1117
DX	325	1-3	B	59	1118-1167
DX	326	4-45	B	60	1168-1267
DX	327	46-234	BD	61	1268-1567
D	328	255-304	BD	62	1568-1717
D	329	235-254	BD	63	1718-1867
		305-479	B	64	1868-2287
D	330	480-584	BD	65	2288-2976
D	331	585-684	BD	65	2977-3176
DX	332	723-772	BD	66	3177-3226
DX	333	773-822	BD	67	9999
D	334	823-922			
D	334	1031-1281	BK	100	301-400
D	334	1282-1416	BK	101	401-582
			BK	102	583-646
DX	348	685-722			
DX	349	1001-1030	K	121	1-149
H	350	1-100	K	122	150
H	351	101-400	K	123	151-300
H	352	401-2000	KX	124	1, 3-13, 15,
H	351	2020 to			17, 18, 20, 22
H	352	2064			29, 31-42, 44-100
Buck	380	1, 2, 3	BC	125	1-100
Drop			BC	126	101-150
			BC	127	206-274
PF	400	1-18	BM	150	1-20
Steel	500	12	BM	151	21-150
Roll off			BM	152	151-175
A	1	13	BR	175	1-50
A	2	16	BR	176	51-100
A	3	17	BR	177	101-125
A	4	30-59			
		70-79			

Figure 160

The details in **Figure 160** are from the information in the index pages of the Container Diagram Book

RAILHEAD DISTRIBUTION FOR INDUSTRIAL PRODUCTS

An insight into railway thinking, following the 1923 amalgamation, is given in this article which appeared in the *Railway Magazine*. It clearly shows how one of the benefits of 1923 was the release of surplus warehouses, which enabled the railhead distribution system to be developed, which in itself lead to the development of containers.

It should be remembered that while containers to carry coal were in use from the earliest days of railways, containers for merchandise were a much later development in the history of railways.

An important development of recent years is the extent to which firms are using depots or railway premises as centres for their local distribution, these centres being served by express freight train facilities from and to the works or headquarters of the firms in question. In most cases, use is made of containers of various types, while railway wagons suitably fitted, are allocated to the service.

LMSR DISTRIBUTION WAREHOUSES

The LMSR, with the advent of grouping at the close of 1922, was enabled to release from their normal function a large number of warehouses at 'key' points throughout the United Kingdom, and these were immediately placed at the disposal of the trading community. Many well-known firms dealing in all kinds of commodities have organised their distribution over the length and breadth of the country by the establishment of railhead depots on the LMS system at points conveniently situated in relation to the consuming areas.

Merchandise is conveyed by express freight trains in bulk from factory or importing centre. On arrival at railhead depot, wagons are unloaded direct to warehouse, after which bulk is broken and goods are sorted. Distribution to customers in the surrounding areas is effected by means of a highly-organised system of road distrbution.

The time factor is today, predominant, and it is therefore worthy of note that railhead distribution enables orders to be met immediately from stock held locally, while each depot is fed by direct express freight trains, undoubtedly the quickest form of goods transport available today. Incidentally, there is also an actual saving of £ s d in respect of freight charges and packing costs, while experience proves that a marked increase in business follows upon the establishment of depots in the heart of the densely populated consuming areas.

Amongst the first firms to take up railhead distribution on scientific lines, mention may be made of S. P. D. Limited, the transport organisation for Lever Brothers and their associated companies, and Cadbury Brothers, the well-known chocolate manufacturers. Cadbury Brothers' London depot, opened nearly six years ago, at Camden Town, may be taken as typical. At this station, premises have been provided which, in addition to rail-side deck space and motor-loading berths, comprise stock room, offices and show room.

Ten covered railway vans, each conveying 6 tons of confectionery, are despatched from Bournville Works at 5.30p.m. daily. These vans arrive at Camden at 2a.m. the following morning, and are in position for unloading when the depot opens at 8a.m.

A special feature of the arrangement is the packing of goods at the factory into 'cages', which are transferred by means of hydraulic lift bogies into railway vans, each van holding 14 'cages'. A special device secures the 'cages' in position and prevents shifting of the load during transit. On arrival at the railhead depot, 'lift bogies' are again used to transfer the 'cages' to the stock room, where the goods are unloaded, sorted, and taken into stock. Empty 'cages' are returned to the waiting railway vans (which are kept in circuit between Bournville and London), and, travelling through the night, arrive at Bournville at 7.30a.m. for reloading — a total of 38 hours for the round trip. Urgent orders for 'speciality' lines not usually stocked at Camden can be obtained from Bournville and delivered to the customer in less than 24 hours.

In the stock room, goods are assembled and packed for individual orders on to trays, and lift bogies are once more brought into operation for wheeling these trays to the fleet of waiting motor vans. Road distribution throughout Greater London is undertaken by Thomas Tilling Limited, from 15 to 20 motor loads, according to the season of the year, being despatched daily.

The success of railhead distribution may be gauged by the remarkable growth in the number of depots opened by the LMSR for individual firms during the last five years. In 1922, sixty three depots were in operation, while today, the figure exceeds 400, embracing many manufacturers whose names are household words.

Commodities as widely divergent as cement, soap, cattle food, preserves, chocolate, groceries, mineral water, toys and even motor cars, are being transported and delivered under this scheme, the advantage of elasticity enabling it to be adapted to any individual requirements.

Reference may be made also to the fact that the LMSR is developing the container system of goods transport to allow of combined road and rail transit. This method permits the following conditions to be realized:-

(1) Door-to-door delivery without unloading and unloading at stations.
(2) Elimination of packing costs.
(3) Reduction in risk of damage or loss by theft.
(4) Saving in time and money.
(5) Speeding up of goods services.

This system is being co-ordinated with the railhead distribution system described above. In conclusion, it may be said that railhead distribution effectively combines the advantages of two modes of transport, each supreme in its own sphere. Cheap and speedy rail conveyance is secured for traffic in bulk over the long haul, while 'door-to-door' distribution is efficiently performed by motor vehicles in the actual consuming areas. Undoubtedly, a big future lies ahead for the co-ordination of rail and road facilities along these lines.

RAIL-ROAD TRAFFIC AND THE LMSR

In connection with the foregoing, reference may also be made to container traffic as it has been developed on the LMSR.

The use of containers in the handling and transportation of merchandise constitutes a question which, in one form or another, has occupied the attention of railway executive officers from time to time in connection with the intensive development of freight operation, but more particularly from the point of view of the possible economies or other domestic advantages to be derived from the consequent saving in time and labour. They have, of course, been used for many years under particular circumstances, as, for example, in the case of luggage and parcels between London and Ireland or the Continent and involving cross-channel services, while in the case of goods traffic an outstanding instance is afforded by the late L&Y (now LMS) Railway in the use of 'flats' — a form of container — in connection with their extensive traffic in cotton goods. From the point of view of the trader, however, the inherent advantages of a system of transport affording 'door-to-door' conveyance of merchandise, thereby avoiding the customary handling at railway depots, are apparent, and the march of progress, coupled with the development of competitive forms of transport has, during recent years, brought this aspect of the question into increasing prominence.

The London Midland and Scottish Railway has, over the past two years, been engaged in an exhaustive programme of research on the subject, accompanied by experiments which latterly have been carried out on a scale sufficiently extensive to afford a practical test of the possibilities of the system and to demonstrate its various features as affecting both the railway and the trader. In the course of these experiments, a sum of £20,000 has been expended, representing a total stock of between 400 and 500 containers, which have in the main been built in the LMSR Carriage & Wagon Works at Derby.

As a result of the experience gained, four types of container have been evolved as standard, two representing the equivalent of the covered van and two the equivalent of the open wagon. The various types are shown in the accompanying illustrations, and details as to dimensions and carrying capacities are given below:-

Closed Containers, Types 'A' and 'B'

Type	Dimensions (interior)			Capacity in		Tare
	Length	Width	Height at Centre	Tons	Cub. ft.	
	Ft. Ins.	Ft. Ins.	Ft. Ins.			Cwt.
'A'	7 0	6 0	6 6	2½	273	16
'B'	13 6	6 0	6 6	4	526	25

Open Containers, Types 'C' and 'D'

Type	Dimensions (interior)			Capacity in Tons	Tare
	Length	Width	Height of Sides		
	Ft. Ins.	Ft. Ins.	Ft. Ins.		Cwt.
'C'	7 0	6 0	3 9	2½	9
'D'	13 4	6 0	3 9	4	17

In arriving at the various types, due regard has been necessary to the normal capacity of cranage and cartage equipment, while at the same time affording the largest possible capacity coupled with the lowest possible tare. Up to the present the containers have been of timber construction, although attention is being given to the possible use of steel or other metal.

The closed type containers are fitted with end doors, comprising a drop door at the bottom and a pair of swing doors above. A certain number are fitted with louvred ventilators in order to provide for traffics of a perishable nature. In the case of the open type containers both sides and ends are detachable, but the inevitable detraction from the strength of the walls has certain disadvantages, and consideration is being given to a new type 'D' container having side drop doors, as in the case of the usual open wagon, and a single drop door at one end. These containers are lifted from eyes fitted at the base of the sides, and in order to prevent 'binding' of the crane chains a 'spreader' has been provided, through the grooved ends of which the crane chains are passed, and which at the same time is adapted to reinforce the strength of the sides. This 'spreader' has formed a convenient foundation for the sheet bow.

Research is being made with the object of evolving a type of container of the roll-off type, i.e. on wheels or castors, to obviate the necessity for a crane for transferring between rail and road vehicle.

With the gradual development of the number of stock in use, some method of control was found to be essential if light running was to be kept down and the stock worked as economically as possible. A system was, therefore, established, the whole of the stock being placed under the control of the Chief Goods Manager at Euston, although a certain amount of local autonomy was accorded the respective District Goods Managers so far as requirements within the limits of their particular districts were concerned. All movements of container stock are telegraphed to the control at Euston, where they are recorded on a wall-board by means of tickets — different coloured tickets being used for the respective types of container.

(Note: The illustrations mentioned above have not been used with this article, but have been included within this volume.)

The wall-board shows at a glance the following information in respect of each district:-

(1) Traffic waiting, i.e. stock required
(2) Supplied for loading
(3) Arrival for delivery
(4) On hand empty

In this way it is possible to meet all shortages to the best advantage, and to manipulate the stock with the maximum of loaded use. In spite of the comparatively limited scale on which operations have been conducted, the proportion of loaded mileage has reached the vicinity of 80 per cent, which speaks highly for the efficacy of the system.

In dealing with this phase, it must be remembered that the development of the container by the LMSR Company has been in the main in the direction of its application as a 'full load' instrument, and movements of stock are, therefore, general and not confined to reciprocating streams of traffic between pairs of points.

Generally speaking, the use of containers is limited to consignments of one ton or over, from one sender to one consignee, although, in suitable circumstances delivery to three or four addresses has been undertaken by special arrangements.

It will be apparent that with a facility of this kind, the operations of the railway company are altogether of a different character from those entailed in dealing with merchandise loaded in ordinary wagons.

The nature of the traffic to be conveyed in containers very largely determines the rates at which the merchandise is carried and conditions as to risk, &c.

The experience of the LMSR Company in regard to claims for damage, &c., has been noteworthy, as the following examples will show:-

400 loads of gas stoves carried for one firm with only six known cases of damage
100 loads of enamel baths carried with three or four isolated damages
Several hundred loads of new furniture, gramophones, &c., carried with almost complete immunity from damage
700 loads of preserves carried for one firm during five months. Claims (which arose mainly in connection with the return empty jars) paid to the extent of 0.22 per cent of revenue.

In all these cases carriage by rail had dwindled to vanishing point, owing mainly to the growth of road transport.

The LMSR Company has found that the container system of railway transport provides the advantages arising from 'door-to-door' service, i.e.:-

(1) Risk of damage or loss minimised
(2) Packing costs reduced
(3) Time and labour saved

It is of interest to note that the use of containers by the LMSR has been the means of enabling a number of British traders to compete more successfully against foreign manufacturers for such traffics as enamelware, baths, &c.

This article is reproduced by courtesy of The Railway Magazine

Plate 146

Plate 147

Chapter Three

An Outline of Livery Practice

The earliest reference to a unified painting procedure to be adopted by the LMS is dated March 1929, the original documet being loaned, to the author, by George Dow. It was felt that this document should be reproduced in full and it will be noted that it refers to carriages, non-passenger coaching stock, wagon stock, various road vehicles, platform trucks and barrows.

LONDON MIDLAND & SCOTTISH RAILWAY COMPANY

Carriage & Wagon Department

DERBY

SCHEDULE OF PAINTS AND FORMULAE FOR SAME FOR THE PAINTING OF THE COMPANY'S ROLLING STOCK

The following methods and formulae for the painting of Carriage and Wagon Stock have been agreed upon by the Paints Standardisation Committee, and no deviation must be made without reference to Headquarters.

Any question relating to quality of materials must be referred to the Chemical Laboratory, Wolverton.

Where the shade is a governing factor, standard samples indicating the agreed standard of shade are being supplied to the factories for their guidance, but it must be distinctly understood that the composition and quality is essentially governed by the specifications.

Carriages

Carriage stock will, in future, receive two coats of priming made in accordance with the following formula:-

Protective White Paint . . . . 112 lb Special Paints Contract
Liquid Driers . . . . 9 to 12 lb Special Contract
White Spirit . . . . 27 lb Item 1, Contract 218
Black-in-oil. . . . . 8 to 12 lb Item 6, Contract 55

After priming this should be followed by three coats of filling to the following formula:-

Enamel Filling. . . . . 112 lb Special Contract
Gold Size. . . . . .7 lb Special Contract
Carriage Varnish. . . . . .7 lb Special Contract
Genuine Turpentine . . . . 6 lb Item 1, Contract 300

Where the filling has been standing for some time in the cask, and some of the oil may have run away, it is recommended in mixing to the formula that an amount not exceeding 4 lb of raw linseed oil be added.

The filling after rubbing down is followed by two coats of lead colour, which will be similar in composition to the formula laid down for lead colour for priming:-

One coat of lake Ground is then applied — made to the following formula:-

Lake Ground, dry. . . . . 30 lb Item 2, Contract 279
Raw Linseed Oil. . . . . 10 lb Item 3, Contract 149

After grinding the following to be added:-

Genuine Turpentine . . . . 22½ lb Item 1, Contract 300
Liquid Driers . . . . 2 to 5 lb Special Contract
Carriage Varnish (inside). . . . . .9 lb Special Contract
Gold Size. . . . . .4½ lb Special Contract

Two Coats of Crimson Lake to the following formula:-

Crimson Lake dry. . . . . 6 lb Item 1, Contract 279
Raw Linseed Oil. . . . . 3 lb Item 3, Contract 149
Genuine Turpentine . . . . 3 lb Item 1, Contract 300

After grinding the following to be added:-

Carriage Varnish (inside) . . . . 3 lb Item 1, Contract 300
Genuine Turpentine . . . . 3 lb Item 1, Contract 300
Liquid Driers . . . . 2 to 3 lb Special Contract

Where necessary all vehicles over 20 years of age to be finished with Engine Lake instead of Crimson Lake and the formula for Engine Lake is:-

Engine Lake, dry . . . . 6 lb Item 3, Contract 279
Raw Linseed Oil. . . . . 3 lb Item 3, Contract 149
Genuine Turpentine . . . . 3 lb Item 1, Contract 300

After grinding the following to be added:-

Carriage Varnish (inside) . . . . .4 lb Special Contract
Genuine Turpentine . . . . 3 lb Item 1, Contract 300
Liquid Driers . . . . 1 to 2 lb Special Contract

Black for picking out mouldings to be in accordance with the following:-

Drop Black, Dry. . . . . 56 lb Item 3, Contract 55
Raw Linseed Oil. . . . . 9 lb Item 3, Contract 149
Liquid Driers . . . . 4 to 8 lb Special Contract
Genuine Turpentine . . . . 9 lb Item 1, Contract 300

Yellow for picking out mouldings:-

Zinc Sulphide White 33% . . . . 20 lb Item 40, Contract 55
Ochre Yellow in Oil. . . . . 7 lb Item 20, Contract 55
Chrome Lemon in Oil . . . . 1 lb Item 20, Contract 55
Liquid Driers . . . . 1 to 2 lb Special Contracts
White Spirit . . . . 1 to 3 lb Item 1, Contract 218

Plate 146   This view, taken at the works of Charles Roberts, shows three stages of wagon painting. To the left we see open goods to D1892 with the first coats of paint. The centre row of wagons is complete as far as the grey paint is concerned, while the right hand line is ready to enter service. In the interior of these wagons, only the ironwork has been painted.

Photograph National Railway Museum

Plate 147   A few photographs exist which show the letters LMS in either dark grey or black. This picture, of an LNWR cattle wagon, is one of the best examples seen by the author and is reproduced to show this livery style. Unfortunately, no explanation can be offered, by the author, for this style.

Photograph Railway Revivals

Vermilion for fine lining:-

Vermilion Genuine Dry . . . . .2 lb Item 34, Contract 55
Gold Size. . . . . ¾ lb Special Contract
Genuine Turpentine . . . . .¼ lb Item 1, Contract 300

VARNISHING — All new work to receive 4 coats of Finishing Body Varnish and repainted jobs 3 coats.

Ironwork

All new Ironwork to be given two coats of Red or Purple Brown Oxide, and the exposed portion of the underframe to be given in addition one coat of black lacquer.

Formula for Red or Purple Brown Oxide:-

Oxide of Iron, Purple Brown in oil . . . 112 lb Item 5, Contract 279
Liquid Driers . . . . .4½ to 8 lb Special Contract
Boiled Linseed Oil . . . . 54 lb Item 1, Contract 149

All ironwork other than bogies to be given one coat of Black Japan, and the solebar to be given one coat of finishing body varnish.

Roofs

The bare wood to receive one coat of lead colour the same as the priming coat for the bodies, afterwards to be stopped up with putty and then jointing paste applied. The canvas then to be stretched on, and after this has been done a mixture of equal parts of boiled linseed oil and jointing paste to be applied, and after this four coats of a mixture of equal parts of Protective White Paint and Tarpaulin Dressing to be applied.

White paint for inside of carriages

The formula for the white paint used as a ground work prior to the enamelling should be in accordance with the following:-

Zinc Sulphide White 33% . . . . 112 lb Item 40, Contract 55
Liquid Driers . . . . .3 to 6 lb Special Contract
White Spirit . . . . 27 lb Item 1, Contract 218

Battery Box

The battery box carried under the underframe to receive one coat of acid resisting black varnish.

Interiors of Passenger Brake Vans

Ceilings to receive three coats of white paint, mixed to the formula for white paint for the insides of carriages, followed by one coat of glossy white enamel. Repair jobs to have two coats of white paint and one coat of enamel. Sides, ends, etc., to have three coats of terra cotta paint made to the following formula:-

Zinc Sulphide White 33% . . . . 112 lb Item 40, Contract 55
Venetian Red, dry . . . . .38 lb Item 27, Contract 55
　　　　　　　　　　　(ground to a suitable consistency)
Vermilion Substitute in oil. . . . . . . .14 lb Item 35, Contract 55
　　　　　　　　　　　(ground to a suitable consistency)
Yellow Ochre in Oil. . . . . .38 lb Item 20, Contract 55
Orange Chrome in Oil . . . . .28 lb Item 13, Contract 55
Boiled Linseed Oil . . . . .18 lb Item 1, Contract 149
Liquid Driers . . . . .9 lb Special Contract
White Spirit . . . . .9 lb Item 1, Contract 218

To be followed by one coat of carriage varnish.

Sundry Passenger Stock Vehicles

The procedure for painting sundry vehicles, i.e., Horse Boxes, Scenery Trucks, Hound Vans, Covered Carriage Trucks, etc., to be as follows:-

Exteriors

One coat of lead colour priming made in accordance with the priming used for carriage stock.

Stopped up.

Two coats of lead colour of the same formula as that used for carriages. (Repairs — one coat)

Two coats of Lake Ground as used for carriages.

Two coats of finishing body varnish.

Interiors
Horse Boxes (New Work)

Ceilings (including Groom's Compartment) to receive three coats of white paint, similar to that used for the insides of carriages, to be followed by one coat of glossy white enamel.

Sides, Ends, etc., of Horse Compartment to be given three coats of Drab Paint mixed to the following formula:-

Zinc Sulphite White 33%. . . . . 112 lb Item 40, Contract 55
Liquid Driers . . . . .6 lb Special Contract
Yellow Ochre in Oil. . . . . .10 lb Item 20, Contract 55
Raw Umber in Oil. . . . . .10 lb Purchased as required
Raw Linseed Oil. . . . . .9 lb Item 3, Contract 149
Boiled Linseed Oil . . . . 27 lb Item 1, Contract 149
Venetian Red dry . . . . .1 lb Item 27, Contract 55
　　　　　　　　　　　(ground to a suitable consistency)

Sides, Ends, etc., of Groom's Compartment to receive three coats of Drab Paint to the above formula, followed by one coat of carriage varnish.

Scenery Trucks, Covered Carriage Trucks, etc.

The whole of the interiors to receive three coats of Drab Paint. (Repairs — two coats)

Wagon Stock

All new wagons to receive three coats of paint in accordance with the following particulars:-

Priming Coat.
The first coat to be made from Zinc Sulphide White 33% mixed with smudge* where available.
　*Smudge is a mixture of old paints used as a priming coat on new timber.
With regard to this first coat, it is difficult to lay down any strict formula owing to the varying consistency of the smudge which may be used, but it must be emphasised it should contain sufficient oil to give it the necessary binding properties.

The second and finishing coat should be to the following formula:-

Zinc Sulphide White 33% . . . . 112 lb Item 40, Contract 55
Boiled Linseed Oil . . . . 60 lb Item 1, Contract 149
Black in Oil . . . . .8 lb Item 6, Contract 55
Liquid Driers . . . . .2 to 5 lb Special Contract
Carriage Varnish (inside) . . . . .9 lb Special Contract

This formula is only to meet the requirements of paint for brush application, and is not intended to apply to those Depots where spray or flow paint is required. It is recognised that in these cases special provisions must be made to suit individual cases.

The tops of all main wagon members should be painted with one coat of acid resisting black varnish of similar quality to that used for battery boxes on carriages. (This applies to repairs only. Wood Frame Wagons).

Paint for lettering

The following should be the paint used for the lettering of wagons:-

White Protective Paint and Zinc Sulphide White 33%, equal parts, and, where necessary to bring it down to suitable consistency, approximately 5% inside carriage varnish may be added.

Roofs

In the case of wooden roofs the same procedure must be followed as in the case of carriage roofs.

Steel roofs to have a priming coat of Red or Purple Brown Oxide to the following formula:-

Oxide of Iron, Purple Brown in Oil. . . 112 lb Item 5, Contract 279
Liquid Driers . . . . 4½ to 8 lb Special Contract
Boiled Linseed Oil . . . . 54 lb Item 1, Contract 149
and to be given three coats of White Protective Paint mixed with equal parts of tarpaulin dressing.

Ironwork

NEW IRONWORK — All new ironwork to be given two coats of Oxide of Iron, Purple Brown, to the same formula as that for steel roofs, and the exposed portions to be given one coat of black lacquer of brushing or dipping consistency.

REPAIRED IRONWORK — To receive one coat of Black Lacquer.

Insides of Goods Brakes

The ceiling to have two coats of white paint mixed in accordance with the formula for white paint used for painting insides of carriages.

New vehicles only to receive in addition one coat of white paint with the addition of 25% of carriage varnish.

The sides, ends, etc., should receive one coat of smudge and one coat of green mixed to the following formula:-

Brunswick Green, dry . . . . 30 lb Item 15, Contract 55
Raw Linseed Oil. . . . . 15 lb Item 3, Contract 149

After grinding the following to be added:-

Liquid Driers . . . . .2 lb Special Contract
Boiled Linseed Oil . . . . 12 lb Item 1, Contract 149
Carriage Varnish (inside) . . . . .4 lb Special Contract
to be followed by one coat of this green with the addition of 25% of carriage varnish.

ROAD VEHICLES

Horse Drawn Goods Lorries — New

The procedure for painting these vehicles to be as follows:-

One coat of lead colour priming (similar to that for coaches).

Afterwards to be puttied up and given one coat of dark lead colour to the following formula:-

Protective White Paint . . . . 112 lb Special Contract
Liquid Driers . . . . .9 lb Special Contract
White Spirit . . . . 27 lb Item 1, Contract 218
Black in Oil . . . (Sufficient to produce the necessary shade, Item 6, Contract 55

These vehicles should then receive one coat of finishing body varnish.

White for Writing

Two coats of white to the same formula as that for the lettering of wagons, to be used for lettering.

Horse Drawn Vehicles — Parcels Vans

To be treated in exactly the same manner as coaching stock up to the filling.

After rubbing down to have one coat of lead colour, to the same formula as that for the priming coat for carriages, and then to have two coats of Lake Ground to the same formula as given for Lake Ground in colours for coaching stock.

The lining to be in accordance with the standard coaching practice, and the whole of the body to be afterwards given two coats of finishing body varnish (outside).

Motor Parcels Vans

The practice to be the standard coaching practice up to the filling, then one coat of lead colour priming to be followed by one coat of lake ground, and then one coat of Crimson Lake similar to that used for coaching stock.

Lining paints to be in accordance with the standard practice for coaches, and finally to have three coats of body varnish (outside).

Goods Motor Lorries

One coat of lead colour priming, puttied up, and to be followed by one coat of dark lead colour, the same as Horse Drawn Goods Lorries, and followed by one coat of Ultramarine Blue to the following formula:-

Ultramarine Blue, dry . . . . .30 lb Item 8, Contract 55
Raw Linseed Oil. . . . . 10 lb Item 3, Contract 149

The above to be ground together and the finished paint to consist of:-

Ultramarine Blue in Oil. . . . . .40 lb As prepared above
White Spirit . . . . .9 lb Item 1, Contract 218
Liquid Driers . . . . .2 to 5 lb Special Contract
Carriage Varnish (inside) . . . . .9 lb Special Contract

The wheels of the chassis to have one coat of priming colour, and to be followed by one coat of vermilion substitute.

The priming colour for the wheels to be as follows:-

Protective White Paint . . . . 110 lb Special Contract
Liquid Driers . . . . .2 to 5 lb Special Contract
Venetian Red in Oil 20 lb . (Prepared by grinding Item 27, Contract
                                55 to suitable consistency)
Raw Linseed Oil. . . . . .9 lb Item 3, Contract 149
White Spirit . . . . 27 lb Item 1, Contract 218

The formula for the Vermilion Substitute to be:-

Vermilion Substitute dry. . . . . 30 lb Item 35, Contract 55
Raw Linseed Oil. . . . . 15 lb Item 3, Contract 149
White Spirit . . . . .6 lb Item 1, Contract 218
Liquid Driers . . . . .4 to 7 lb Special Contract

The vehicles should receive two coats of finishing body varnish.

Interiors of Horse Drawn and Motor Road Vehicles

The interiors of Horse Drawn and Motor Road Vehicles should be given three coats of paint mixed to the following formula (Repairs — 2 coats):-

Protective White Paint . . . . .56lb Special Contract
Brunswick Green in Oil. . . . . .9lb Item 16, Contract 55
Yellow Ochre in Oil. . . . . .33lb Item 20, Contract 55
Lemon Chrome in Oil . . . . .4lb Item 11, Contract 55
Venetian Red . . . . .1½lb Item 27, Contract 55
Liquid Driers . . . . .4 to 7lb Special Contract
White Spirit . . . . .4½lb Item 1, Contract 218
this to be followed by one coat of carriage varnish (inside).

Platform Trucks and Barrows

Two coats Red or Purple Brown Oxide to formula as for steel roofs, given under wagon stock painting.

It is realized that small quantities of colours other than those mentioned in this schedule will be required from time to time. As these will in all probability only be used in extremely small quantities such as touching up etc., it is not thought desirable to include these.

Derby,
March 1929

This schedule was kindly loaned and reproduced by courtesy of George Dow

---

The LMS adopted what was, as far as locomotives and carriages were concerned, the old Midland railway livery. In the circumstances, it would have been surprising if the company had used anything other than the basic Midland livery for its wagon stock. The basic facts are that the LMS used two colours, grey prior to 1936 and bauxite thereafter. The main problem is that more than one shade of grey appears to have been used. Midland practice in 1921 was to use a light shade for new construction and a dark grey, called smudge, for repaired wagons.

The 1888 specificiation for Midland Railway grey appears in an *Illustrated History of Midland Wagons, Volume One,* Chapter 2, and the author believes that this specification was not changed until 1929 when the LMS issued a new one which has been reproduced in full. The reader's attention is drawn to the third paragraph which suggests that the composition is more important than the shade.

The other paint specification in this chapter is the one which appeared in the 1935 edition of the official LMS paint schedule and the parts referring to wagons is reproduced in full.

The grey specified in the 1929 schedule would have been darker than the 1935 colour since Mix 5 called for 8lb of black in oil as against 3—4lb, while the ultramarine was omitted. Photographic evidence confuses the issue still further since some photographs taken before and during 1928 clearly show some vehicles, brake vans and refrigerator vans in particular, in a much darker colour.

A study of **Plate 91** shows that the line of wagons clearly ex-works have the cattle wagons in a much lighter shade than the refrigerator van. Since the latter vehicle is brand new, the others being repaints, it would appear that the Midland policy was in this instance completely reversed. The author freely admits that he has not been able to throw any further light on the subject, and has been unable to find an example of this dark grey in anything other than a vehicle which has been part of the background view.

The official change to bauxite in May 1936 was preceeded slightly by a change to what was to become the more standardised type of insignia and some new construction, outshopped in the grey body colour, was lettered in the new style before bauxite became general for all bodywork. Even so some vehicles were re-lettered but not repainted, so that until after 1948 it was possible to see vehicles in a weathered grey body colour carrying the post-1936 lettering style. Some of these vehicles even had traces of the pre-May 1936 lettering still visible.

During the War a further livery change occurred, many wooden-bodied vehicles being built without the benefit of paintwork on the woodwork except where lettering was placed, and here painted patches were used with the insignia detail of numbering and letters painted on to the bauxite painted patches.

Below solebars everything was painted black but the solebar itself was painted the relevant body colour. Above the bottom of the solebar there were exceptions to this rule. Buffer heads and shanks, couplings hooks, links and brake lever guards were painted black; a patch giving oiling date and district numbers was painted slate grey.

Roof Colour

The colour of van roofs is quite a problem and readers are referred to the available written evidence. The LMS carriage and wagon department, schedule of paints and formulae, states:-

In the case of wooden roofs the same procedure must be followed as in the case of carriage roofs.

Before 1935 the specification differed in that the final operation was to apply four coats of a mixture of equal parts of protective white paint and tarpaulin dressing and although the 1935 specification shows an aluminium colour type paint was used, this is rather misleading since after a short time in service, weathering conditions would rapidly turn the ex-works root colour muddy grey, darkening as the time lengthened from leaving the works.

Service Vehicles

While the foregoing applied to revenue earning vehicles, there was also a considerable amount of service stock. The LMS did not add to this to any great extent for several years, and LMS livery policy for this stock needs clarification. Indeed, researchers could be forgiven if they believed no such policy existed. Nowhere within the available written evidence is there any mention of a livery for service stock, and photographic evidence suggests the existence of at least three other colour schemes. Because the number of vehicles was fairly small and their duties were of a humble nature, they seem to have almost escaped notice. This summary, while not conclusive, is believed to be fairly accurate.

PLOUGH BRAKE VANS — Probably slate grey body.
BALLAST WAGONS — Wartime constructions unpainted but earlier construction had red oxide bodywork.
SLEEPER WAGONS — As ballast wagons.
LOCO COAL WAGONS — Normal freight stock livery.
BOGIE HOPPER COAL WAGONS — Normal freight stock livery.
CHAIRED SLEEPER TROLLIES — Normal freight stock livery.
CRANE MATCH WAGONS — Some black all over, others slate grey body and black underframes.

Painting Methods

Although the painting of goods stock did not receive quite so much attention as contemporary coach stock, nevertheless the 1935 painting schedule is still comprehensive and shows that the painting methods, at least for new stock, was not as haphazard as is often supposed. The main points of divergence between the two were that fewer operations were involved in the case of goods stock, and no set time was specified between the operations. Furthermore, this later specification was much more comprehensive than that in the 1929 instructions.

Wooden Bodied Wagons

Before assembly started, all of the previously prepared timber received one coat of primer (mix 1) on all edges which were inaccessible after assembly. This was allowed to dry hard before any further work was done. Similarly, all steel details had rust, scale etc. removed by chipping, scraping and wire brushing. Oil and grease were then removed with white spirit and one coat of bauxite (mix 2) applied immediately. Where welding was employed, the weld was first freed from all slag, and the adjacent areas were wire brushed; after examination an area extending for two inches on each side of the weld was given one coat of primer (mix 3A) followed by one coat of bauxite (mix 2) all over.

After assembly, all of the exterior woodwork was given one coat of knotting to all knots. This was followed by one coat of primer (mix 1 or 4A) and any imperfections in the woodwork were stopped up with putty. All of the exterior ironwork was touched up where necessary with mix 2, and

this was followed by a further coat of the same mixture or one coat of mix 2A. Finally the exterior of the body, solebars, headstocks and buffers was given two coats of grey (mix 5), or one coat if flow painted. After 1936 this operation was carried out using bauxite (mix 2B). While the specification does not detail flow painting, this term was used by London Transport to describe a method used to paint buses. The paint was poured into a distributor which allowed it to flow out on to the top edge of the bus. The paint then flowed down the bus sides into recovery drains.

The undergear and inside faces of the frame received one coat of bauxite (mix 2A), followed on the undergear by one coat of finishing black enamel.

The exterior of the roof on covered vehicles first had one coat or primer (mix 1 or 4A) applied; it was then stopped up with putty and one coat of jointing paste applied. The canvas was next stretched on and bedded down. One coat of a mixture consisting of equal parts of boiled linseed oil and jointing paste was then applied, followed by three coats of roof paint (mix 6).

It will be noticed that nothing is said in the foregoing specification regarding the interiors of vehicles, and in fact the only instance where such information is quoted is in respect of the brake vans, which after having the treatment already described had a coat of knotting applied to all interior knots. The ceiling then had two coats of white undercoat (mix 7), followed by one coat of finishing white (mix 7A). The sides and ends were given one coat of primer (mix 1) followed by one coat of green undercoat (mix 8) an and one finishing coat of green (mix 8A). The lettering was then applied, in all cases using white paint (mix 9). The specification states that this was to be done by spraying, though much of this work was in fact hand applied.

It will be noted that the specification does not mention the painting of wooden underframes, probably because when it was issued new vehicles of this type were fairly rare. It does state that repaired vehicles of this type were to have one coat of acid resisting black enamel on the top faces of all main members.

On the matter of repaints, the specification is equally vague, merely stating that the condition of the wagon and the facilities available must be taken into account when determining methods to be used, which perhaps serves to show that the subject did not receive quite so much attention as did passenger stock.

Steel-Bodied Wagons

The procedure adopted here was very similar to that already described for the steel details of the wooden-bodied wagons. The only point to be noted is that the interior of hopper wagons was finished in one of two ways. The first specified that one coat of bauxite (mix 2) and one of bauxite (mix 2A) was to be followed by one coat of finishing black enamel. The second method was to apply one coat of bauxite (mix 2) followed by two coats of bituminous paint (mix 10). An exception to this rule applied to grain hoppers, which were to be left unpainted.

Containers

Although the painting methods for containers were given in a completely separate part of the specification, it is hardly surprising that much of the information duplicated that already given for wagon stock. Unless otherwise stated, the information already given applies equally to this section.

Open containers were painted grey, or after 1936 bauxite, the only point to be noted being that the steel type was given one coat of steel primer (mix 3) inside and out, followed by two coats of grey (mix 5) on the exterior and one coat on the interior surfaces. The underside of the floor was given one coat of primer, followed by one coat of acid resisting black enamel, the wooden type receiving the enamel only, apparently without the benefit of a priming coat.

The specification for covered containers was divided into four groups, viz., wood or steel construction, painted white or lake. Taking the white painted wooden type first, the specification stated that after the preliminary operations one coat of white undercoat (mix 7) was to be applied, followed after stopping up by two further undercoats. Two coats of glossy white enamel followed, after which the lettering was applied using black air drying enamel. The lettering was then varnished using carriage stock exterior finishing varnish. The underside of the floor was given one coat of acid resisting black enamel, while the interior received two coats of knotting.

The lake liveried wooden containers received one coat of primer (mix 4A), stopping up being done with hard stopping (mix 11). One coat of lead colour undercoat (mix 4) was followed by one coat of lake undercoat (mix 12) and one of standard lake (mix 13). The specification stated that lettering was then to be carried out using yellow paint (mix 14), (but see livery details regarding this point). Finally the exterior was varnished with two coats of carriage stock exterior finishing varnish, flatted down lightly between coats with pumice dust. The underside was dealt with as described above, while the roof in both cases was dealt with exactly as already described for the wagon stock.

The covered steel containers had a somewhat different treatment, the first part of which can be considered for both liveries. All of the steel panels were covered with panel wash (mix 15), which was left for 30 minutes and the panels were then washed in warm water and thoroughly dried. This process had to be carried out at least one day before proceeding further. One coat of steel primer (mix 3) was then applied to both surfaces. The white containers were painted exactly like the wooden variety; the lake containers, however, only had one coat of lake undercoat (mix 12) followed by one coat of lake (mix 13), lettering and varnishing being as for the wooden variety.

The interior, where it was unlined, was given two coats of white synthetic enamel; where a wooden lining was present the interior of the shell was given one coat of bauxite (mix 2), the plywood panelling being given two coats of knotting.

Where the roof was of galvanised material it was given a coating of zinc wash (mix 16); this was allowed to dry and wiped clean. Where mild steel was used it was treated as already described for the side panels, after which in both cases two coats of steel primer (mix 3) were applied to the outside and one to the inside. The exterior of the roof was then given two coats of roof paint (mix 6). The underside of the floor received one coat of steel primer (mix 3) and one coat of acid resisting black enamel.

Paint Specifications

MIX 1 SMUDGE PRIMER

No quantities were specified for this item. It consisted of smudge and zinc white, composite pigment, in oil and suitably tinted.

MIX 2 BAUXITE PAINT (UNDERCOAT)

Boiled linseed oil	8 lb
White spirit	6—10 lb
Liquid drier	2—4 lb
Bauxite residue in oil	82 lb

MIX 2A BAUXITE PAINT (SECOND COAT)

Mixture number 2	100 lb
Black in oil	6 lb

MIX 2B BAUXITE PAINT (FINISHING COAT)

This is not shown in the specification, but its probable composition is given below:

Mixture number 2A	90 lb
Mixing varnish	10 lb

MIX 3 PRIMER FOR STEEL

Oxide of iron, in oil, type R (red shade)	88 lb
Zinc oxide white in oil	2 lb
Aluminium powder (fine varnish powder)	10 lb
Raw linseed oil	10 lb
Mixing varnish	26 lb
Genuine Turpentine	16—20 lb
Liquid drier	not more than 4 lb

MIX 3A PRIMER FOR WELDED JOINTS

Mixture number 3	80 lb
Aluminium powder (fine varnish powder)	10 lb
Mixing varnish	10 lb

MIX 4 LEAD COLOUR UNDERCOAT

Protective white paint paste	112 lb
Liquid drier	9—12 lb
White spirit	26—30 lb
Black in oil	9—10 lb
Raw linseed oil	4 lb

MIX 4A WOOD PRIMER

Mixture number 4	80 lb
Aluminium powder (fine varnish powder)	10 lb
Mixing varnish	10 lb

MIX 5 LEAD COLOUR FOR WAGONS

Zinc white, composite pigment in oil	112 lb
Boiled linseed oil	60 lb
Black in oil	3—4 lb
Liquid drier	2—5 lb
Mixing varnish	9 lb
Ultramarine blue in oil	3—4 lb

MIX 6 ROOF PAINT

Protective white paint paste	56 lb
Thickened linseed oil	4 lb
Boiled linseed oil	7 lb
Mixing varnish	7 lb
White spirit	8—12 lb
Black in oil	8 lb
Aluminium powder (fine varnish powder)	7 lb
Liquid drier	not more than 4 lb

MIX 7 WHITE UNDERCOAT PAINT

Zinc white, composite pigment in oil	112 lb
White spirit	27 lb
Paste driers in oil	3 lb
Mixing varnish	4—7 lb

MIX 7A WHITE PAINT FOR INTERIORS

Mixture number 7	90 lb
Mixing varnish	10 lb

MIX 8 GREEN UNDERCOAT FOR GOODS BRAKES

Green, middle brunswick, in oil	36 lb
Raw linseed oil	10 lb
Liquid drier	2 lb
Boiled linseed oil	12—16 lb
Mixing varnish	4 lb

MIX 8A FINISHING GREEN FOR GOODS BRAKES

Mixture number 8	90 lb
Mixing varnish	10 lb

MIX 9 WHITE PAINT FOR LETTERING

Zinc white oxide in oil	60 lb
Titanium white in oil	150 lb
Zinc white, composite pigment in oil	230 lb
Raw linseed oil	10—20 lb
Paste driers in oil	40 lb
Gold size, type B (light)	10—30 lb
Mixing varnish	40—60 lb
White spirit	40—50 lb

MIX 10 BITUMINOUS PAINT

Blown bitumin	50 lb
White spirit	50 lb

MIX 11 HARD STOPPING

Enamel filling	112 lb
Gold size, type A (dark)	4 parts
Genuine turpentine	1 part
(sufficient to bring to suitable consistency)	

MIX 12 UNDERCOAT FOR LAKE

Oxide in iron, in oil, type R (red shade)	100 lb
Liquid drier	4—6 lb
Mixing varnish	28—30 lb
Genuine Turpentine	12—14 lb

The above mixture produced a brown undercoat, this was taken and mixed as below to produce the lake undercoat.

Mixture as above	95 lb
Black in oil	5 lb

MIX 13 STANDARD LAKE

Standard LMS lake (paste form)	12 lb
Mixing varnish	4 lb
Genuine Turpentine	3—5 lb
Liquid drier	1—3 lb

MIX 14 YELLOW PAINT FOR LETTERING LAKE CONTAINERS

Zinc white, composite pigment, in oil	2 lb
Lemon chrome in oil	12 oz
Liquid drier	2—3 oz

MIX 15 PANEL WASH FOR STEEL PANELS

Phosphoric acid	2 gallons
Methylated spirit	8 gallons

MIX 16 ZINC WASH FOR GALVANISED PANELS

Methylated spirits	6 gallons
Toluol	3 gallons
Spirits of salts (hydrochloric acid)	½ gallon
Carbon tetrachloride	½ gallon

Numbering

The pre-grouping companies in general had no real system of wagon numbering. In most cases they merely started at one, and numbered their stock consecutively, without any regard for type, while new vehicles often took the numbers vacated by withdrawals. There were exceptions; both the LNWR and MR, for example, appear to have allotted the lowest numbers in their wagon fleets to the brake vans. At the time of the grouping the LMS took over about 305,000 wagons from its constituent companies, and renumbered them, in most cases by a straight addition to their old numbers, thus perpetuating the random numbering system. A point of interest here is that some vehicles were renumbered without being repainted, these vehicles often retaining their pre-grouping livery well into the 1930s.

At first, new construction continued to take vacant numbers within the range thus laid down, some vehicles being allocated in small blocks of numbers, while some of the early brake vans took block numbers higher than any previously allocated. In 1934 the block numbering system was adopted for all new construction, the lowest number under this scheme being 400000. Unlike coaching stock, which was completely renumbered at this time, existing wagons were not affected. The probable reason for this was that to trace and replace the cast iron numberplates of all the wagons was considered to be too mammoth a task even for the tidy minded LMS Railway.

Unfortunately a large number of wagon records were destroyed by a fire at Derby works some years ago, and it is not possible to give complete numbering details in this volume. Even if it were possible, it is felt that few readers would be interested in looking at a list of over 54,000 numbers for one type of open wagon. In these volumes a selection of the numbers carried by these vehicles is given, the block numbers being quoted in full as far as is possible.

Outline of LMS Wagon Numbering Scheme 1923

Midland Railway

Retained original numbers within the block 1—129000*
*This statement requires qualification, inasmuch as Midland brake vans carried an M prefix to their numbers, this practice being dropped after grouping.

Lancashire & Yorkshire Railway

Renumbered by the addition of 130000 to their original numbers, between 130001—169999.

Glasgow & South Western Railway

Renumbered by the addition of 170000 to their original numbers, between 170001—191999.

London & North Western Railway

Renumbered by the addition of 200000 to their original numbers, between 200001—278999 with the following exceptions: 279000 added to the numbers of service vehicles up to 279999; 280000 added to the numbers of brake vans up to 281999; 282000 added to the numbers of service vehicles up to 284999.

Caledonian Railway

Renumbered by the addition of 300000 to their original numbers between 300001—352999, with the exception of brake vans and service vehicles, which were renumbered by the addition of 353000 to their original numbers up to about 356999.

The smaller companies' stocks were renumbered into blocks, in this case no account being taken of their former numbers. The vehicles were renumbered as they became available, taking the lowest number vacant within the block, the scheme for these vehicles being:

North Staffordshire Railway

Numbered between 192000—199999.

Furness Railway

Numbered between 285000—291999**.
** This number block presumably also included Maryport & Carlisle stock.

Highland Railway

Numbered between 292000—299999.

After nationalisation, LMS vehicles retained their numbers, prefixed with the letter M, service vehicles being prefixed DM. Some vehicles of LMS design built after 1948 were given BR lot numbers, and appeared in the BR

diagram book. These vehicles were given numbers in the BR series with a B prefix.

Insignia Details

Unlike passenger stock, where most insignia were applied by transfers, those on the goods vehicles were painted on, in most cases by hand. It is hardly surprising that considerable variations existed, both in the shape and positioning of the characters.

This was particularly true during the earlier part of the period under review, for with the change to bauxite livery a standard position for each item of insignia was laid down. The following paragraphs attempt to describe the insignia used, and the standard positions used after 1936, supplementing the notes with each diagram for the various types of vehicle involved.

Company Initials

During the period when grey livery was in use, company initials were of several different sizes. In general each type of vehicle employed a particular size of letter, the largest of which was 18in. high. The shape and sizes most used are shown in **Figure 161**, but considerable variation of shape occurred, particularly in respect of the S.

With the change to bauxite livery 4in. letters became the rule, the standard position being at the left hand end of the body, above the carrying capacity and running number. As a wartime measure the height of the letters was reduced still further to 3in.

Vehicle Number

The vehicle number was carried on the cast plates and in addition was painted on the body. On the majority of vehicles they were 4in. high, but on the brake vans at first they were 5½in. high, and were painted on a black panel having a white surround, see **Figure 161**. This latter practice was of MR origin, and it is worth noting here that it was not universally carried out on the brake vans of pre-grouping origin; LNWR vehicles in particular seem to have had plain numbering from the start. The 1936 standard position was at the left hand end of the body, below the company initials and carrying capacity. Wartime measures again stated that they were to be reduced to 3in. in height.

Carrying Capacity

On the majority of vehicles this appears, at first, to have been confined to the cast number plates. There were naturally exceptions, and in these cases the usual marking appears to have consisted of the capacity in figures, followed by the word Tons in full. With the introduction of the bauxite livery, the capacity in figures was followed by the letter T, both being 3in. high. It was again stated that this was to be reduced to 2in. as a wartime measure, the standard position being at the left hand end, between the company initials and vehicle number.

Tare Weight

On brake vans, this was at first given as the weight in figures, followed by the word Tons in full. This was later abbreviated to the letter T only. On the other vehicles the weight was given in figures only, as tons, cwts and quarters with a small hyphen between each figure. The 1936 specification stated that the weight was to be given as tons and cwts only, the standard position being at the right hand bottom corner of the body, or on the solebar for vehicles without a body. Height of figures was 3 in. reduced to 2 in. as a wartime measure.

Non-Common-User

This was confined to vacuum fitted stock and special wagons and took the form of a letter N 4 in. in height, (3 in. in wartime), the standard position being at the lower edge of the body at each end.

Vacuum Fitted Stock

The first marking for these vehicles took the form of a large letter X generally 12 in. in height. The date of introduction of this symbol is uncertain, but it dates from Midland Railway practice. Reference should be made to an *Illustrated History of Midland Wagons, Volume One,* Chapters 5 and 6; it should not be confused with the same symbol which was used by some pre-grouping companies to denote common user vehicles. This marking was supplemented by a seven pointed star, placed by the vacuum release cord. The initial shape of this star was as shown in **Figure 161** being modified later to have much blunter points. The X was later replaced by the marking XP; this was 4 in. in height, the standard position being above the wheelbase markings at the right hand end of the body.

Wheelbase

This took the form of the letters WB followed by the wheelbase in figures for feet and inches. It appears to have been little used before 1936 and thereafter was used mainly

on fitted stock. Height of the symbols was 2 in. the standard position being at the right hand end of the body, under the XP marking.

Brake Overhaul, Lifting and Painting Dates

These were stencilled on the solebars in 1 in. high figures, being prefixed BO, L and P respectively. These were followed by the date in figures, i.e., 11-10-34 and suffixed by a number which indicated the works involved. The brake overhaul date was applied near to the vacuum cord star, the other two items being at the left hand end.

Oiling Date

This took the form of a black painted panel 10 in. x 5½ in. positioned on the solebar above the right hand wheel. Painted on it in white letters were the words Date Oiled and District No., the relevant information then being stencilled on.

Wagon Code

This was painted at the left hand end of the solebar, height of the figures being 2 in. It does not appear to have been very much used before 1936, although some vehicles had metal plates with the code on before this date.

Metro Gauge Mark

This again appears to have been little used on the wagon stock; it is illustrated in **Figure 161**, and indicated that the vehicle concerned could work over the so-called Widened Lines of the London Transport Metropolitan route.

In addition to the foregoing, various descriptive words such as Banana, Gunpowder etc., were used, while there were also some special symbols on such vehicles as mineral wagons. Examples of these markings will be found with the diagrams which cover the vehicles concerned.

A Selection of LMS Goods Vehicle Insignia.

Figure 161

Colour: white.   Scale: ½ inch to 1 foot.

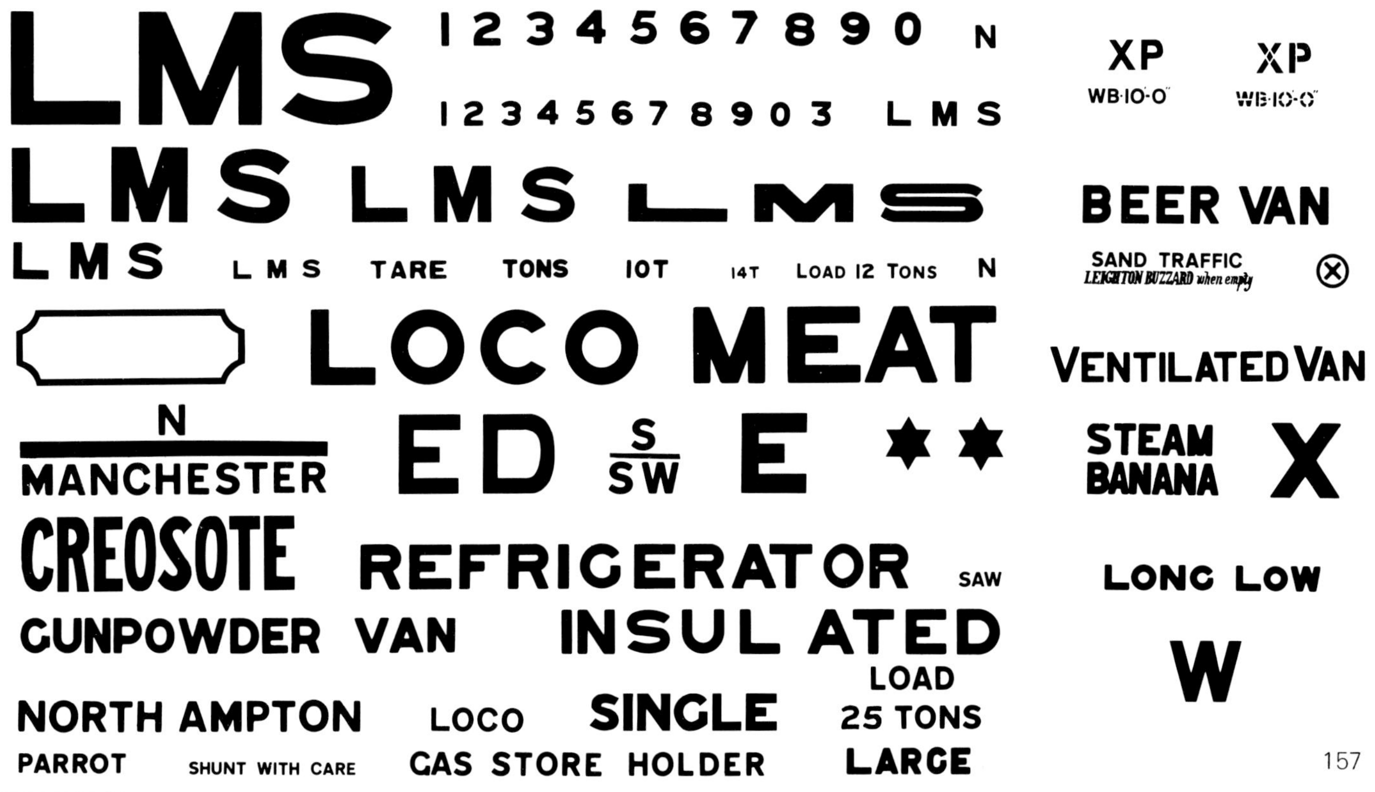

LMS

1 2 3 4 5 6 7 8 9 0   N

1 2 3 4 5 6 7 8 9 0 3   L M S

XP
WB·IO·O"

XP
WB·IO·O"

LMS **LMS** **LMS**

BEER VAN

LMS   L M S   TARE   TONS   IOT   I4T   LOAD I2 TONS   N

SAND TRAFFIC
LEIGHTON BUZZARD when empty

⊗

LOCO MEAT

VENTILATED VAN

N
MANCHESTER

ED $\frac{S}{SW}$ E   ★★

STEAM BANANA   **X**

CREOSOTE   **REFRIGERATOR**   SAW

LONG LOW

GUNPOWDER VAN   **INSULATED**

LOAD

W

NORTH AMPTON   LOCO   **SINGLE**   25 TONS

PARROT   SHUNT WITH CARE   **GAS STORE HOLDER**   **LARGE**

Plates 148 & 149 have been selected
illustrate early LMS sheets. **Plate 149** sh
an LMS sheet on a GWR open goods wa
and the picture is dated 1924–26, wh
suggests this was the early LMS style
sheet or a relettered sheet of pre-gr
origin, but one which was not ex-Midl
Railway. The small LMS lettering sho
be noted. A larger 'LMS' is where
number is located on No. 68789 and
dates are in the same place on both she
There is no sign of a number on the sheet
Photograph Roger Cox Collect

Plate 148 (top) This ex-LNWR low go
wagon clearly displays the early style
LMS sheet which measured 21 ft. x 1
4 in. when made up and when new,
black in colour with white lettering.
LMS standard sheets were made at
Midland Railway Works near Trent.
Photograph British

Chapter Four

Extracts from General Appendix

This section contains a series of extracts taken from a copy of the General Appendix to the Working Timetable which was dated March 1937. In addition, three amendments from 1943 and 1944 have been placed in sequence.

It is believed that these official instructions will be of interest to railway enthusiasts in general, but will be particularly valuable to modellers who wish to accurately reproduce authentic railway operation on their layouts.

INSTRUCTIONS RESPECTING THE WORKING OF TRAINS

CONVEYANCE OF FOUR-WHEELED, ETC. VEHICLES BY PASSENGER TRAINS

Four-wheeled vehicles such as horse boxes, carriage trucks, refrigerator vans, meat vans, etc., with a wheelbase of not less than 9 ft. (altered to 10 ft. in 1939) may be worked on express passenger trains (except those trains specially prohibited), but they must be marshalled in the following positions only:-

(1) In the rear of all bogie vehicles provided for the conveyance of passengers, but where this is impracticable, in traffic working, may be marshalled next the engine.

NOTE: When marshalled in front of a train, four and six-wheeled vehicles may be intermixed provided they are all attached in front of bogie vehicles.

(2) On special trains conveying theatrical parties, four-wheeled vehicles with a wheelbase of not less than 9 ft. may be marshalled according to destination. Every effort must be made to maintain the steam heating apparatus through to all loaded passenger-carrying vehicles. Vehicles with a wheelbase of 15 ft. or over, provided they are fitted with oil axle-boxes, automatic brakes or through pipes, screw couplings and long buffers, and with a minimum tare of 6 tons, may be marshalled in any position on the train.

Open fish and open carriage trucks of less than 21 ft. body length, also four-wheeled vehicles with a wheelbase of less than 9 ft., are prohibited from working on express passenger trains.

Bogie freight vehicles, and empty one-plank freight wagons fitted with vacuum automatic pipe, are prohibited from being attached to passenger trains.

The restrictions in the first paragraph do not refer to glass-lined milk tanks.

Certain express passenger trains are prohibited from conveying 4-wheeled vehicles. Details of the trains concerned will be shown in the Passenger Train Marshalling circulars as issued by the Division Superintendents of Operation from time to time.

MIXED TRAINS

(1) 'Mixed' trains for the conveyance of freight and passengers, in which the freight wagons are not required to have continuous brakes, may be run, subject to the following conditions, namely:-

(a) That the engine, tender and passenger vehicles of such 'mixed' trains shall be provided with continuous brakes worked from the engine.

(b) That the freight wagons shall be conveyed behind the passenger vehicles with brake van, or brake vans, in the proportion of one brake van with a tare of 10 tons for every 10 wagons, or one brake van with a tare of 13 or more tons for every 15 wagons, or one brake van with a tare of 16 or more tons for every 20 wagons, or fractional parts of 10, 15, or 20 wagons respectively.

(c) That the total number of vehicles of all descriptions of any such 'mixed' train shall not exceed 30, except in the case of a circus train when the number shall not exceed 35.

(d) That all such trains shall stop at stations, so as to avoid a longer run than 10 miles without stopping, but nothing in these regulations shall require a stop to be made between two stations should the distance between them exceed 10 miles. The distance

over which a circus train may run without a stop may be increased to a maximum of 50 miles.

(2) Upon lines where the maximum speed of trains is limited to 25 miles per hour, all trains may be 'mixed'.

Upon lines where no trains are booked to travel between stations at an average speed of more than 35 miles per hour, half of the total number of passenger trains may be 'mixed'. Authority to work a larger proportion of 'mixed' trains must be obtained from the Minister of Transport.

Upon lines where trains are booked to travel between stations at an average speed exceeding 35 miles per hour, the like authority must be obained before any 'mixed' trains are run.

Circus trains may be run without such authority during the period from March 31st to November 30th in any year whether the maximum average speed of trains run on the section of line concerned is limited or not.

In no case must the speed of a circus train exceed 30 miles per hour.

(3) Trains for the conveyance of horses, cattle or other stock, when vehicles are added for the conveyance of passengers, shall be subject to the same regulations and conditions as apply to 'mixed' trains, but drovers, grooms or other persons travelling in charge of such stock shall not be deemed to be passengers.

A passenger vehicle provided for the special accommodation of persons travelling in charge of stock must, however, be marshalled next the engine, and be provided with the continuous brake worked from the engine.

(4) When, in addition to one goods brake van at the rear of a 'mixed' train, a passenger brake vehicle is included as part of the continuously braked stock, it will not be necessary for a guard to ride in the passenger brake vehicle. If the composition of the train necessitates a second (or third) goods brake van, a second (or third) guard will be necessary, unless communication between the vans is such as to enable one guard to operate efficiently the hand brakes on the vans.

All trains booked to be run as 'mixed' will be so shown in the Working Timetable, and the foregoing regulations will apply to such trains.

The expression circus train means a 'mixed' train in which live-stock, traction engines, trailers, caravans, tenting and other equipment and circus employees belonging to a touring circus are exclusively being conveyed.

NOTE: The above regulations do not apply to troop trains.

Amendment
CONVEYANCE OF FOUR-WHEELED, ETC., VEHICLES BY PASSENGER TRAINS

Four-wheeled vehicles such as horse-boxes, carriage trucks, refrigerator vans, meat vans, etc., provided they are fitted with automatic brakes or continuous pipes may be worked in passenger trains under the following conditions:-

Express Passenger Trains
(except those trains specially prohibited from conveying four-wheeled vehicles)

Open fish and open carriage trucks of less than 21 ft. body length are prohibited from working in express passenger trains.

Four-wheeled vehicles with a wheelbase of less than 10 ft. are prohibited from working on express passenger trains, and all vehicles of 10 ft. wheelbase and over which may be conveyed by express passenger trains are stencilled in white lettering XP with the wheelbase dimension immediately beneath these letters.

Four-wheeled vehicles with a wheelbase of 10 ft. and under 12 ft. must be marshalled at the back of express passenger trains in the rear of any bogie vehicles, but where this is impracticable in traffic working such vehicles may, when so authorised by the Divisional Superintendent of Operation in England or the Operating Manager in Scotland, be marshalled next to the engine.

Four-wheeled vehicles with a wheelbase of 12 ft. and under 15 ft. must be marshalled at the back of express passenger trains in the rear of any bogie vehicles, but where this is impracticable in traffic working, they may be placed next to the engine.

NOTE: When marshalled in the front of a train four and six-wheeled vehicles may be intermixed provided they are all attached in front of bogie vehicles.

Passenger Trains, other than Express Trains

Four-wheeled vehicles with a wheelbase of less than 15 ft. may work in passenger trains other than express trains, but must not be conveyed between bogie stock, except in the following circumstances, when they may, if absolutely necessary, be marshalled in the positions indicated in paragraphs (a), (b) and (c) below, BUT THE SPEED OF THE TRAIN MUST NOT EXCEED 60 MILES PER HOUR AT ANY POINT.

Guards, when giving drivers particulars of the tonnage of their trains, must advise them in every case when they are conveying four-wheeled vehicles marshalled as shown hereafter, in order that a speed of 60 miles per hour may not be exceeded at any point:-

(a) Between bogie non-passenger carrying vehicles, when such are marshalled behind the last vehicle conveying passengers on the train.
(b) Between empty bogie passenger-carrying vehicles and the rear brake van.
(c) Vehicles conveying theatrical, naval military or air force traffic may be marshalled according to destination.

FREIGHT, ETC., TRAINS

EQUIPMENT OF GOODS GUARDS AND GOODS GUARDS' BRAKE VANS

Equipment of goods guards' brake vans: Referring to Rule 129 (iii); all goods brake vans must be equipped with:-

1 standard padlock (for locker)	1 shovel
3 sprags	1 brakestick
1 tail lamp and 2 side lamps	1 shunting pole
1 hand brush	

When giving up charge of a brake, the guard must examine the equipment in the locker, and, if not complete, in good condition, and locked up, he must give particulars on the form provided, i.e. Brake Van Equipment Deficiency Report, and hand it to the person in charge of the sidings where the brake is left.

When taking charge of a brake, a guard must examine the equipment in the locker. If he does not find it complete and in good condition, also properly padlocked, he must give particulars on the Brake Van Equipment Deficiency Report, and leave it with the person in charge of the sidings from which the train is working.

When a guard is relieved he must, in the event of the equipment not being complete and in good condition, hand a form duly signed to the guard taking charge, who will countersign it.

It will be noted it is the duty of a guard to examine the equipment both on taking charge and on giving up charge, but that if it is complete and in good condition, it is not necessary to make out a certificate.

Goods guards' personal equipment— The personal equipment of a goods guard (to be carried by him to and from his brake van) includes:-

Equipment bag	12 detonators in case
Working Timetable (or Sections)	Watch
Appendix, etc.	Whistle
Fortnightly Notices	Hand signal lamp
Wrong line order forms	Key to padlock of locker
Drivers' slips	Can of oil (where necessary), and such other articles as ordered from time to time
Brake van deficiency reports	
Rule Book	
2 flags (red and green) and sticks	

Goods guards are held responsible for seeing that their equipment is maintained complete and in good condition.

In the event of a guard handing a Deficineicy Report to the person in charge of the sidings, when taking charge or giving up charge of a brake, the Yard Master, or other person responsible for the supervision of the sidings, must take such steps as are necessary for making good the deficiencies in accordance with the customary procedure, and must also follow the matter up immediately with a view to ascertaining where the loss occurred, afterwards reporting the circumstances through the usual channels.

It is very essential that when brakes are out of use, the Yard or Station Master, or other person responsible for the supervision of the line or sidings where brakes are standing, should satisfy himself that all possible steps are taken to safeguard the equipment in the brake vans, and in this respect it must be emphasized that the responsibility is the same as in the case of any other of the Company's property.

In the event of any obvious systematic losses or suspected pilferages, suitable steps must be taken without delay, and the circumstances reported to headquarters.

Cleaning of Brake Vans

Goods guards must see that the screws of the brakes in their brake vans are cleaned and oiled. They will also be held responsible for keeping the brake vans clean except at places where special staff is kept for this purpose.

Marshalling of Trains composed of Cattle Boxes, Cattle Trucks Etc., with Livestock and Men

Trains by which men in charge of livestock are carried and which are formed of vehicles, some of which are fitted with the vacuum brake and some of which are not so fitted, must, when practicable, be so marshalled that the vehicles which are fitted with the vacuum brake will be next to the engine and connected to it, and those which are not fitted with the vacuum brake must be marshalled in rear.

FREIGHT TRAINS INDICATED BY THE DISTINCTIVE SIGN IN THE WORKING TIMETABLES

The freight trains, except those worked by standard class 7 (0-8-0) engines, against which is shown the distinctive sign✱ must have four fully fitted vehicles connected up to the engine. Should there by less than this number, the driver must be advised, and he must reduce the speed of the train as may be necessary to enable him to properly control it with the brake power at his disposal.

When these trains are checked by distant signals or are pulled up for any reason by the application of the vacuum brake, the tender brake must be put hard on and not taken off until it is certain that the vacuum brake has been released throughout. Enginemen must be particularly careful not to put steam on to take the train forward until the vacuum has been fully created again on the vehicles connected with the engine, and all brakes released.

Yard inspectors, foremen and shunters must see that the couplings on such vehicles connected to the engine are closely screwed up in all cases to prevent them becoming uncoupled from any cause.

'INSTANTER' COUPLINGS ON FITTED OR PIPED FREIGHT VANS AND CATTLE WAGONS

A number of LMS fitted or piped freight vans and cattle wagons are fitted with the 'Instanter' coupling instead of the screw shackle.

Below is a diagram of the coupling when extended for shunting purposes or when used in slow freight trains and the position in which it is to be placed when marshalled on fitted or piped freight trains, and when cattle wagons are attached to any train.

Shunters and others concerned to see that the coupling is placed in its short position in such circumstances.

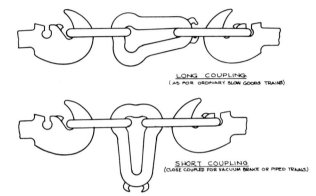

LONG COUPLING.
(AS FOR ORDINARY SLOW GOODS TRAINS)

SHORT COUPLING
(CLOSE COUPLED FOR VACUUM BRAKE OR PIPED TRAINS.)

Should it be necessary at any time for vehicles fitted with 'Instanter' couplings to be conveyed by loaded passenger train, the 'Instanter' coupling must not be used, but only the screw couplings of the other vehicle or vehicles.

VEHICLES FITTED WITH SPECIAL GW CO.'S SHORT LINK COUPLINGS

Vehicles fitted with the special Great Western short link couplings may be conveyed on fitted trains.

MARSHALLING OF HIGH-SIDED VEHICLES ON FREIGHT TRAINS

High-sided vehicles must not be marshalled next to the guard's brake van if it is practicable to avoid this.

FORTY-TON ARMOUR-PLATE WAGONS

Two comparatively light wagons must be marshalled between loaded forty-ton armour-plate wagons, unless contrary instructions are given.

WAGONS WITH LONG LOADS, LNE RAILWAY TO GW RAILWAY

Loads of poles, bars of iron and other traffic resting upon more than one wagon, intended for the GW Railway, must be short coupled with the special short three-length coupling or screw connection, and vehicles must not be accpeted from the LNE Co. unless so coupled.

ENGINE HEAD LAMPS

All LMS engines, whether working over the LMS or other Companies' lines, and the engines of other Companies working of the LMS lines, must, unless instructions are issued to the contrary, carry white head lights arranged as under, and trains must be signalled by the bell signals shown on **page 162.**

Page 45—Add— **TAIL LAMPS ON LIGHT ENGINES**

Tail lamps on light engines must be carried on the centre lower bracket.

(Amended January 1943)

Add—ENGINES AND BRAKE VANS COUPLED TOGETHER

When necessary to facilitate workings an engine may be coupled to the rear of an engine and one or two brake vans or an engine and brake vans may be coupled to an engine and brake van, on any section of the line.

(Amended July 1944)

SIGNALLING OF TRAINS CONVEYING SPECIAL HORSE OR PIGEON TRAFFIC

Where instructions are given in the Special Train Notices for trains conveying special horse or pigeon traffic and composed of coaching stock to be signalled by the bell signal of 5 beats (given 3 pause 1 pause 1), such trains must carry No. 3 headlights and take precedence of all other trains except express passenger trains, breakdown van trains going to clear the line, light engine going to assist disabled trains, or fire brigade trains.

TAIL LAMPS AND SIDE LIGHTS ON TRAINS

Referring to Rule 120; the following instructions apply to trains working over the LMS Railway:

Mixed trains with a freight train guard's brake van in rear must carry side lamps as laid down for freight trains.

Except where instructions are issued to the contrary, all freight trains or engines with freight train guard's brake van or vans must carry side lights on the rear brake van as follows on **page 162.**

Tail lamps on passenger trains: The guard, or rear guard where there is more than one, must see that the tail lamp is properly fixed before signalling the train away. This will not, however, relieve from responsibility any of the platform staff who should affix tail lamps.

Station Masters and inspectors must pay special attention when vehicles are attached or detached, and see that the tail lamp is in its proper position.

A clean trimmed tail lamp must be carried inside the rear van of all trains provided with gas tail lamps, and in each portion where there is more than one van provided with gas tail lamps.

LNE Railway (GE Section) coaching stock brake vans with fitted tail lamps: When one of these brake vans is the rear vehicle on a train, the fixed tail lamp must not be used and an ordinary oil tail lamp must be carried both by day and by night.

Extinguishing lights in side and tail lamps: At the completion of the train journey and, after the train is shunted into a siding clear of the running lines, the guard, before leaving the train, must, unless instructions are issued to the contrary, extinguish the lights in the side and tail lamps.

Freight, etc., trains, assisted in rear—Tail and side lamps: Referring to Rule 133; when a freight train is assisted in rear by an engine or by an engine propelling one or two brake vans, the guard of the freight train must remove his tail lamp. When the train is assisted by an engine drawing one or two brake vans, the guard of the freight train must, in addition to removing the tail lamp, remove his side lamps, and side lamps must be carried on the rearmost brake van attached to the assisting engine.

Description of train	Bell Signal	Head light
1) Express passenger train, or break-down van train going to clear the line, or light engine going to assist disabled train, or fire brigade train	4	
2) Ordinary passenger train, or break-down van train not going to clear the line	3—1	
Branch passenger train (where authorised)	1—3	
Rail motor or motor train with engine leading (When running with driving compartment leading rail motors or motor trains will carry the headlamp on the same bracket as used for the tail lamp)	3—1—2	

NOTE: For arrangements in regard to electric trains see the various electric line instruction books

Description of train	Bell Signal	Head light
3) Parcels, newspaper, fish, meat, fruit, milk, horse, or perishable train, composed of coaching stock	1—1—3	
4) Empty coach stock train	2—2—1	
Fitted freight, fish or cattle train with the continuous brake in use on NOT LESS than on-third the vehicles	5	
5) Express freight or cattle train with the continuous brake on less than one-third the vehicles, but in use on four vehicles connected to the engine indicated by ✠ in the Working Timetables	2—2—3	
Express freight or cattle train not fitted with the continuous brake, or with the continuous brake in use on LESS than four vehicles	3—2	
6) Through freight train, or ballast train conveying workmen and running not less than 15 miles without stopping	1—4	
7) Light engine, or light engines coupled together	2—3	
Engine with one or two brakes	1—3—1	
8) Through mineral or empty wagon train	4—1	
9) Freight train stopping at intermediate stations, or ballast train running short distance	3	
Branch freight train (where authorised)	1—2	
Ballast train, freight train, or officers' special requiring to stop in section or at intermediate siding in section	1—2—2	
10) Shunting engines working exclusively in station yards and sidings	Must, while in those sidings, carry one red head light and one red tail light	

The lamps must be carried in position day and night

NOTE: Local exceptional arrangements are shown in the respective Sectional Appendices

When a train running on the LMS Railway is worked by two engines attached in front of the train, the second engine must not carry head lamps

TAIL LAMPS AND SIDE LIGHTS ON TRAINS

(a) On main lines where there are only two lines and on single lines — One red tail light and two red side lights

(b) On main lines where there are three or four running lines:-
 (i) On the fast line — One red tail light and two red side lights
 (ii) On the slow, goods, or loop lines — One red side light on the side of the van furthest away from the fast line, one white side light on the side of the van nearest the fast line, and one red tail light (see Note)

(c) On goods or loop lines adjoining four main lines — One red tail light only. Side lamps must be removed when the train has passed into the loop

NOTE: Certain brake vans are provided with side lamps which cannot be turned, or which, when turned to show a white light to the rear, show a red light to the front. In these cases the instructions in paragraph (b) (ii) will not apply, and the side lamp instead of being turned must be removed. A signalman will not be required to send the 'Tail or side light out, or improper side light exhibited' signal when a train passes his box with side light removed as directed

Where side lights are shown to be carried the side lamps must, except in the case of local trips, be carried on the rear brake van during daylight as well as during darkness.

The instruction in clause (a) of Rule 120 respecting the carrying, cleaning, trimming, and lighting of tail lamps also apply to light engines.

When the assisting engine or assisting engine with one or two brake vans leaves the train at a signal box, the tail lamp or tail lamp and side lamps, as the case may be, must, where practicable, be replaced within view of the signalman to remind him of the assisting engine or engine with one or two brake vans, and to prevent the train being signalled as having passed without the prescribed tail and side lamps.

Should, however, the assisting engine or engine with one or two brake vans, from any cause, leave the train between two signal boxes and the train proceed without it, the guard must replace the side lamps, if these have been removed, but must take care not to replace the tail lamp until the train has passed out of sight of the signalman at the next box, and he must use every endeavour to intimate to the signalman at such box that the assisting engine or engine with one or two brake vans, as the case may be, has been left in the section.

A white light must be placed on the leading end of the brake van when attached in front of the assisting engine, or leading brake van in case of two brake vans being attached, immediately the assisting engine with one or two brake vans has left the train, whether at a signal box or between two signal boxes.

VEHICLES FITTED WITH GREASE AXLE BOXES

Vehicles fitted with grease axle boxes must not be conveyed by the following trains:-

    Express passenger trains
    Parcels, newspaper, fish, meat, fruit, milk, horse or perishable
    trains composed of coaching stock
    Fitted freight, fish or cattle trains with the continuous brake
    in use on NOT LESS than one-third of the vehicles

Freight wagons and vans of over 10 tons capacity, unless fitted with oil axle boxes, must not be attached to express freight trains.

Private owners' wagons, whether running on account of the owners or hired by Railway Companies, must not be worked on express freight trains unless fitted with oil axle boxes.

CONVEYANCE OF CERTAIN TYPES OF SPECIALLY CONSTRUCTED VEHICLES ON EXPRESS FREIGHT TRAINS

In order that there may be no misunderstanding with regard to the carrying out of Rule 158, the following instruction respecting conveyance of specially constructed vehicles must be observed:-

Specially constructed vehicles, if fitted with oil axle boxes, given in the following list, may be worked on express freight trains unless the load on the vehicle is such as to come within the interpretation of Rule 158:-

Type of vehicles	Conditions under which may be conveyed on express freight trains
Deal wagons, 20-ton plate and tube wagons	Loaded or empty
Economiser wagons	Load not to exceed 7 tons
40 and 50-ton armour plate wagons	Empty
Bogie bolster trucks	Empty
Flat trucks	Loaded or Empty
Traction wagons	Loaded or Empty
Glass wagons up to 15 tons capacity	Loaded or Empty
Starred tanks	Loaded or Empty
Gunpowder vans	Loaded or empty
20-ton bulk grain wagons	Loaded or empty

Specially constructed vehicles not included in the above list, whether fitted with oil or grease axle boxes, must not be conveyed on express freight trains.

Goods wagons and vans of over 10 tons capacity, unless fitted with oil axle boxes, must not be worked on express freight trains.

Private owner's wagons, whether running on account of the owners or hired by railway companies, must not be worked on express freight trains unless fitted with oil axle boxes.

Conveyance of wagons on fitted freight (No. 2) trains

Deal wagons and tube wagons (both loaded and empty) may be worked on these trains, but privately owned wagons must not be conveyed.

Gunpowder vans fitted with oil axle boxes may be conveyed on these trains provided the vehicles are attached next to the fitted portion of the train and a screw, or instanter, coupling is used.

INSTRUCTIONS RESPECTING THE SHUNTING AND MOVEMENT OF VEHICLES

1) Care to be exercised — Shunters, guards and others concerned must exercise great care in the shunting of vehicles in order to avoid the breaking or chafing of goods. Inspectors and others concerned must keep a sharp look-out for any cases of rough shunting, and report them promptly.

2) Wagons containing acids, oils, and other traffic of a corrosive or inflammable nature — Inspectors, foremen, guards, shunters and others concerned must exercise great care in dealing with these wagons, which may or may not bear special labels indicating the nature of their contents. Carboys containing acids are particularly liable to breakage by rough shunting, and leakage arising in such circumstances not only involves considerable loss by the value of acids, but entails risk of injury to the staff and damage to the rolling stock. The shunting of such wagons should always be performed with discretion, and on the trains the vehicles should, as far as possible, be marshalled in such a position as to reduce the risk of accident to a minimum.

3) Loose shunting of vehicles — Wherever it can be avoided, vehicles must not be loose shunted into loading docks, stages, warehouse platforms etc., unless the brakes are so arranged that they can be applied without risk to the men operating them. Where it is necessary for a vehicle with a brake lever on the wall side of a loading dock, warehouse stage, etc., to be run by gravitation, into such a loading dock, etc., it must be previously brought to a stand clear of the wall and pushed into position by hand. Except at those places where special instructions are issued to the contrary, boiler trollies and other specially constructed vehicles to which it has not been found practicable to fit a hand brake must not be moved unless attached to an engine. Loose shunting of brake vans of ballast trains conveying workmen is strictly prohibited.

4) Moving of vehicles over crossings, etc. — When vehicles are to be moved over a level crossing, roadway, or other similar place, the person in charge of the movement must post an assistant at a point where any person or vehicles approaching can be seen, and they must be prevented from crossing until the movement has been finished.

5) Stabling of carriages in sidings on falling gradients — When stabling carriages in sidings situated on falling gradients, guards and shunters must apply the hand brake where provided at both ends of the train, and must satisfy themselves that the brakes are hard on before closing up to the carriages with other vehicles or an engine.

6) Shunting of coaching stock — Great care must be exercised during frosty weather when shunting coaching stock into sidings to stand. The buffers must not be pushed up but most stand so that the brake pipes may be left as nearly as possible in their ordinary or running position. When the buffers are pushed up, the hose pipes are bent, and in frosty weather they often crack and are rendered useless.

7) Shunting of electric stock by locomotives — Drivers and shunters must exercise extreme care when shunting electric stock in order to guard against the coupling link of the coach working off the drawbar hook of the engine.

8) Shunting by horses — The chains must be attached whenever practicable to the side loops of the vehicles and not to the drawbar hooks or couplings, and men must not pass in front of vehicles in motion to unhook them. Men in charge of shunting horses must exercise the greatest care in seeing that they are not called upon to start unreasonably heavy loads. The sides of rails must be kept clear of dirt, etc., so as to ease the draught of the horses.

9) Shunting poles — All persons whose duty it is to couple or uncouple wagons must be in possession of a shunting pole. Shunting poles are not to be used as brake sticks, or for any other purpose than that for which they are intended. Guards and shunters taking shunting poles with them in passenger trains must place them in the guard's van.

10) General instructions — The person giving hand signals to drivers of engines engaged in shunting operations must place himself in such a position that the signals will not be taken by any other driver than the one for whom they are intended. If two or more engines are standing in such a position that the driver of one might mistake a hand signal intended for the driver of another engine, such hand signal must not be given, but the shunter or other person in charge of the operations must convey this instruction to the driver verbally. Drivers must satisfy themselves before making any movement in response to a hand signal that such signal is itended for them. During shunting, the driver must work only to the signals given by the guard, shunter, or other person in charge of the operation. Where fixed signals, other than siding signals, are provided for running purposes, drivers must consider they are under the control of the signal applying to the operation they are performing, whether they are in rear of such signal or not, and, unless they receive verbal instructions from the signalman or person in charge of the operation, they must not move their engines until the siding signal is off. Where signals are provided some distance from the points to which they apply, drivers, after drawing over the points towards the signal, must not move their engines back until the fixed signal has been taken off.

GRAVITATION SHUNTING

Shunters, guards, and all concerned must exercise great care in shunting at gravitation sidings, to prevent injury, damage or loss. In shunting special loads, wagons labelled with 'Brittle Goods', 'Fragile', or 'Shunt with Care' labels, also special vehicles, a man must, when necessary, accompany the vehicles throughout, controlling their movement into the sidings to avoid them coming into sharp contact with the stop blocks or vehicles already in the sidings. The same care must be observed to avoid subsequent shunts from colliding sharply with the special loads.

Referring to Rule 110, clause (b), live stock must not be shunted at gravitation sidings if it is possible to avoid it. In all cases where it is necessary to shunt live stock traffic at gravitation sidings, it must be attached to an engine, otherwise a man must accompany the vehicles, which must be worked at a walking pace, from the summit until brought to a state of rest in the sidings.

Yard Masters, Station Masters and inspectors in charge must frequently satisfy themselves that these orders are being carried out.

FLY SHUNTING

Fly shunting (i.e., making a run with the engine in front of the wagons and uncoupling the latter while in motion to follow into a siding other than that into which the engine is turned) is prohibited except at places where there are no other reasonably practicable means of performing the work. The foreman or person in charge of the shunting operations must decide when fly shunting shall be performed.

SHUNTING AND BANKING ENGINES PERFORMING LOCOMOTIVE DUTIES

Drivers of shunting and bank engines which require coal or to perform other loco. services must give as much notice as possible to the person in charge. When shunting and banking engines have to stand for other engines to work, etc., they must be sent to the coaling point or water tank for locomotive purposes, if necessary. When requested by the person in charge to resume work, the drivers must do so at once unless the engine fire is being cleaned, or some other duty which cannot be interrupted is in hand.

CONVEYANCE OF LIVE STOCK

General treatment of live stock — In dealing with live stock (horses, cattle, sheep, pigs, and goats, poultry, etc.) care and patience must be shown, not only in loading and unloading, but also during transit, and in and about the yards, pens, sheds and stations, in order to avoid fright or injury and consequent suffering on the part of the animals. If, during transit, cows appear to be suffering pain or discomfort, they must be milked without delay.

All staff concerned with the movement of live stock are hereby impressed with the importance that such traffic should receive the quickest possible transit. The instructions as to telegraphic or other advice, which has to be given in advance to all concerned, including the District Controllers, of the forwarding of live stock must be carefully observed in order that the best arrangements can be made for working the traffic forward. When any mishap occurs to either cattle or other live stock in transit or whilst on a train, guards must in all cases give the number of the wagon, with sending station and destination, when making out their reports.

Marshalling of trucks containing live stock — Care must be taken to see that trucks containing live stock are placed on the trains in such a position as to admit of the minimum amount of shunting, and when two or more such wagons are on the same train the coupling should be tightly screwed up.

Examination of live stock while in transit — Foremen, shunters, guards and others concerned must examine wagons containing live stock as frequently as possible, in order to ascertain whether any of the animals have fallen down, or require to be watered, fed or milked. If any of the animals are down, unless the staff are satisfied the animal is only resting and not in danger of being trampled upon by other animals, arrangements must be made to get them on their feet, although this may necessitate the wagons being taken off the train and put in the cattle dock. When an animal is obviously seriously injured, arrangements must be made in conjunction with the Goods Department to call in the services of a veterinary surgeon, and the injured animal must not be sent on without his authority. If it is clear that the animals are due to be watered, fed, or milked, the wagons should be detached and put in the cattle dock and the Goods Department advised, or other suitable arrangements made for the necessary attention to be given to the animals. No longer period of time than 24 consecutive hours should elapse during any portion of the transit without watering, except in the case of sheep which may be left 36 consecutive hours without watering, and also in the case of cattle or swine where, by extending the period to 27 hours, the animals could be worked through to destination station during that period. In cases of the latter description, the animals must be watered at destination station immediately after arrival thereat. Particulars as to when and where watering or feeding takes place on the journey must be shown on the live stock label (specimen given below). Any expense incurred in connection with feeding and watering must be charged forward to destination to be collected from consignee.

London Midland and Scottish Railway Company.

LIVE STOCK.

Loaded.   Time   Date   19
From
To
Via
Consignee
*Watered and
(or) Fed at }   Time   Date
Ditto   Time   Date
Require to be Milked
not later than   Time {   Date

WAGON No.		PAID.		TO PAY.	
	CARRIAGE CHARGES.	£ s. d.		£ s. d.	

NOTE.—*The word "watered" or "fed" to be deleted as may be necessary.

LABELS TO BE RETAINED BY RECEIVING STATION.

GOODS CONVEYED IN TARIFF VANS

Packages of goods conveyed in tariff vans must be properly labelled, and invoices made out and handed to the guard. Guards must not accept traffic for the road vans unless the goods are labelled and the invoices accompany them. The Goods Department staff must load the vans in station order, and traffic to be unloaded first placed next the doors. Guards working trains conveying tariff vans must report full particulars on their journals of cases where this is not done.

SECTION IX OF THE RULE BOOK

(A) GENERAL REGULATIONS FOR WORKING THE VACUUM BRAKE

1 — Description (a) The operation of the vacuum brake depends upon the creation and maintenance of a vacuum of not less than 19 inches and not more than 21 inches on the engine, and not less than 17 inches in the brake van in the rear of the train where the vacuum gauge is fitted.

b) The vacuum brake is continuous throughout the fitted and piped portions of the train, the amount of vacuum available in the train pipe for operating the brake being shown on the gauges on the engine and in the brake vans on passenger trains, and in some cases in the brake vans used on complete vacuum fitted freight trains. On all engines a vacuum gauge is provided to register the amount of vacuum in the train pipe, but on some engines and in certain vans the gauge has two pointers, one indicating the amount of vacuum in the train pipe and the other the amount in the reservoir.

A 'fitted' vehicle must be understood to mean a vehicle which carries its own brake apparatus connected by a branch pipe or pipes to the train pipe, and on which the brake blocks are operated by the vacuum brake.

A 'piped' vehicle must be understood to mean a vehicle which is equipped with a continuous pipe only, i.e., without brake blocks operated by the vacuum brake.

c) The vacuum train pipes at the ends of 'fitted' vehicles are painted black; the vacuum train pipes at the ends of 'piped' vehicles are painted red.

2 — Operation of Brake — a) The brake is applied by admitting air into the train pipe and is taken off by closing the air valves and restoring the vacuum to the required amount.

b) The brake is ordinarily applied by the driver, but it can also be applied by the guard. A partial application of the brake can also be made, in case of emergency, by pulling the passenger communication chain.

When a freight train is being worked with only a portion of the vehicles fitted with the vacuum brake, the driver, after being advised by the guard of the number connected to the engine, must, as soon as possible after starting, test the vacuum brake power by applying it sufficiently to satisfy himself that it has been properly connected and is in working order.

c) Care must be taken that the proportion of vehicles fitted with pipes only and not with brake apparatus does not exceed one in four in any passenger train running a distance of ten miles or under without a stop, nor one in six in any passenger train running more than ten miles without a stop.

For the purpose of this instruction, the number of vehicles forming a passenger train must be counted as follows:-

Horse box, carriage truck, fish van, or
   other 4-wheeled vehicles not carrying
   passengers . . . . As ½ vehicle
Coaching vehicles, 4 or 6-wheeled. . . . . .As 1 vehicle
Coaching vehicles, 8 or 12-wheeled . . . . As 2 vehicles
Articulated coaching vehicles, each bogie . . . . .As 1 vehicle
Tank engine, 4 or 6-wheeled coupled. . . . . As 2 vehicles
Tender engine, 4-coupled . . . . As 3 vehicles
Tender engine, 6 or 8-coupled. . . . . As 4 vehicles

d) Should the brake not be in operation on any vehicle conveying passengers formed behind the rear brake van, such passengers (unless in charge of livestock) must be transferred to the vehicles in front of it unless another fitted vehicle on which the brake can be applied by the driver is attached in rear.

Chapter Five   Loading Gauges

The LMSR issued a booklet which detailed the loading gauges for each section of the Company. Later documents tended to show all the sections on one drawing and these are perhaps confusing to read and not helpful if one wishes to model a particular loading gauge. This chapter, therefore, contains reproductions of the thirteen sections as detailed below.

Note: These diagrams are the Load Gauges for the various Sections. Any variation from same are shewn in the 'Special Instructions relating to Goods, Mineral and Live Stock Traffic' (Pink Pamphlet)

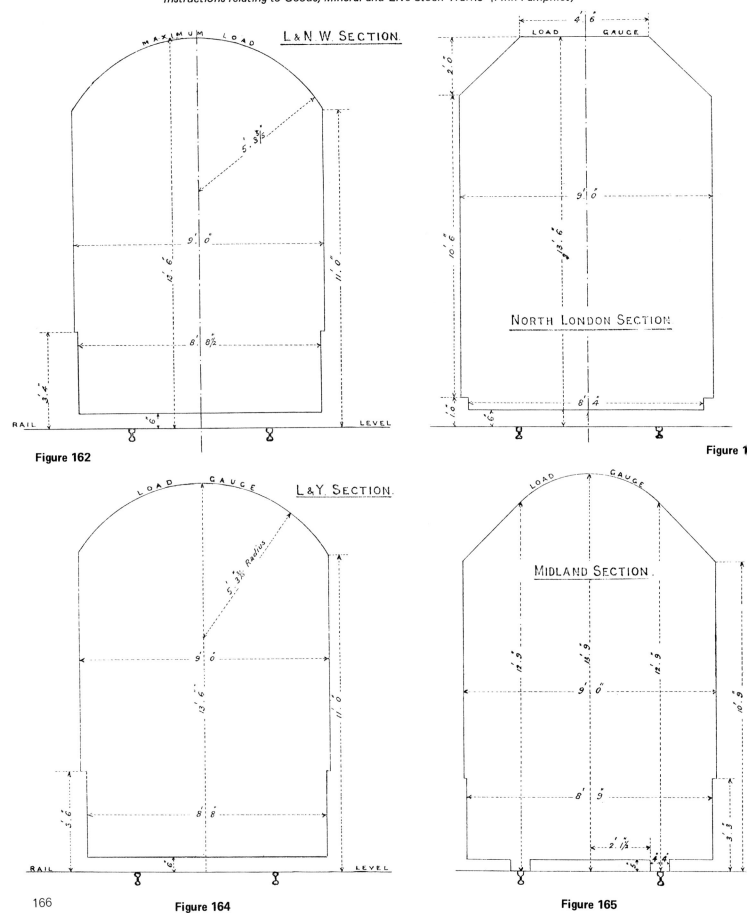

Figure 162

Figure 163

Figure 164

Figure 165

166

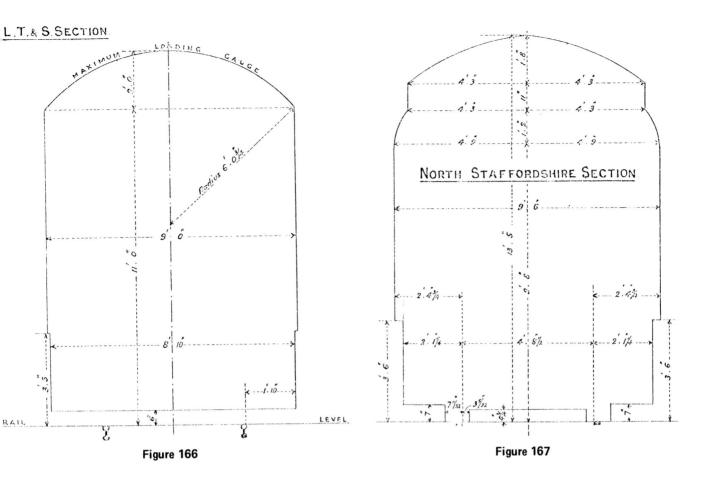

Figure 166

Figure 167

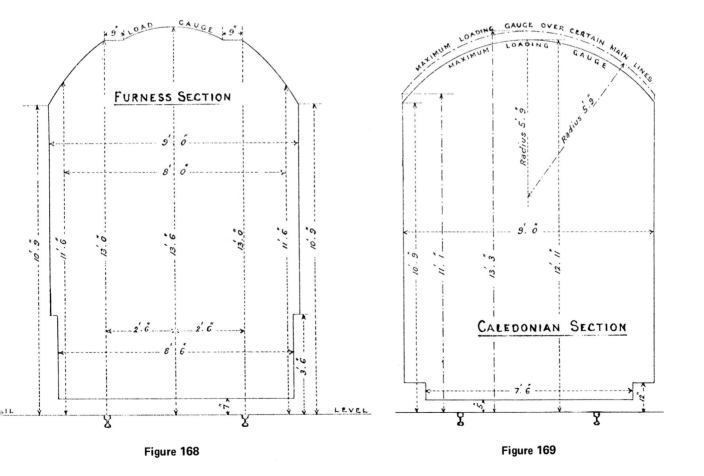

Figure 168

Figure 169

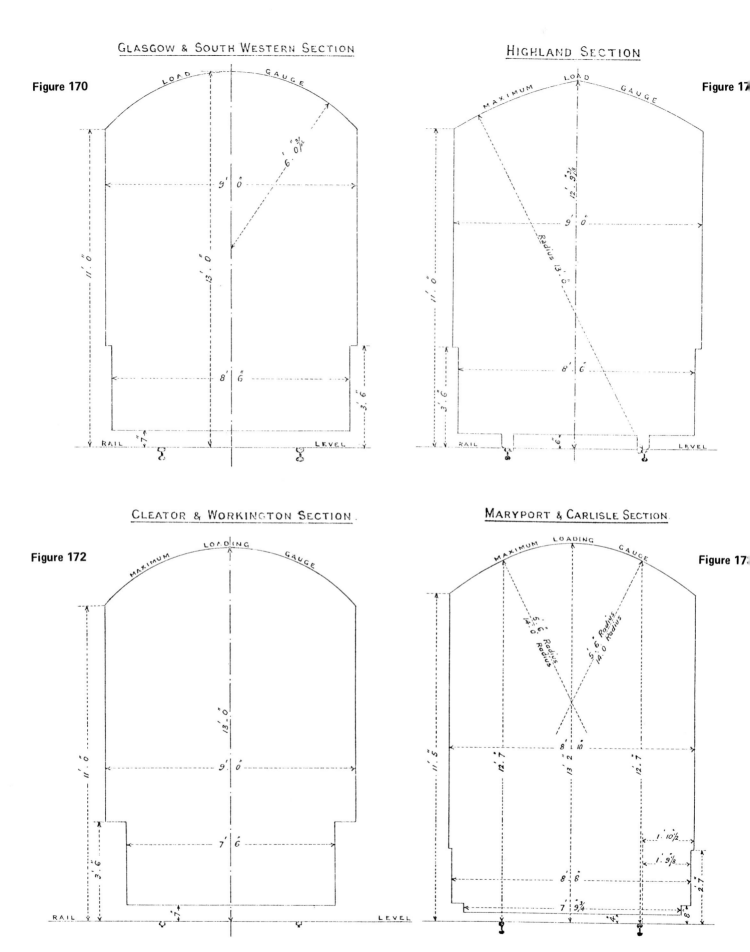

GLASGOW & SOUTH WESTERN SECTION

Figure 170

HIGHLAND SECTION

Figure 171

CLEATOR & WORKINGTON SECTION.

Figure 172

MARYPORT & CARLISLE SECTION.

Figure 173

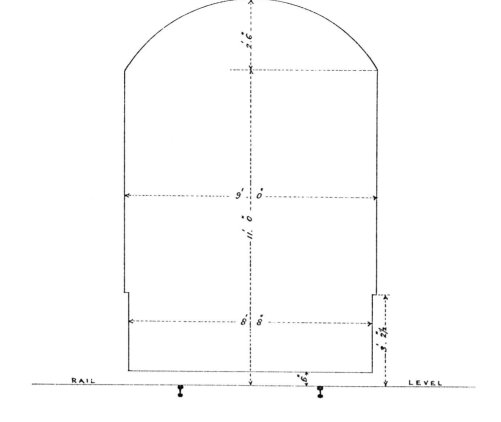

Figure 174

STRATFORD-UPON-AVON & MIDLAND J\. SECTION

Chapter Six

Axlebox Diagrams

In an *Illustrated History of Midland Wagons, Volume One,* page 47, there were illustrated all the Midland Railway axleboxes which were included in the LMS axlebox diagram book. Almost all the remaining axleboxes have been included in this chapter to complete the story.

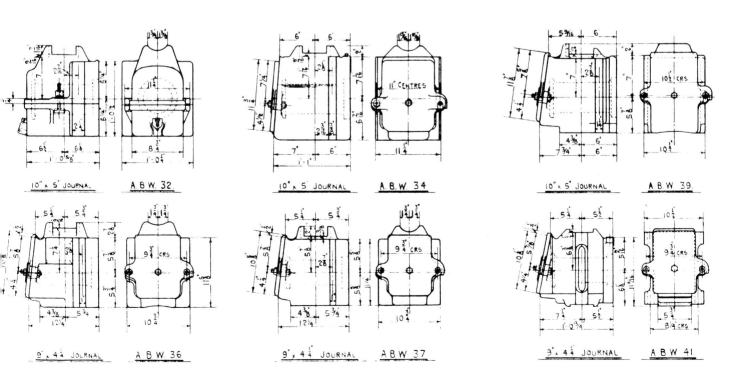

10" x 5" JOURNAL   A.B.W. 32   10" x 5" JOURNAL   A.B.W. 34   10" x 5" JOURNAL   A.B.W 39

9" x 4¼" JOURNAL   A.B.W 36   9" x 4¼" JOURNAL   A.B.W 37   9" x 4¼" JOURNAL   A.B.W 41

169

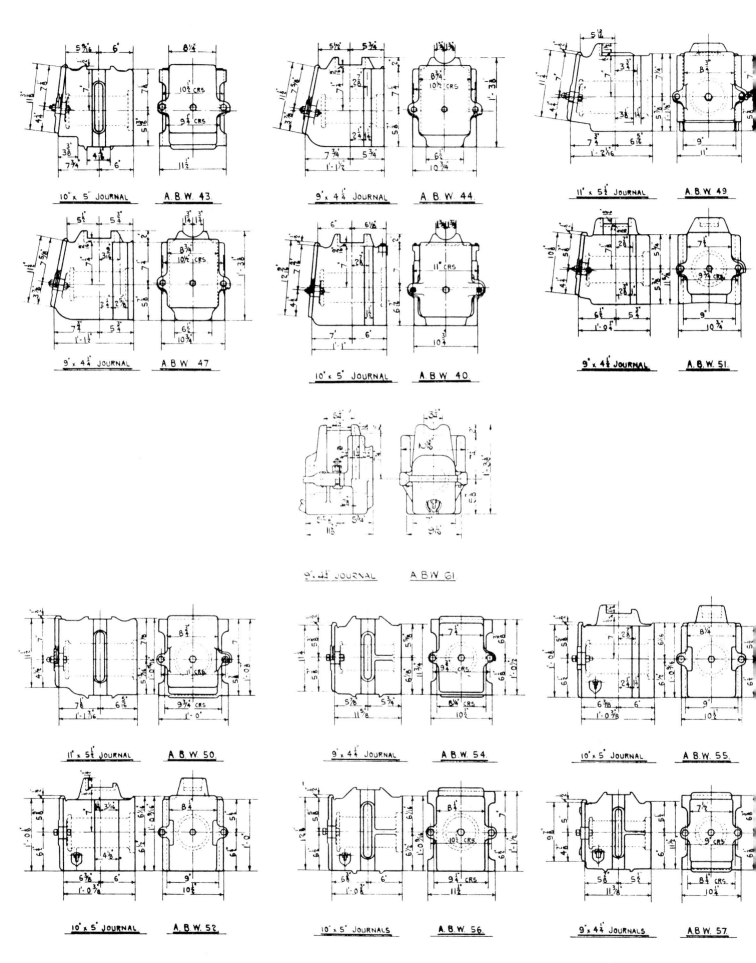

10" × 5" JOURNAL   A.B.W. 43.

9' × 4¼" JOURNAL   A.B.W. 44.

11' × 5½" JOURNAL   A.B.W. 49

9' × 4¼" JOURNAL   A.B.W. 47

10' × 5" JOURNAL   A.B.W. 40.

9' × 4¼" JOURNAL   A.B.W. 51.

9'× 4¼' JOURNAL   A.B.W. 61.

11' × 5½" JOURNAL   A.B.W. 50.

9' × 4¼" JOURNAL   A.B.W. 54.

10' × 5" JOURNAL   A.B.W. 55.

10' × 5" JOURNAL   A.B.W. 52.

10' × 5" JOURNALS   A.B.W. 56.

9'× 4¼" JOURNALS   A.B.W. 57.

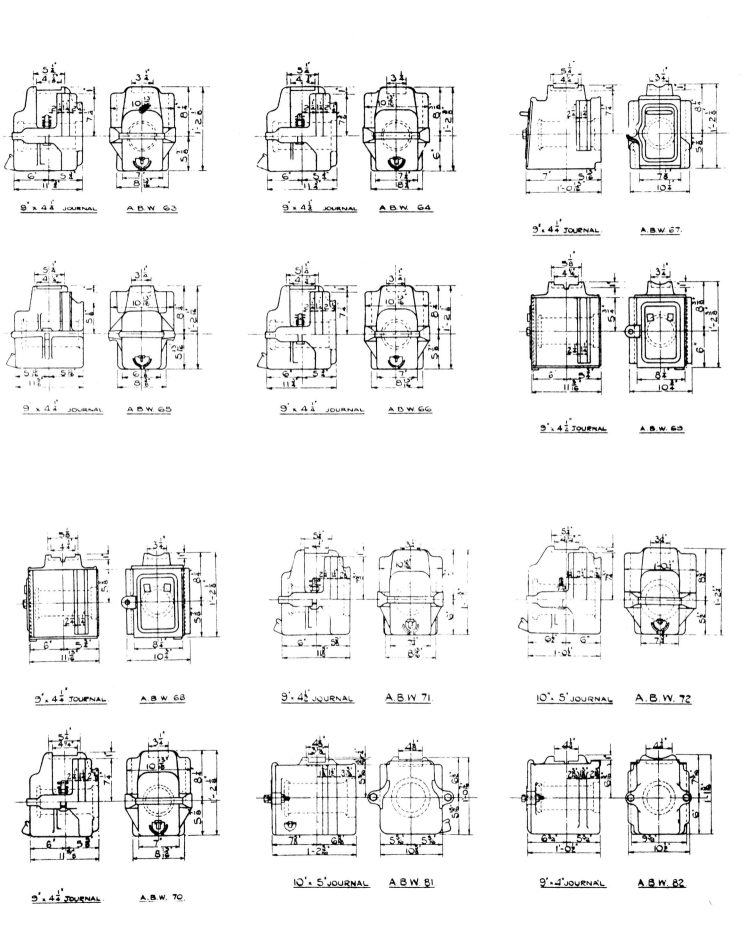

9" x 4¼" JOURNAL   A.B.W. 63

9" x 4¼" JOURNAL   A.B.W. 64

9" x 4¼" JOURNAL.   A.B.W. 67

9" x 4¼" JOURNAL   A.B.W. 65

9" x 4¼" JOURNAL   A.B.W. 66

9" x 4½" JOURNAL   A.B.W. 69

9" x 4¼" JOURNAL.   A.B.W. 68

9" x 4½" JOURNAL   A.B.W. 71

10" x 5" JOURNAL   A.B.W. 72

9" x 4¼" JOURNAL.   A.B.W. 70.

10" x 5" JOURNAL   A.B.W. 81

9" x 4" JOURNAL   A.B.W. 82

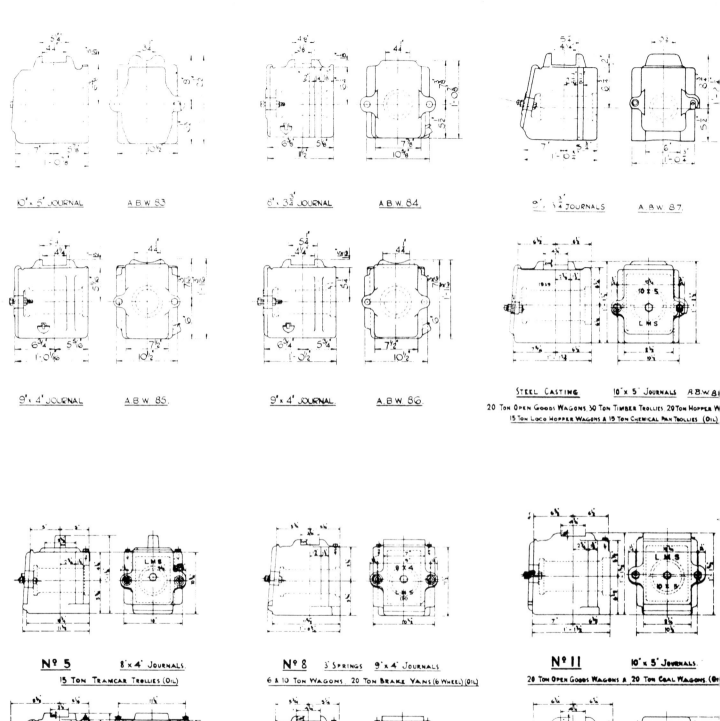

10" x 5" JOURNAL   A.B.W. 83

8" x 3¾" JOURNAL   A.B.W. 84.

9" x 3¾" JOURNALS   A.B.W. 87.

9" x 4" JOURNAL   A.B.W. 85.

9" x 4" JOURNAL   A.B.W. 86.

STEEL CASTING   10" x 5" JOURNALS   A.B.W. 8
20 TON OPEN GOODS WAGONS, 30 TON TIMBER TROLLIES, 20 TON HOPPER W
15 TON LOCO HOPPER WAGONS & 15 TON CHEMICAL PAN TROLLIES (OIL)

No 5   8" x 4" JOURNALS.
15 TON TRAMCAR TROLLIES (OIL)

No 8   3" SPRINGS   9" x 4" JOURNALS
6 & 10 TON WAGONS, 20 TON BRAKE VANS (6 WHEEL) (OIL)

No 11   10" x 5" JOURNALS.
20 TON OPEN GOODS WAGONS & 20 TON COAL WAGONS (O

B 4   8" x 3¾" JOURNALS.
10 TON WAGONS (OIL)

No 8   4" SPRINGS   9" x 4" JOURNALS.
6 & 10 TON WAGONS. 20 TON BRAKE VANS (6 WHEEL) (OIL)

No 15   11" x 6" JOURNALS
20 TON & 40 TON TROLLIES (OIL)

172

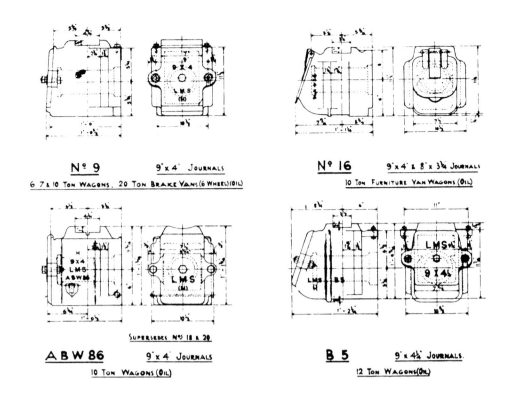

Nº 9 9" x 4" JOURNALS

6 7 & 10 TON WAGONS, 20 TON BRAKE VANS (6 WHEEL) (OIL)

Nº 16 9" x 4" & 8" x 3¼" JOURNALS

10 TON FURNITURE VAN WAGONS (OIL)

SUPERSEDES Nºˢ 18 & 20.

A B W 86 9" x 4" JOURNALS

10 TON WAGONS (OIL)

B 5 9" x 4½" JOURNALS.

12 TON WAGONS (OIL)

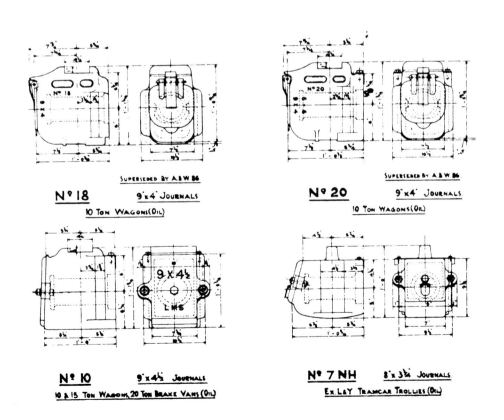

SUPERSEDED BY A B W 86

Nº 18 9" x 4" JOURNALS

10 TON WAGONS (OIL)

SUPERSEDED BY A B W 86.

Nº 20 9" x 4" JOURNALS.

10 TON WAGONS (OIL)

Nº 10 9" x 4½" JOURNALS

10 & 15 TON WAGONS, 20 TON BRAKE VANS (OIL)

Nº 7 NH 8" x 3¼" JOURNALS

Ex L&Y TRAMCAR TROLLIES (OIL)

Chapter Seven Wagon Building ~ Details for the Modeller

By K. R. Morgan

The underframes of ordinary goods wagons, and the running gear of all wagons was very standardized. For this reason, it is possible to give very full details in written form, which cover most of the main features of these items.

The LMS built ordinary goods wagons on both wooden and steel underframes, the vast majority being to the RCH 1923 specification for 12 ton wagons, 17ft. 6in. long over headstocks on a 9ft. (later 10ft.) wheelbase.

The wooden underframe (**Figure 176**) consisted of longitudinal members, the outer pair of which were known as solebars. Lateral members connected the longitudinal members together, of which the end pair, carrying the buffers, were known as headstocks. Diagonal members were also incorporated in the outer end panels to give additional rigidity. The solebars and all lateral timbers were 12in. deep by 5in. thick; secondary longitudinal and diagonals being 12in. deep by 3½in. thick.

The floor planks, laid crosswise, were generally 7in. wide by 2½in. thick, they were shorter than the full width of the wagon, their outer ends being protected by a longitudinal piece of timber known as a curbrail. This timber was notched out where it sat on top of the headstocks, so that its top edge was level with the top of the floor planks, its lower edge being below floor level to enable bolts to be passed through it and through the solebars, short packing pieces at the bolt positions between the two members enabling the whole to be pulled up tight. The floor planks were thus sandwiched between the two curbrails. Some wagons were, however, built without this refinement, allowing the ends of the floor planks to be easily seen **(Vol. 1: Plates 137 & 138)**.

The various timber members were secured to one another by metal brackets, bolts being passed through timber and bracket, with nuts on the inner ends to tighten up the assembly. Most of the metalwork was hidden under the wagon. The bolt heads were, however, prominent on the outer edges of solebars, headstocks and curbrails.

Many thousands of open goods wagons were built on this standard wooden underframe, while other wagons, which employed virtually identical wooden underframes, though of differing lengths were:

Calf Vans and Cattle wagons	19 ft 1 in over headstocks	11 ft wheelbase
Mineral wagons	16ft. 6in. over headstocks	9ft. wheelbase
Single Bolsters	15 ft 6 in over headstocks	8 ft wheelbase

The equivalent standard 12 ton steel underframe was also extensively used by the LMS. This employed a similar layout of frame members, although as will be seen in **Figure 175** extra diagonals were incorporated, the outer end secondary longitudinals being dispensed with. In this case, all the frame members were made from steel channels 9in. deep by 3⅛in. wide by ⁷⁄₁₆in. thick. The members were again secured where they met, by metal brackets, in this case rivets being used instead of nuts and bolts. This, to a large extent, overcame the problem, associated with wooden frames, of bolts and nuts slackening off in service.

In the 1930s, the LMS undertook experiments with welded steel underframes. These were described as lightweight frames, for, by eliminating many of the brackets and rivets, an appreciable saving in weight was achieved, while, at the same time, a considerable gain in strength resulted.

The standard 12 ton steel underframe was used for many of the later open goods wagons, and also on all the covered goods and the associated vans for the more specialized traffics such as bananas, meat, etc. In a shortened (16ft. 6in.) form, it was employed under gunpowder vans and also on the later mineral wagons, whilst in still shorter (15ft. 6in.) form, it was used for single bolsters. An otherwise standard frame, in stretched form, was to be found under cattle wagons (18ft. 6in.) and 12 ton ballast and sleeper wagons having the rather odd length of 20ft. 8in.

The various 20 ton capacity wagons also had steel underframes of generally similar construction. In this case the majority employed a channel section 10in. deep by 3⅜in. wide; exceptions being the brake vans which employed a 12in. deep section. Other wagons which employed this 12in. section were the long low wagons to D2083 and the ballast hoppers to D1804. On steel underframed wagons, a steel angle was used, in many cases, to protect the outer ends of the floor planks. This angle was known as a curb iron but was not universally employed even on wagons of the same general type. **Plate 141 (Vol. 1)** shows a curb iron very clearly, whilst **Plate 153 (Vol. 1)** just as clearly shows a wagon without this feature.

A number of the four-wheeled and bogie special wagons also used steel underframes of very similar type, although, in these cases, they were considerably longer than those outlined above and, in many cases, incorporated angle iron trusses below the frame to provide additional rigidity. Many of the special wagons, however, did not have a separate underframe, consisting instead of an integral steel structure which formed a combined body/underframe to which the running gear was attached. Of the running gear details, the first item requiring attention is the wheels. On the majority of the stock these were, nominally, 3ft. 1½in. diameter over tread. It will be noted, however, that the brake van diagrams show a diameter of 3ft. 2in., which is hardly a significant variation. Some of the earlier batches of covered goods vans had 3ft. 6½in. diameter wheels, this practice being common on the Midland Railway in pre-grouping days, for fitted vans of this type. Some special wagons such as traction trucks had wheels of 2ft. 8½in. diameter, permitting a lower floor level to enable the vehicle to carry loads which would otherwise foul the loading gauge.

The wheels, themselves, were of several different types, namely split spoke and solid spoke having eight spokes and, for heavier duties, solid spoke with ten spokes were employed. In addition, there were three hole pressed steel disc type. Little guidance can be given as to which type was used with any particular type of wagon, since official photographs of the wagons, when new, often show wagons of the same type with differing types of wheel. In later

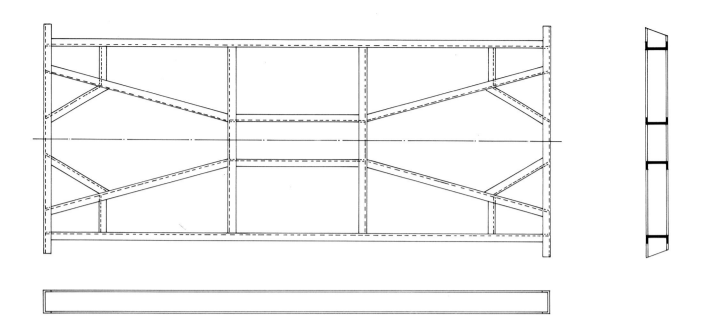

Figure 175

STANDARD STEEL UNDERFRAME

Drawing K. R. Morgan

Headstock Solebar Curbrail Longitudinal Tiebar Diagonal Floor Planks

Curbrail Spacer

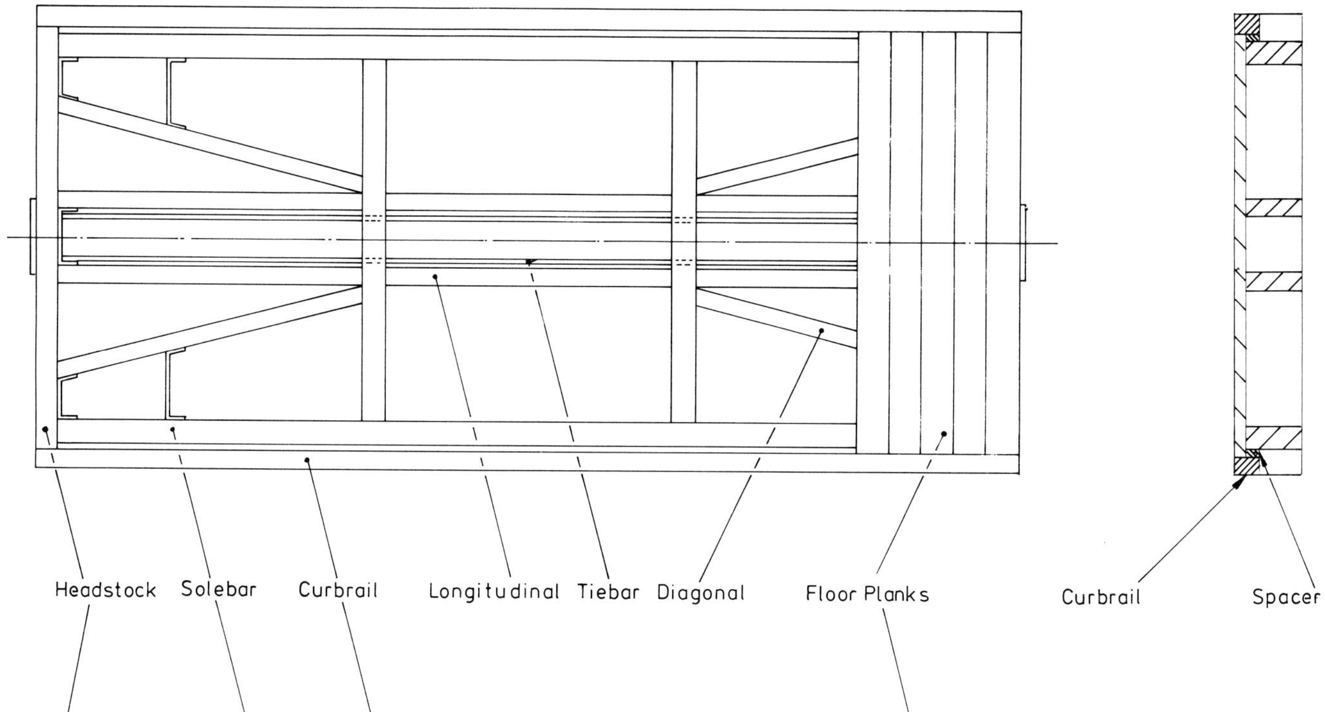

Figure 176

STANDARD WOODEN UNDERFRAME

Drawing K. R. Morgan

days, wagons with one pair of spoked and one pair of disc wheels became commonplace, although it is thought that this practice only started with World War II, when shortages, and a general state of 'make do and mend' became the order of the day.

The wheels were mounted on to axles, the size of which, particularly as regards the journal or bearing which ran in the axlebox, varied to suit the carrying capacity. The difference in size is not apparent in photographs, the most important difference, that of the journals, being hidden within the axlebox. In practice, wheels were reprofiled from time to time until their diameter was reduced to a predetermined size. The earlier wheels, with separate tyres, would then be re-tyred to the 'as new' condition. In latter years, one piece three hole disc wheels were produced, the wheel being scrapped once minimum diameter was reached.

The axles were also re-turned on the journals when wear developed. 'Wasting', through rust, also reduced the exposed portion of the axle. Here, again, minimum diameters were laid down at which point the axle would be scrapped.

The axleboxes of the period had plain bearings in which the axle journals ran and were of the oil-filled type. These, again, had certain standardized dimensions as laid down by the RCH, particularly on the bearing size and on the guides by which the axlebox was located. A limited number of types were, at first, produced to suit various capacity ratings, these being updated from time to time as improvements were made. The main types of axleboxes used by the LMS are shown in **Chapter Six**. On the majority of the ordinary wagons, the axleboxes were mounted in 'W' irons of the normal open pattern. The two middle legs of the 'W' were, in fact, parallel, and the axlebox was free to slide up and down in these. The 'W' irons were only about 1 in. thick, and while this was adequate for the 12 ton wagons, on the heavier vehicles cast steel angle pieces were riveted to the vertical legs to give a wider bearing surface, while many of the 'W' irons were of solid plate to give additional stiffness. On the special wagons, without separate underframes, similar angle pieces or 'horncheeks' were riveted directly to the side frames of the wagon, the 'W' irons thus being dispensed with altogether.

The buffers were, again, very standardized and the length of the buffer, extending beyond the headstocks, was 1 ft. 6 in. on unfitted stock and 1 ft. 8½ in. on piped and fitted wagons. Several types were used, again, dependent mainly on carrying capacity and these are illustrated in **Plates**

162—164.

The drawgear, on the ordinary stock, was of the continuous type (**Figure 177**). The drawhook, which carried the coupling, had a square shank to prevent rotation and passed through a matching hole in a plate attached to the headstock. The inner end of this shank was then attached to a circular shaft which extended nearly to the longitudinal centre line of the wagon. In the centre of the wagon, there was a cradle of box-like shape but without top or bottom. The circular shafts from the drawhooks passed through the ends of this cradle, and one of them was fitted with washers and there was a nut to secure it. The other shaft had a heavy compression spring passed over it, a washer and nut then securing the outer end. When this was assembled, the spring was tensioned by screwing up the nut, so that the drawhooks were held firmly against the headstocks. They were thus, in effect, helping to hold the wagon together. When a load was applied to the drawhooks, the spring was able to compress further, thus giving a cushioning effect to the shocks transmitted throughout a train on starting. It will be seen from this, therefore, that the wagon was, in effect, pushed along by the hook furthest away from the engine, keeping the underframe in compression, instead of trying to tear it apart as was the case with older wagons without this type of drawgear. On the special wagons with lowered floors, continuous drawgear was not possible. Here, however, the wagon itself was of much more solid construction and was, thus, more able to take the strains imposed upon it.

The couplings were of three main types, namely three link, screw or, more rarely, instanter. The three link type was used universally on all unfitted stock. They were termed 'loose' couplings since they did not hold the buffers in contact with one another. A train joined with such couplings, makes it presence felt when stopping, or starting, by a cacophony of crashing and banging along its length. Screw couplings, which can be adjusted to draw adjoining buffers together, were confined to the piped and fitted wagons, while the instanter type, which has three links of which the centre one is shaped to allow close or loose coupling, as required, was much more rarely found on LMS stock.

The springs which controlled the rise and fall of the axleboxes, were of the leaf type. The number of leaves varied dependent on the carrying capacity. On unfitted stock, the ends of the spring merely rested in brackets secured to the

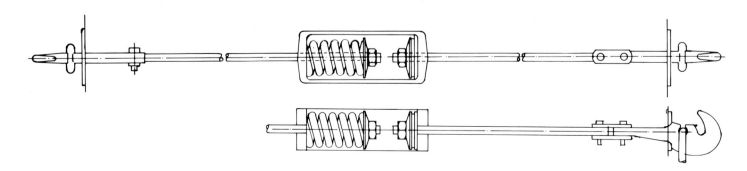

       Continuous Drawgear   *Drawing K. R. Morgan*   **Figure 177**

lower edge of the solebar, the centre of the spring being secured to the axlebox in a pocket with a 'U' shaped bracket over it. This relatively crude arrangement was also to be found on some of the earlier piped and fitted stock. On later fitted vehicles, a more sophisticated type of springing was used. The same type of fixing was applied at the axlebox but the outer ends had a vertical rod passed and pivoted in an 'eye' formed on the end of the longest leaf. Secured to the lower edges of the solebars were brackets which resembled a 'J' in side view. The vertical rod from the spring passed through these 'J' hangers and resilient pads were placed over the rod and against the hanger, being secured by washers and nuts on the ends of the rods. A variation of this type is to be found on the brake vans where a short swing link connects the hanger to the spring.

The subject of brakes on goods wagons is a fairly complex one. Where the wagon only had handbrakes, it was said to be 'unfitted' since these brakes could only be applied whilst the wagon was stationary or moving very slowly. Such brakes were, therefore, of no assistance when working a train although, at the top of steep inclines, trains of unfitted wagons were stopped while a proportion of the brakes were 'pinned down'. This, then, helped to retard the speed down the incline. Once the bottom was reached, the train had to be stopped again whilst the brakes were again released. This laborious and time consuming practice is now a thing of the past. It was, however, commonplace on all of the railways in this country during the steam era.

Where a wagon had, in addition to the handbrake, a vacuum or Westinghouse brake, it was said to be 'fitted' whilst if it had both, it was said to be 'dual fitted'. Such wagons, if connected to the engine brake pipe, were under the driver's control, which actively assisted the stopping of the train. The fitted wagons were augmented by 'piped' vehicles. These, as the name implies, had an automatic brake pipe with hose connections at each end, but did not have the actual brake cylinder. Such wagons, though not under the control of the automatic brake themselves, could maintain continuity of the system to adjacent fitted vehicles.

Regulations introduced in 1911 for future new construction, stated that all wagons must incorporate handbrakes capable of being applied from both sides of the wagon. The operating position was also standardized to be at the right hand end of the wagon when facing it.

The early LMS construction had two completely independent sets of brake gear. The type, known as 'double brake gear' was easily distinguishable by the two 'Vee' hangers, one on each side of the solebar on both sides of the wagon. This type is well shown in **Plate 129 (Vol. 1)** and in **Figure 178**. As many of the components of this type of brake were common to other varieties to be described later, they can conveniently be detailed here to save repetition.

The brake blocks were of cast iron. They were of symmetrical type, having suspension holes on the side of the centre line, so that they could be used for either right or left hand

positions. They were machined to the radius of the wheels, the back portion being machined to give a loose fit around the wheel flange, a lug going behind the flange preventing sideways movement. The blocks were hung on suspension links which passed each side of the block. The upper end of these links pivoted on pins which passed through brackets secured to the underframe, whilst at the lower end, a pin was passed through links and blocks to give pivoting at this end also.

On the centre line of the wagon, the two 'Vee' hangers had a short horizontal shaft which passed through them. At the inner end of this shaft, a short lever was secured at right angles, in such a way as to give an equal lever each side of the shaft centre line. Push rods, comprising two steel plates with wooden spacers between them connected the ends of the short levers to the brake blocks. The push rods were attached at both ends by means of pivot pins, those at the inner or 'Vee' hanger end having a number of hole positions to give adjustment as the brake blocks wore away.

To safeguard against breakage of the various pivot pins, with a subsequent fouling of the track, safety straps were fitted near to the outer ends of the push rods. At the inner end, in the case of pivot pin breakage, the upper push rod, of the two, would drop down on to the lever shaft and was thus quite safe. To safeguard the lower push rod, a further safety strap was provided which was hung from the upper push rod.

The brakes were applied by a long side lever. This was secured to the 'Vee' hanger cross shaft at its inner end, while at the outer end, the lever was supported in a guard, as shown in **Figure 178**. When not in use, the lever was retained in the guard by the small lug shown in the end view. On occasions, if the lever had been hastily replaced after use, it would jump this lug and drop down into the guard. It was quite commonplace to see and hear a wagon with the brake lever banging about in the guard as the brake blocks 'picked up' on the wheels.

To apply the brake, the side lever was, at first, pushed down, either by hand pressure or with the assistance of a shunting pole or brake stick. A pin, attached to a short length of chain, whose other end was secured to the small lug shown at the side of the guard, was then pushed into the most convenient hole in the guard above the lever to hold the lever in position; hence the expression 'pinning down'. As can be seen, this was a two handed job and was not easy whilst the wagon was moving. **Plate 128 (Vol. 1)** shows a brake 'pinned down' in this way.

The double brake, whilst it satisfied the condition of being capable of application from both sides of the wagon, was wasteful of components inasmuch that only one set of gear would be in use at any one time. Except for vehicles with bottom doors, the solution adopted by the LMS was to make use of the type of brake generally known as the 'Morton' in future construction.

With this type of brake, only one 'Vee' hanger on each side of the wagon was employed, these being secured to the

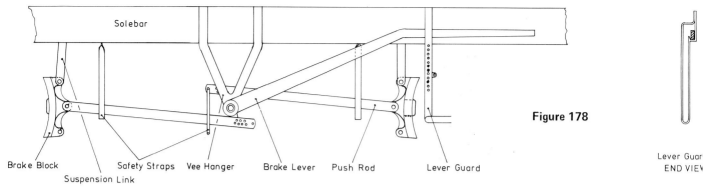

Solebar

Brake Block Safety Straps Vee Hanger Brake Lever Push Rod Lever Guard

Suspension Link

DOUBLE BRAKE

Figure 178

Lever Guar
END VIEW

Drawing K. R. Morga

inner face of the solebars. Between the 'Vee' hangers, a long cross shaft ran the full width of the wagon. This carried the short lever to which the push rods were attached. In this case, however, only one full set of brake gear was provided. This acted on both axles on one side, provision for operating it from either brake lever being achieved by the simple, but ingenious, mechanism shown in **Figure 180**. This shows the essential operating parts of the gear, the 'Vee' hangers being omitted for clarity. The nearer brake lever is shown removed from the cross shaft for clarity. In fact, it was mounted on, but not secured to the cross shaft, being retained in place by a washer and nut on the end of the shaft. Inboard of the lever was a clutch, the end of the brake lever being formed into a mating and similar clutch as shown. When this lever was used to apply the brakes, the two halves of the clutch met, thus rotating the cross shaft to apply the brake. On the far side, a similar clutch was attached to the cross shaft, the brake lever being mounted above it, as shown, on a separate stub shaft attached to the 'Vee' hanger on that side. Study of the drawing shows that whichever lever is used to apply the brake, it will make the opposite clutch separate from its brake lever. Where this type of brake was used on fitted stock, a lever was secured to the cross shaft as shown. The outer end of this lever was slotted to allow the vacuum cylinder piston rod to pass through. The end of the piston rod had a short cross rod attached to it, which, when the vacuum brake was applied, pulled the lever upwards, whilst when the handbrake was applied the vacuum brake lever was free to slide up the piston rod.

Some of the later fitted stock and all of the brake vans had clasp brakes. These had two brake blocks per wheel on all wheels and necessitated the rather complicated gear as

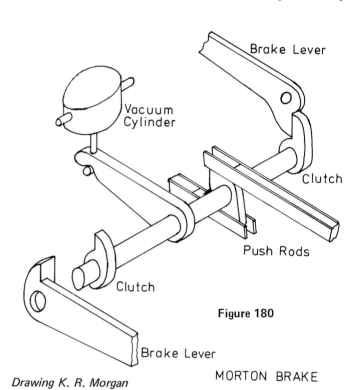

Brake Lever

Vacuum Cylinder

Clutch

Push Rods

Clutch

Figure 180

Brake Lever

MORTON BRAKE

Drawing K. R. Morgan

shown in **Figure 179**. The brake blocks were suspended, as before, but were connected by a cross shaft (A). This shaft had to subsidiary shafts welded to it in the form of a shallow 'Vee' (B) at the apex of which, on the centre line, were mounted levers (C). These were pivoted, as shown, and were connected by link (D). The right hand lever (C) was suspended from the underframe by link (E) while the left hand lever (C) was pivoted from bracket (F) which was, in turn, secured to the underframe.

On the centre line of the wagon, the arrangement was as for the 'Morton' brake (**Figure 180**) and was connected, as shown, by pull rod (H). The whole of this arrangement was repeated for the other end of the wagon.

When the brake was applied, the pull rod (H) moved to the left and thus started to pull the cross shafts (A) together. As soon as one pair of brake blocks touched the wheels, the linkage compensated to bring the other pair of blocks into contact. Both pairs then tightened on the wheels with a uniform pressure. The arrangement on the brake vans was similar. In this case, however, a vertical shaft extended from inside the van, where the brake hand-wheel was situated, to below the van floor where it was connected, via a screwed nut, to two bell crank levers to which the pull rods were attached.

Figure 179

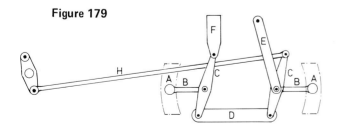

F E

H A B C C B A

D

TYPICAL CLASP BRAKE

Drawing K. R. Morgan

The existence of some photographs taken at Wolverton **Plates 150—153** and those probably taken at Wolverton **Plates 154—156**, has enabled the author to illustrate some aspects of wagon construction. The Wolverton pictures show various stages in the construction of 12 ton covered goods vans, while **Plates 154—156** show varying stages of construction of 16 ton mineral wagons.

Photographs British Rail

Plate 150

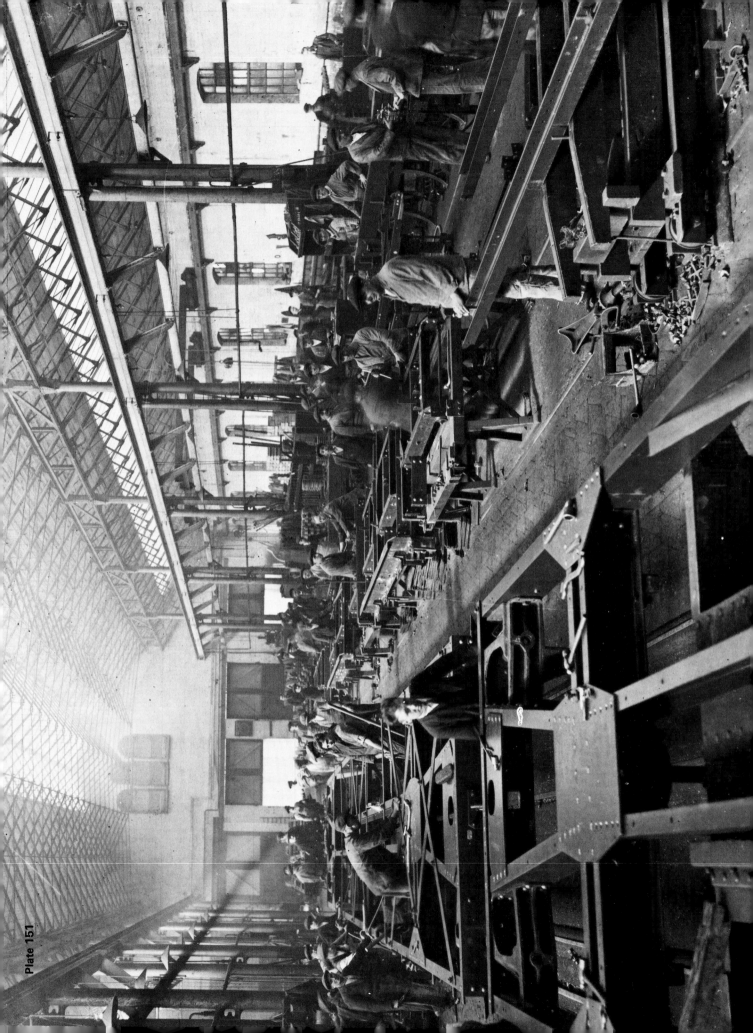

Plate 151

Plate 152

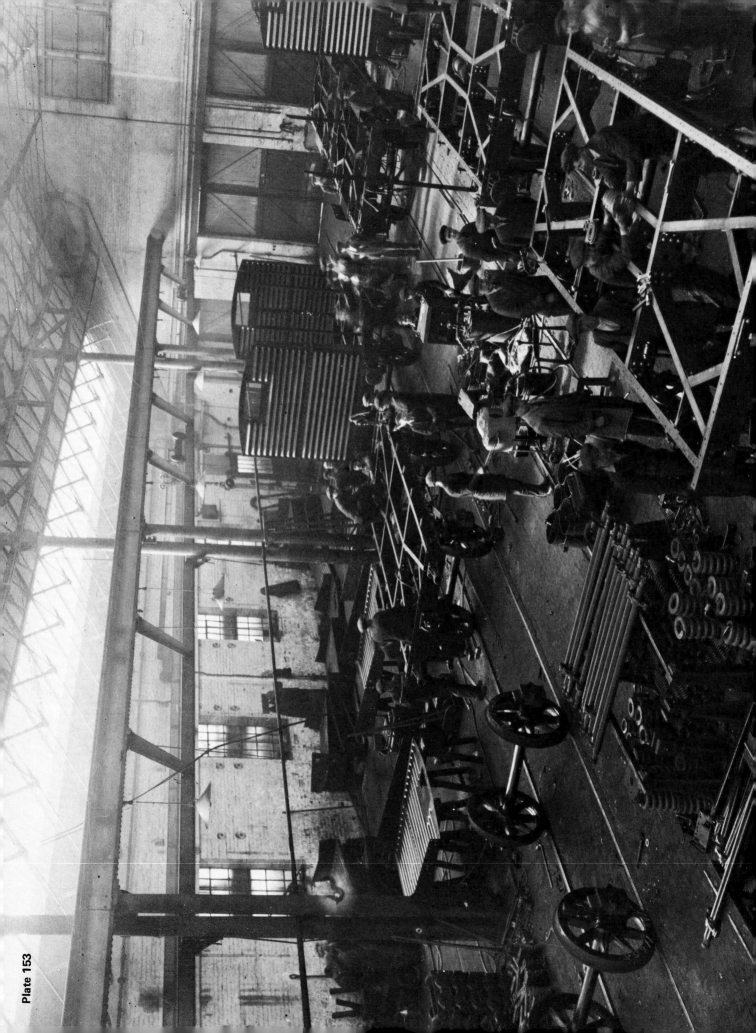

Plate 153

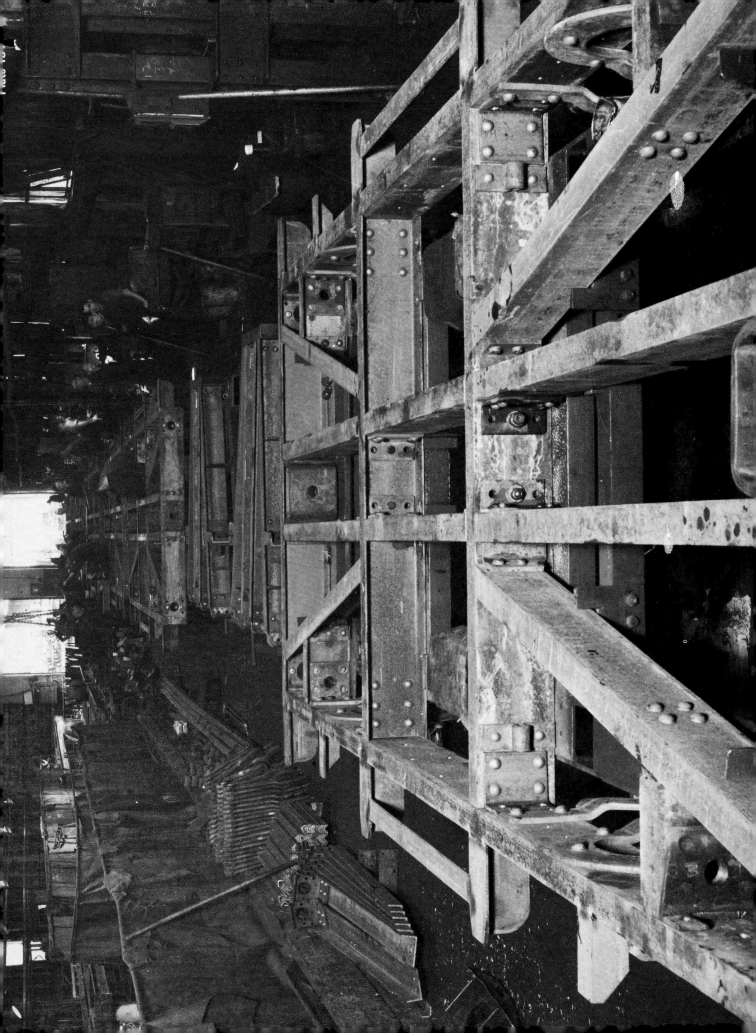

Plate 155

To assist modellers with these elusive detailed pictures, **Plates 157—172** have been included.

Plate 156

Plate 157 A close up of the brake lever in the off position.

Photograph V. R. Anderson

Plate 158 This shows the brake pinned down.
Photograph V. R. Anderson

Plate 160 Another view of a 12 ton mineral wagon brake gear. This picture shows the ironwork against which the door fell.

Photograph A. E. West

Plate 159 A double 'V' brake hanger on a wooden solebar mineral wagon. Note the twin push rods and safety loop to prevent the lower push rod from falling. Also of interest is the hook on the solebar which secures the tarpaulin sheet.

Photograph V. R. Anderson

Plate 161 A wagon label clip and a 'Not to go' label. Other cards were used to indicate traffic. Class 1 was for coal, class 2 for other minerals, class 3 for goods and the number was printed clearly so that the staff would know what type of traffic was being carried, thus enabling them to calculate the weight of the train.

Photograph V. R. Anderson

Plates 162 to 164 These are close up photographs of buffer guides. **Plate 162** is the open door end on a mineral wagon, **Plate 163** is the fixed end on a mineral wagon, while **Plate 164** is another buffer guide used by the LMS.

Photographs V. R. Anderson

Plates 165 & 166 These show axleguards.
Plate 165 shows a simple wagon type axle-
guard and spring, while Plate 166 shows a
more sophisticated arrangement of a swing
link used on a goods brake van.

Photographs K. R. Morgan and
Author's Collection

Plate 167 A three link coupling on a 13
ton mineral wagon.

Photograph V. R. Anderson

Plate 168   A solebar and number plate on No. 726037, a double bolster wagon to D2029.

Photograph Author's Collection

Plate 169   Brake gear detail on a tube wagon to D1675, No. 499541.

Photograph A. E. West

Plate 170 Brake gear detail on a long low
wagon to D1924, No. 497545.

Photograph Author's Collection

Plate 171 An LMS standard wagon
number-plate.

Photograph V. R. Anderson

Plate 172 An LMS wagon works plate.
When built, it was lettered 'LMS' but under
B R ownership the L and S have been
removed to leave M representing the London
Midland Region.

Photograph V. R. Anderson

Following the tradition of the Midland Railway which used 'runners' or shunters trucks but never recorded their existence, the LNWR also used them but did acknowledge, by way of a diagram reference, that they existed. These two pictures have been included to illustrate what the LMS did with this type of vehicle, and concludes this volume.

Plate 173 Photographed in 1960, this shows No. M154005 which was lettered 'Upperby Runner' and was in use as a shunters truck at Carlisle. It was presumably a conversion from an existing previous standard wagon.

Photograph Don Rowland

Plate 174 This 1966 Derby view illustrates No. M127494 which is a more elaborate design and follows the tradition of the early Midland vehicles described in an *Illustrated History of Midland Wagons* published by O.P.C. Unfortunately, no other information is available.

Photograph Author's Collection

Title page	The covered goods van, No. 298159 was built at Wolverton in April 1924 to D1664.
Frontispiece	It was not correct to say that there were no pre-grouping liveries visible. A wagon in MR livery and one in NER livery can be seen in the picture.
Figure 4 — D1890	Additional number, 295987 still running in June 1982, painted olive green.
Figure 17 — D1661	Some lot numbers were omitted from the text. These are Nos 194—198 and 279—286.
Figure 23 — D1663	The caption suggests that a packing piece was used to increase the length of the buffer body. This was not entirely correct. It was Midland practice at one time to use an elm washer to increase the length of the buffer body but the LMS 'packed out' by using two different lengths of buffer body, one for non-fitted stock and a longer body for those vehicles which were fitted and equipped with screw or instanter couplings.
Figure 24 — D1832	Additional number 157754, tare: 7 tons 8 cwt.
Plate 59	The vehicle is fitted with a through pipe and not an automatic vacuum brake.
Figure 26 — D1830	Additional number, 140659. AVB.
Plate 63	This is a further example which suggests errors in the lot book and upon reflection, it would seem that this vehicle was built with an AVB.
Plate 65	The use of black patches, upon which the wagon number etc. was painted during the BR period, applied mostly to grey painted non-fitted vehicles and was not a normal practice on bauxite painted fitted vehicles.
Figure 30 — D1828	Additional number, 181145.
Figure 31 — D1830	Incorrectly captioned. Should read D1829.
Figure 36 — D2031	Lot number 1340 was omitted.
Figure 40 — D2074	Should read 5ft. 3in. gauge.
Figure 47 — D1665	Additional number, 287838. Also lot 709 was numbered 299031—50.
Plate 123	This was not in original condition but as modified by British Railways.
Figure 49 — D1666	Additional numbers: 111145, 132255, 137649, 184026, 192349, 214769, 257719, 305964, 336355, 336361, 337377, 337432 and 356405.
Figure 51	A picture of one in early LMS livery is to hand and illustrates No. 403697 when almost new. The tare weight, 6 tons 8 cwt. 3 qrs, is on the bottom plank at the right hand end. What is interesting is the fact that, unlike the vehicles illustrated in *Plates 137 & 138*, this wagon has a short rib 'RCH' buffer body.
Figure 55 — D1667	Some lot numbers were omitted from the text. These are Nos. 56—58, 173—180, 268—276, 440 and 476. Additional numbers are 87067, 159310, 289482.
Figure 56 — D1839	Additional number, 4427.
Plate 182	The following are listed as 'Limestone' in 1961 and are presumably as **Plate 182**. Nos. M690132, M690230/33, M690401/23/88/97, M690797, M690844, M690928, M691210/69, M691316/72, M691449/54, M691617/89, M691811/78.
Plate 186	The following are listed as converted 'Lime' hoppers in 1961 for traffic from Creigiau and G.K.N., East Moors. They were lettered 'TO WORK BETWEEN CREIGIAU (QUARRIES) AND GUEST KEEN IRON & STEEL WORKS' CARDIFF'. Nos. M690171, M690298, M690327/86, M690645/69/70, M690764/99, M690804/33/35/81, M691077, M691138/41/61, M691251, M691320/50, M691416, M691544, M691639, M691710/13.
Figure 81 — D1671	Additional numbers are 55568, 173034/9, 190303, 227165, 262132, 261296, 324279.
Plate 193	The caption is not clear. The bottom doors illustrated were indicated on the outside of the wagon by the white stripes **(see Plate 198)**.
Plate 199	For hopper bottom read bottom door.
Figure 82 — D2049	3,489 vehicles to this diagram were running in 1951.
Figure 96 — D2077	333 vehicles to this diagram were running in 1951.
Figure 97 — D2080	42 vehicles to this diagram were running in 1951.
Figure 103 — D1676	Additional number 125572. Tare: 7 tons 2 cwt.
Figure 106 — D1798	Additional numbers are 43334 and 45300.
Figure 111 — D1689	Lot number 373 covers Nos. 168851—60. Lot number 402 covers Nos. 168861—75. Lot number 723 covers Nos. 299021—30 and lot number 755 covers Nos. 298648—62.
Figure 112 — D1871	A picture exists which illustrates a beer van, No. 195405 which suggests that numbers outside of those allocated may have been used.

And so to LMS Trains . . .